ROYAL FORTUNE

Tax, Money & the Monarchy

PHILLIP HALL

BLOOMSBURY

First published 1992

Copyright © 1992 by Phillip Hall

The moral right of the author has been asserted.

Bloomsbury Publishing Ltd, 2 Soho Square, London W1V 5DE

A CIP catalogue record for this book is available
from the British Library.

ISBN 0 7475 1098 9

Typeset by Hewer Text Composition Services, Edinburgh
Printed in Great Britain by Richard Clay Ltd, Bungay, Suffolk

CONTENTS

**TO THE MEMORY OF MY MOTHER,
ROSALIE HALL**

Acknowledgments

Many people have helped with this book. Considerable thanks are due to Mike McKenna, Harry Tait, Colette Smyth and John Griffith for reading it in draft and providing constructive comment. Laurie Flynn provided occasional dialogue and stimulation. Roy Bartlett of Exeter University gave some advice about royal taxation matters. Steve McSweeney assisted on translating the data provided by the West German Embassy on the costs of the Federal President. Janet Hickman, Alf Woods and Martin Hughes helped on the Queen's racehorses. Lord Carnarvon, the Queen's friend and racing manager, was good enough to find time to speak to me. Brian Cox of the Transport and General Workers' Union and Colonel Richard Mackeness of the National Trainers' Federation gave somewhat diverging views on the pay and conditions of stable staff. Nick Savvides helped dig out other sundry information. Anthony Howard discussed the Queen's purchase of Gatcombe Park from R.A. Butler. Suzy Menkes discussed with me several of the issues surrounding the royal jewels. Alun Howkins similarly provided interesting comments on the history of Norfolk agricultural labourers, including those who worked at Sandringham. Interviews with the MPs Michael Foot and Tony Benn were helpful as background. Jim Nichol, Professor Fred Halliday and Paul Lashmar have also been of help in various ways.

There were also many spokespersons at Buckingham Palace, government departments, the Bank of England, the Inland Revenue, the Department of the Environment, the Duchy of Lancaster and elsewhere, who, whilst in my opinion often preserving far too much secrecy about the monarchy, were able to give me some relevant information. The list of

ACKNOWLEDGMENTS

archives and libraries consulted is a long one, but I am principally indebted to librarians at the British Library, University of London Library, the Public Record Office, House of Lords Record Office and the Bodleian Library, Oxford. Naturally, the interpretations provided here are the author's responsibility, as are any errors or omissions.

When I started out to write a projected Ph.D. on the monarchy in the early 1980s, Alan Swingewood and Jean Seaton gave their time and encouragement. More recently, Liz Calder at Bloomsbury has provided patience at its slow genesis. Reg Davis-Poyntor, my agent, has shown similar forbearance and given much support, though also administering some gentle prodding.

Phillip Hall
London, July 1991

Introduction

Double Standards

In 1842, Sir Robert Peel's government reintroduced income tax, which had been abolished in 1816 following the conclusion of the Napoleonic Wars. Unsurprisingly, the return of this tax was not popular amongst those who had to pay it, but Peel hoped to make it somewhat less unpopular by an announcement he made in the House of Commons in March 1842:

> Her Majesty, prompted by those feelings of deep and affectionate interest in the welfare of her people which she had ever manifested, stated to him [Peel] that if the financial condition of the country was such that, in a time of peace, Parliament should think it necessary to subject all incomes to a certain charge, it was her determination that her own income should be subjected to a similar burden.

And pay she did.

The July 1988 edition of *The Monarchy in Britain*, a reference pamphlet produced by the government's Central Office of Information, bluntly described how matters stand now: 'As part of the royal prerogative the Queen does not pay tax – either on her private wealth and income, or on the Queen's Civil List – unless Parliament decides otherwise.' Parliament has not so far decided otherwise, though if it had been better informed by government and monarch during this century, it most probably would have.

In other respects, the above pamphlet echoes the common claim that the British monarchy has adapted to the modern world. But in successfully reviving tax privileges, it has gone backwards not forwards. More usually the trend in recent times has been to end tax exemptions that have been based on ancient and questionable right. The Swedish King now pays tax on his private income. The Japanese Emperor became liable to income tax in 1945. As the Emperor was once considered a divine being in Japan, this rather poses the question, if an ex-deity can pay tax why not the British monarch? Neither could celestial connections protect the Vatican in 1968, when the Italian government ended the Vatican's exemption from tax on its investment income.[1]

The *Mail on Sunday* in a March 1990 editorial entitled 'How can we justify a tax-free monarch?' found no satisfactory reason why the Queen should not pay tax on her 'vast fortune'. The editorial also argued, like many people before, that removing the Queen 'from the vicissitudes of everyday life', like taxation, distances the monarch from the people. No convincing argument has ever been put forward for granting this extraordinary bounty to Britain's richest person, when even those below the official poverty-line have to pay income tax.* The very existence of this tax exemption was for as long as possible and until relatively recently kept secret, which demonstrates how little faith monarch and government had in its justification. Indeed, this exemption has gone against the trend over this century, which has been for more and more people to pay income tax.

It is no wonder that a 1991 opinion poll found that 79 per cent thought the Queen should pay tax on her private income.[2] The royals are commonly described as not just sharing the best characteristics of the nation, but actually setting us a good example. It was for this reason that 140 years ago Sir Robert Peel, the Prime Minister, persuaded Queen Victoria to pay the income tax when he reintroduced it.

A sizeable portion of this book reveals the long and hitherto hidden history of royal tax-paying and the devious and secretive ways by which it was brought to an end. The account of royal taxation and other aspects of royal finances has been pieced together from a lengthy process of detective work in various archives. It offers a very different view of monarchy than is usually available. It is fully documented and does not depend upon

* In the latest bout of controversy over the Queen's tax immunity in June–July 1991, some argued that the Queen was entitled to her immunity because she had voluntarily relinquished the income from the Crown Estate. This argument and the whole status of the Crown Estate is dealt with in Chapter 6.

anonymous and uncheckable sources. References are given at the back of the book.

Nobody likes paying income tax, and it might be said that the Queen is just like everyone else in this respect, the only difference being that she has got away with it. However, her exemption is claimed on the grounds that she is not like everybody else. Rather, she is a special person, embodying 'the Crown' and above the common herd, so that she should not be subject to the same standards as people with much lower incomes. Part One of this book argues that the basis for the Queen's immunity from taxation is unfounded. Nevertheless, even if on an invalid basis, it has been agreed by the government and therefore does not of course fall within Princess Anne's strictures against tax evasion and fraud. Tax-dodgers, Her Royal Highness claimed, 'cost people like you and me money . . . usually it is the most vulnerable who suffer.'[3]

In public, the large majority of media and politicians declare the monarchy good value for money, claiming that members of the royal family receive only what is necessary to do their job. Yet reading through the diaries, letters and memoranda in the archives, one sees a different side. In private, politicians and civil servants constantly refer to this or that aspect of royal finance as 'delicate' or 'sensitive', something about which not too much should be known. Thus the secretiveness about the Queen's personal fortune is protecting not so much her privacy as her image.

The Queen's investments are protected from the public gaze by special arrangements built into successive company acts, which otherwise were designed to reveal more about company shareholders. Again, the Queen and her family are going against the modern trend, which is towards more and more disclosure of the real owners of shares.

Often, following the fortune of royal finances means understanding the monarchy's special relationship with the Treasury, the department responsible for stopping any excesses in public expenditure. But there is a double standard which pervades governments, covering most areas of national expenditure and of society generally: low pay for nurses alongside high drug-company profits from sales to the National Health Service; redundancy payments for employees and 'golden handshakes' for chief executives; stringent cost-cutting in education and social services in the name of efficiency versus loose monitoring of the expense of defence contracts. And when it comes to incentives, governments mostly view them as working differently, depending on whom they are applied to. J.K. Galbraith once noted the contradiction in the free-enterprise ethic. The rich needed more money in the form of tax cuts (or 'sweeteners' in the case of British Aerospace's purchase of Rover) if they were to invest, whilst the poor, for their own good, should not be 'featherbedded' lest they lose the incentive to work and become dependent on the welfare state.

This double standard certainly covers royalty. In 1936, a top Treasury civil servant described why Edward VIII had to be given a larger Civil List than he would spend. The King, he said, could thus accumulate money, using the surplus to provide for his grandchildren or other relatives, for whom no provision is made by Parliament, 'and who even if they may under modern conditions be expected to enter a gainful profession, cannot *decently* be left to adjust their standard of living according to their individual earning capacities' (my emphasis).[4] No mention of this was made by the Chancellor of the Exchequer when he recommended the Civil List to the Commons, while an earlier Chancellor had specifically denied that the Civil List should provide any such surplus.[5]

It was not even very likely that the new King would ever have grand-children. Edward VIII was 41 and still unmarried (and in fact his marriage to Mrs Simpson did not produce any children). But in any event, grandchildren of monarchs have, this century, never been remotely in need of this sort of funding. When it came to the unemployed in the 1930s, the Conservative-dominated National Government, with the enthusiastic support of the Treasury, had no qualms about the decency of imposing the hated Means Test.

It was this same double standard which offended Richard Crossman in 1971, at the time of a royal request for a larger Civil List income. Crossman had been a senior Cabinet Minister in the Labour government of 1964–70. He had met the Queen regularly in his capacity as Lord President of the Council. His published diaries reveal his great pains to be considerate and friendly towards her. He had the odd republican sentiment, but felt on the whole that the monarchy was a defensible institution, even if some changes were desirable. However, in 1971 he found there was something about the 'royal pay increase' which he could not stomach, especially in view of the monarch's tax privileges. Crossman, in a widely publicized article, talked about the unspoken premise that 'different social categories deserve fundamentally different treatment from the state, and that lack of money – or the ability to make it – implies inferior moral rights'.[6] In other words, different classes of people need different amounts of money to live 'decently'.

When confronted with the idea, which indeed was implemented, that Prince Philip should receive enough to save for his old age, Crossman thought that for someone 'married to the richest woman in the country, this seems an unnecessary refinement of royal social security'.[7] (It should also be remembered that royals in their old age continue to receive their annuity in full.) Such measures are considered necessary 'to support the dignity of the Crown'; others receive less dignity at the hands of the Department of Social Security.

Some writers have stated that the great British public does not begrudge the royals the money. Walter Bagehot's *The English Constitution* is invariably quoted by monarchists to show that if you are going to have a monarchy, then it cannot be done on the cheap: 'There are arguments for not having a Court and there are arguments for having a splendid Court; but there are no arguments for having a mean Court.'[8] Palaces, footmen in fancy dress and other ingredients of pageantry which create the whole theatre of monarchy, all cost money. The argument against a 'cut-price monarchy' smacks of double standards, employed as it is by those who are relatively untroubled with the increasingly cut-price services of the welfare state. Moreover, a great deal of the pageantry is for the benefit of politicians and the privileged. It is they who get to drink the fine wines and to eat off gold plate, served by liveried footmen.

Bagehot himself, who was writing in 1865, did not argue for a 'splendid Court' and against a 'mean Court'. He was not at all against pageantry, but in the passage quoted from he was presenting views of those who wanted the British Court to be as splendid as that of the French Emperor, Louis Napoleon. Bagehot disagreed, stating that 'we have voluntary show enough already in London; we do not wish to have it encouraged and intensified, but quieted and mitigated'.[9] One would not make an issue of this misquotation of Bagehot were it not so very common. In any case, making sufficient provision for pageantry does not necessarily involve tax exemption. Even royalists recognize that the Queen receives enough from the state without that added bonus.

A common response to those criticisms of royalty that do surface is that no one should envy them their role – they can't help being royal, they didn't choose it, they have to put up with the press, they are hard-working and have to endure boring repetitive public functions during which they always have to smile and be gracious. There is an element of truth in this point of view, yet when stated sufficiently vigorously ('I wouldn't like to have their job') it seems to lead to the conclusion that we should abolish the monarchy to save the royals from further suffering. The 'pity the poor royals' stance, however, is based on a judgment of the public face of royalty. One obviously does not see the privacy which they must enjoy at Balmoral, Sandringham, Highfield, Gatcombe Park, aboard the Royal Yacht or on the Royal Train, or in the royal counting-house. If, instead, all that was provided was an average middle-class standard of living, they might indeed choose not to be royal.

How hard-working, in fact, the royals are is difficult to measure. The number of their public engagements is sometimes cited, but these can range in time from a few minutes to a lot longer. They may include events they would attend anyway, like the opera. So to say that a member of the royal family undertakes two or three hundred engagements per year is not a very good guide. Also, one needs to count up their holidays – for instance, Charles takes a five-week break at the start of the New Year, during which he goes skiing, in addition to a summer and other holidays. Similarly, there is time for polo, hunting, fishing. Many other categories of people are undoubtedly very hard-working without receiving anything like the same level of reward.

The monarchy meets with general acceptance, scoring in recent years about 85 per cent approval in opinion polls. Therefore it might be suggested that the working class perceive no double standard in the government's treatment of the royals. Opinion polls do not, however, generally provide a breakdown by social class; where they do, a class difference emerges in response to the issue of royal finance. Working-class respondents are generally much less in favour of increases in Civil List payments to the royals and more disapproving of the Queen's wealth.[10]

On the other hand, the truly wealthy are not scandalized by the Queen's wealth and the opulence of royalty. In fact, wealth, privilege and snobbery are the very things that they require the monarchy to enshrine. If the monarchy did not symbolize what they wished to preserve in society, then the wealthy would be about as enthralled with royalty as they are with the Pearly Kings and Queens of Cockney London. Generally, the rich are not really too concerned as to whether royalty is hard-working or not, or whether or not the monarchy earns foreign currency by boosting tourism and trade. (The argument about the royals earning money for Britain is examined in Appendix A.) Given Britain's enormous balance of payments deficit (£20 billion in 1989, including a £2.5 billion deficit on tourism[11]), monarchists might question how effective the royal family's contribution really is.

Backward as the monarchy as an institution undoubtedly is, it must be remembered that contemporary capitalist society has one thing in common with its feudal predecessor: a concern with inherited wealth, something which affects all those with wealth, not just those who inherit a title. On the one hand, the individualism at the core of modern capitalist thinking suggests that ability and hard work should be valued above inherited social position. On the other hand, the same philosophy decries any interference with a person's rights to bequeath and inherit wealth. So the modern bourgeois might agree with Tom Paine that a hereditary monarch is as absurd as the idea of hereditary mathematicians or hereditary poets. But in fact he or she tends not to, because there is nothing too drastically old-fashioned about monarchy in a society where the most likely way to attain wealth is still through birth.

The royals are often said to be inexpensive. For instance, *Royalty Monthly* in March 1987 answered a reader's query about the cost of the monarchy to the tax-payer by referring to the 'total cost to the country for the royal family in 1985 of £4,838,200'. The magazine, one of those glossy products which have appeared in the 1980s for the royalist market, confidently stated that 'at this sum many countries operating a republican system would regard the cost of our royal family as constituting something of a bargain'. Yet the above figure is only the tip of the iceberg. Once the costs, borne by the government, of running the Royal Yacht, *Britannia*, the Royal Train, aircraft, palaces and so on are included, the total rises to more than £50 million per annum.* The constant expense of *Britannia*, which is in fact an ocean-going liner, should perhaps be contrasted with the way in which the state has left the operation of lifeboats from Britain's coasts to be funded by charity.

The idea that the monarch is cheaper than supporting a president of a republic like West Germany or Italy is plain silly. The annual costs of *non-executive* presidencies are a fraction of those of the British

* To see how this figure is calculated, see Chapter 8.

monarchy.* Nor do they bear the hidden cost of the Queen's tax exemption on her private income. Even with the cuts in higher-rate taxation in the 1980s, this may still be one of the greatest costs of all. Whilst the West German President does not pay tax on the sums provided for the expenses of the presidency, he does pay tax at the top rate on his salary and any other income. Also, none of his family receive anything from the state; there is no presidential ocean-going liner or any other vessel, nor even a presidential train. Therefore, all the various costs of the West German presidency come to the much lower figure of about £10 million a year.[12]

Some argue that, even if the monarchy costs upwards of £50 million a year, this is a drop in the ocean of state expenditure, coming to about £1 per head of population per year. Undeniably, there are other ways in which the state is much more profligate with our money. Quite regularly the Commons Public Accounts Committee points out the loose monitoring on spending on contracts for military hardware. Spending on the development of the Nimrod early warning system, for example, reached no less than £1 billion before the decision was taken to cancel the project totally and buy the American AWACS.[13] However, there are other statistical ways of portraying the expenditure on the monarchy than the £1 per head figure. One can calculate how many income-tax payers it takes to generate £50 million a year, which does not include the undisclosed cost of police protection for the royals, the value of the tax exemption or what public bodies may spend locally to prepare for royal visits – official receptions, fresh coats of paint, new flowerbeds etc. As the average tax-payer in 1989–80 paid £1,861 in income tax,[14] one can state that it takes over 26,000 people at work to produce sufficient revenue to maintain the monarchy. Or one can compare the income of a charity like Save the Children Fund with the cost of the monarchy. In 1988–9, the Fund spent £38 million to help needy children in no fewer than fifty-four countries.[15] This sum represents about the difference in cost between the British monarchy and the West German presidency.

Thus, how much the royals cost is far from being negligible, in terms of the actual money spent. But it is also significant in the way that it

---

* Comparisons of the monarchy with the American presidency, which is an executive presidency, should not be made. The US President is the head of the government, not just the head of state. Many of the presidency's costs are therefore the costs of government.

is part of the double standard operated by government and the wider society. Much of the effort put in to justify and celebrate the monarchy derives from that fact. The monarchy, as the symbol of 'national unity', legitimizes the status quo within which these double standards operate.

A Note on Prices

From time to time, sums mentioned in the text are converted into present (1991) figures, following conventional practice. It might be helpful for readers to know that this involves prices from 1850 to 1914 being multiplied by between 43 and 55, depending on the precise year; those from the 1920s and 1930s by between 20 and 34; those from 1950 by about 15, from 1960 by about 10, from 1970 by about 7 and from 1980 by about 2.

It should be borne in mind that the longer the period of time over which one tries to make this conversion, the more approximate the results will be. Also, to understand what it is to receive a particular figure as income in, say, 1900, it is not just necessary to know what it would buy today, but where it stood in relation to the average income in 1900. Comparisons with incomes and expenditures of the time are perhaps more illuminating, as they allow us to understand what the figures would have meant in the society of that time. Also, the calculations which go to make up the retail price index today include items like televisions, electrical goods and frozen food. They have no clear equivalent in 1900 to enable one straightforwardly to chart the rate of price increases from then to the present day. Statistical comparisons over this length of time are therefore necessarily very approximate, though from time to time such comparisons are given.

Chronology

1698 Parliament votes William III Civil List of £700,000 p.a., raised from Hereditary Revenues to cover civil government, Royal Household and royal lifestyle.

1702 Clause in Queen Anne's Civil List Act forbids the monarch's sale of remaining Crown Lands.

1727 Walpole persuades Parliament to grant George II any surpluses over £800,000 from Civil List revenues.

1760 Various tax revenues and also Crown Lands revenues hitherto directly received by monarch now surrendered to Parliament; George III receives fixed sum of £800,000 p.a. On that proving insufficient, certain civil government expenses hitherto paid from Civil List funded by Parliament.

1799 Income tax introduced to pay for Napoleonic Wars.

1800 Crown Private Estate Act gives monarch private financial status, allowing him to make a will and to own land privately, on which he was made liable to tax.

1816 Income tax ends after conclusion of Napoleonic Wars.

1830 William IV's reduced Civil List, allotted purely for 'the personal dignity' of the King and Queen, no longer for any civil government items. King surrenders Smaller Branches of Hereditary Revenues to Parliament.

1842   Peel reintroduces income tax; Victoria 'offers' to pay on her own income. Pays on private income, the Duchy of Lancaster and on Civil List Classes I (Privy Purse) and III and, from 1871, on savings on Class II, transferred to Privy Purse.

1862   Act passed to allow Victoria to inherit Balmoral from Prince Albert and laying down that monarch's will need not be published.

1873   Third Crown Private Estate Act; issue of disclosure of monarch's personal wealth agreed by Solicitor-General as relevant in determining Civil List.

1894   Liberal government introduces Estate Duty. (Monarchs never paid this or subsequent versions, Capital Transfer Tax or Inheritance Tax.)

1901   Edward VII tries to escape income tax on Civil List; government 'advises' he should keep paying but takes over cost of postage and some pensions. Chancellor of Exchequer, Hicks-Beach, gives King's lack of personal fortune as reason for higher Civil List.

1904   Edward VII tries to escape paying income tax on Civil List.

1910   Lloyd George relieves Civil List of income tax. In return, George V pays for costs of visiting heads of state and own return visits. Solicitor-General says monarch liable for estate duty on Balmoral and Sandringham (never implemented).

1913   Annuities of Victoria's remaining children made tax-free.

1916   George V pays back £100,000 from war-time Civil List savings to Exchequer.

1920   George V asks for increased Civil List.

1920–1   Over 90 per cent of annuity of Alexandra, Edward VII's widow, made tax-free.

1921   Prince of Wales's Duchy of Cornwall escapes tax on rental income; hitherto paid income tax (Schedule A) and supertax. Pays lower 'voluntary contribution' instead.

1922   80 per cent of annuities paid to George V's children made tax-free; made public only in 1926.

1933 George V, after accepting cut of £50,000 p.a. in Civil List (1931–5) during currency crisis, asks for and gets exemption from tax on Duchy of Lancaster rental income.

1936 George V dies, leaving no money to future Edward VIII, who receives larger Civil List than required for current expenditure, to accumulate money for grandchildren. Government relieves Civil List of all employee pensions.

1937 George VI's Civil List. Starts to reclaim tax on private investment income some time between 1937 and 1952.

1944 PAYE (Pay As You Earn) system introduced to cope with vast increase in numbers liable to income tax.

1947–51 Government departments relieve Civil List of various costs including upkeep of Buckingham Palace Gardens, fuel, lighting, phone bills. Refund of Purchase Tax allowed on some expenditure.

1948 George VI makes donations of £100,000 from war-time Civil List savings at same time as Princess Elizabeth, following marriage, receives increased (and 90 per cent tax-free) annuity of £40,000. Duke of Edinburgh receives £10,000.

1952 Butler tells Commons that 'naturally' the Queen is free from tax, except when specified by 1862 Act. Elizabeth II's Civil List relieved of wages bill for industrial staff engaged on maintenance of Royal Palaces. Civil List set with built-in inflation allowance intended to cover entire reign.

1960–1 Civil List relieved of cost of Royal Train and Royal Visits abroad.

1962 Queen's Gallery, Buckingham Palace, opened to public; profits to maintain royal works of art, relieving Civil List of cost.

1963 Schedule A tax altered to become tax on person of landlord, not property; Queen becomes free from tax, apart from local rates, on Sandringham and Balmoral.

1965 Capital Gains Tax introduced by Labour government. Queen does not pay.

1966   Labour government specifies that Queen should pay new Selective Employment Tax on staff employed by her. Tax abolished in 1971.

1967   Criminal Justice Act removes right of Duchy of Lancaster to receive fines imposed in courts of Quarter Sessions; compensation of nearly £200,000 paid to Duchy.

1969   Prince Charles, on reaching age of 21, makes voluntary contribution of 50 per cent of profits of Duchy to Exchequer. Previously more had been deducted 'in lieu of tax'.

1970-1   Revenues of Duchy of Lancaster used to meet Civil List deficits.

1971-2   Queen requests larger Civil List as Civil List fund for inflation runs out. Under new arrangement, Civil List payments increased with built-in inflation allowance to cover next five years or so. Select Committee states officially for first time that Queen pays no tax. Queen forgoes £60,000 Privy Purse. Revealed that Princess Margaret, Queen Mother and Duke of Gloucester receive 100 per cent tax relief on annuities, Princess Anne nearly 95 per cent. Prince Philip granted enough to save for old age.

1973   Companies Bill gives companies power to force shareholders to identify themselves when holding shares in name of nominee. Special clause inserted exempts Queen and some others from disclosure. (Clause retained by Labour when becomes Act in 1976.)

1974   Civil List relieved of paying for Buckingham Palace Press Office.

1975   After rise in inflation to over 20 per cent, Labour government increases Civil List and sets system of yearly upratings, voted by Parliament. Queen relieves government 'for time being' of paying annuities to her three cousins.

1981   Prince Charles on marriage to Diana reduces voluntary contribution to 25 per cent of profits of Duchy of Cornwall.

1988   Duchy of Lancaster Act removes some statutory restrictions imposed by 1702 Act, to allow property development.

1989-90   Queen exempt from Poll Tax but pays for some staff; pays increased Uniform Business Rate at Balmoral and Sandringham.

1990   Chancellor of the Exchequer, John Major, removes Stamp Duty on stocks and share transactions, one of Queen's few remaining taxes. Civil List increased sharply but to remain stationary thereafter for ten years, ending annual publicity over increases.

1993   Queen will probably have to pay at least the property element (half) of the proposed Council Tax.

I

Before the Present Reign:
William III to George VI

1

William III to Victoria:

The Separation of Government Finance from Royal Control

To understand the workings of an institution, it is generally necessary to examine its history. In no case is this more essential than with royal finances, particularly in grasping how questionable is the tax exemption enjoyed by the Queen today.

Until the seventeenth century, national government centred unambiguously on the person of the monarch. The finances of the King were the finances of government. 'The Treasury' was originally no more than a chest containing his money.[1] Thus the King received rents from the Crown Lands and various taxes, from which he paid the expenses of government together with the bills for his own personal expenditure and that of his household. It was difficult to distinguish between the King's personal expenditure and government expenditure. For instance, many positions of government went with being a personal servant in the Household of the King. Similarly, palaces were maintained not just for the comfort of the King and his family, but also as places where government business was transacted.

On the Continent, this identification of the state with the King culminated in the absolutist state. With a large standing army to enforce his will, the absolute monarch did not need the consent of Parliament to levy taxes; in fact, he did not need Parliament at all. Louis XIV of France could say with reason, 'L'état, c'est moi.' The same principle applied to the income of the French government: that also was his alone.[2] High taxes were necessary to maintain the standing army, a centralized bureaucracy and also to supply the luxuries demanded by an absolutist king. The cost of building and fitting out Versailles was far beyond the purse of an English king.

Generally speaking, the propertied in England did not want an absolutist king imposing high taxes on them which would often be spent in ways counter to their interests. The full-blown absolutist state did not come about in England for various reasons, not least of which was the Civil War of the 1640s. In that conflict, to oversimplify, the 'middling sort' of people pushed a section of the gentry and wealthier merchants to join the fight against the King. It became a fight to the finish, despite the fact that, if he had accepted various constraints on his powers, Charles I could have remained on the throne. It was his refusal of that option, as improper for a monarch to accept, that led to his execution in 1649.

However, after eleven years without a king, his son, Charles II, was recalled in 1660 by the propertied, who had become reunited in their desire for a king to restore order, even though they still did not want an absolutist king. Yet Charles II had not abandoned absolutist pretensions. Moreover, his brother, who succeeded him as James II, was much more determined not to have to depend upon Parliament, even a relatively tame one. This proved his undoing, and he was forced to flee to France in 1688.

James had received greater revenue than earlier kings, over £1.9 million a year,[3] and was not personally extravagant like his brother. This financial situation enabled him to gather a standing army, but not the allegiance of the propertied, who turned to Holland for help, in the form of James's nephew, William of Orange, and his army. With their arrival, James's political support, such as it was, together with his army, melted away.

The 'Glorious Revolution' of 1688 had profound consequences for the monarchy. From then on it was to be much more 'limited' in its powers. As with his two predecessors, Parliament voted William an annual sum to be paid for the duration of his life, but this amounted to only £700,000 a year. The very sensitive area of the military budget was to be voted annually and funded directly by Parliament, who thus controlled the size of the army. This control was particularly vigilant in peace-time, to ensure that only a relatively small army existed, thus denying the King the means of large-scale internal repression. The term Civil List, which is still used today to describe money the government gives the Queen, originated with William's £700,000, and was intended to designate the expenses incurred in operating the *civil* side of government, plus maintaining the Royal Household and a royal lifestyle. The new arrangements, by limiting the King's discretion over government money, produced for the first time a distinction, financially and politically, between the King and the state.

When this arrangement was finalized for William in 1698, he was allowed to receive certain specific rents and taxes, deemed to be Hereditary Revenues,[4] which would provide the £700,000. These had always been received by the monarch in one form or another and were considered his property, by hereditary right. But in William's case he was clearly King and receiver of these and other revenues by approval of Parliament.

Even in earlier times, 'hereditary right' was never that clear. It could never be traced back that many generations before one saw its origin in violence. The Norman Conquest ended King Harold's hereditary right at the Battle of Hastings, and several subsequent kings gained the throne by murdering existing kings or defeating them in battle. William himself, very much the soldier, had brought over a large army in 1688. It had not been used in battle against James II's forces in England, but its presence and the threat of its use was the decisive factor in the overthrow of James. The wealthy, wanting no such threat to the existing order as had occurred in the 1640s and 1650s, had been determined to avoid the involvement of the lower orders in the task of ridding themselves of James. William's Dutch army was thus to do the job instead. It was soon to be employed elsewhere, in the war against France, and therefore William had no basis for establishing absolutist rule.

In 1702, Parliament passed a measure which rectified an old grievance felt by those who wished to limit the power of the monarch. A clause was introduced in Queen Anne's Civil List Act which forbade her and her anticipated Hanoverian successors from selling off the remaining Crown Lands. One major reason for this was the fear that the monarch might make herself independent of parliamentary control by gaining income in this way. Any such money might be used illegally to help finance a standing army. In such measures as this and the general arrangements of the Civil List, Parliament still sought to banish the spectre of absolutism, while not exercising a detailed control over how the Queen and her ministers spent the money they did receive.

After Anne came the first two Hanoverian Georges. They received under the same system of royal finance a rather better deal. This was particularly true of George II (reigned 1727–60), who was allowed to receive any surpluses over his allotted £800,000 a year deriving from the various tax and rental income which made up the Civil List revenues. This was engineered by the arch-fixer, Sir Robert Walpole,[5] who realized that only if he could promise and deliver a large Civil List to George II on his accession would the King retain his services as Prime Minister, leaving him to preside profitably over the general corruption of the day.

Regulation was not just exercised by Parliament over the monarch and his or her ministers. The Commons was in turn subject to 'influence' from the Crown, and members could be induced to support the ministers chosen by the monarch, for instance by being given sinecures, government contracts, honours etc. The King's Civil List was also put to this use, through the pensions and positions that it funded. Nor was the electoral process, which determined who were to be Commons members in the first place, free of influence from the Crown and all manner of other influences from those with money. Nevertheless, despite its great imperfections as a representative body (of even the minority who could vote), the House of Commons did ensure that there was a limited monarchy, which did not impose high taxes to maintain an absolutist state.

The accession of George III in 1760 saw a further step towards the separation of royal and government finances, though it was not as big a step as is sometimes portrayed (see Chapter 6). The arrangement between the King and Parliament was that the tax and Crown Lands revenue which had been received by George II, directly, would now be paid into the government's 'Aggregate Fund'. From this fund the King would receive a *fixed* sum of £800,000 a year for his Civil List; this arrangement was intended to last for the duration of George III's reign. Any surpluses above this £800,000 yielded by the revenues which had previously funded the Civil List now accrued to Parliament. This was a poor deal for the new King compared to that enjoyed by his predecessor, but since he had previously criticized George II and his ministers for extravagance, and preached the virtues of economy, he felt obliged to be content with the £800,000 a year.

George III was still responsible for civil government expenditure – the salaries of the Civil Service, Diplomatic Service, judges etc. What really changed the relationship between royal finances and government was that with Britain's growth as a world power, the £800,000 Civil List became insufficient to maintain the trappings of the Court and the expanding civil side of government. Two things happened as a result. Firstly, certain expenses (for instance the salaries of colonial administrators) were funded by Parliament voting the money annually. Parliament did

6

not wish to increase the Civil List for the purpose, as this would give the King more influence at a time when there was a substantial opposition to his existing powers. So increasing amounts of civil expenditure, as well as all of military expenditure, were funded *directly* from Parliament, and not via the Civil List. These 'miscellaneous supply grants' from Parliament rose from £177,000 in 1770 to £848,000 in 1799.[6] Secondly, the Civil List under George III accumulated debts far greater than those in previous reigns. When the King's ministers asked Parliament to pay off these debts, it gave the Commons a lever with which to extract some degree of scrutiny over how the Civil List was spent.

Previously, Parliament had fixed the annual amount at the beginning of the reign, for the duration of the reign. Yet any accountability as to how the money was spent was resisted on the grounds that it was the King's own money, from his Hereditary Revenues, and therefore none of Parliament's business. Amongst the leading parliamentary opponents of the personal powers of George III at this time was Edmund Burke. In 1782 his measure was passed by Parliament, requiring audited accounts of Civil List expenditure to be submitted to Parliament, though in practice the measure had little effect and the King still accumulated debt on his Civil List.

The King's Privy Purse, which was considered to be more in the nature of his personal income, was not to be subject to scrutiny. A distinction, for the purposes of accountability, was being made between the King's more personal finances and his public financial role. However, this public financial role was still maintained, salaries of civil servants, judges, ministers etc. being paid out of the Civil List. And even beyond the areas financed by the Civil List, the government was still the King's government in much more than name, so much so that the year after Burke's Act, George III was able to dismiss his ministers and appoint Pitt the Younger as Prime Minister.

The scale of the Napoleonic Wars in the 1790s meant sharply increasing civilian expenditure, even if it did not rise as fast as military expenditure. By 1800, Parliament was responsible for far more of civil government finance than was the King through the Civil List. This, of course, was one of the reasons for the decline of the powers of the monarch, as government ministers became more dependent upon Parliament than the King for finance. More important was the fact that, as a result of the gradual abolition of sinecures and the removal of other abuses, the executive had fewer powers of patronage with which to control Parliament and make the state more efficient. The decline of royal power would have occurred anyway, even if George III's mind had not become so afflicted. The 'limited' monarchy of 1688 became more limited still.

The separation of government expenditure from the King's personal expenditure at last became formalized in 1830, with William IV's Civil List, which was allotted purely for the benefit of 'the dignity and state of the Crown, and the personal comfort of their Majesties'. It did not have to finance any government expenditure, except for some negligible amounts, and was therefore much reduced from that of George IV's Civil List, granted in 1820. William IV's was the first modern Civil List and is similar to the one received by the Queen today,[7] though up until 1841 the monarch still provided election funds from the Privy Purse, as had George III, to support the party of his or her choice. Queen Victoria's provision of £15,000 to the Whigs seems to be the last example of this.[8]

The Birth of the Monarchy's Private Financial Status and Private Fortune

The gradual parting of the still small, but expanding, state from the finances of the King and his Household manifested itself in another way. In this case the King himself initiated the change, by asking for a *private* financial status. It required a special Act of Parliament in 1800 to produce this additional status. Up until then, even after 1688, the monarch and the state had been so much entwined that the King really only had a *public* legal identity, as head of the government. For instance, it was not certain legally if he could make a valid and binding will.[9] It was argued that he did not own property, landed and otherwise, as a private person but as King. Therefore when he died his worldly goods should go to his successor, regardless of his wishes.

The 1800 Act allowed George III to make a will and also to own landed property privately. Previously his problem was that lands he had bought, hoping to own them privately,[10] instead became Crown Lands. This was very disadvantageous to the King, for the Crown Lands and their profits had been placed in government hands, under the Civil List arrangements of 1760. Any rents he derived from estates he wished to buy privately would have to go to the Crown Lands. Though he might otherwise enjoy his privately acquired estates whilst alive, on his death, because of the problem with monarch's wills, such estates would become merged into the government-controlled Crown Lands. Nor could he sell such estates before he died, because of the 1702 Civil List Act preventing Crown Lands from being sold or otherwise alienated. The purpose underlying the 1800 Crown Private Estates Act was to allow the King to become a private person in the sphere of ownership, as well as a public person who was head of the government.

So he could now make a will to dispose of all his private wealth, as opposed to wealth* he owned purely as King, like the Palaces. To facilitate this, with regard to land, the Act made a distinction between estates owned privately by the King and the old Crown Lands, whose connection with the King was becoming more and more tenuous and which became purely nominal after 1830. As this new private legal identity of the monarch was starting to be created, it was considered absolutely proper that he pay tax on any income from personal landed property. In fact the wording of the 1800 Act could not have been clearer – that he was to be taxed in respect of his private real estate, as if it 'had been the Property of any Subject of this Realm'.

Income tax had just been introduced, in 1799, to finance the Napoleonic Wars. Its application to George III's landed property constituted a new departure. Hitherto the King, who was the focal point of government and who still received tax revenue to meet the expenses of civilian government, had never paid any of the existing government taxes. For him to have done so could be regarded as simply moving the money from one of his pockets to another. And, until 1800, in relation to the monarch, the law did not distinguish a private pocket from a public pocket. Of course, not all Civil List income went on judges and civil servants' salaries and the like; about half went on the expenses of the Court. But the Court was still very much bound up with government, even if Opposition politicians in the late eighteenth century had tried to change that. The 1800 Crown

---

* Nonetheless, there was much confusion over George III's will, made fifty years before his death. It was valid despite being drawn up before the 1800 Act, because the Act was retrospective. But most of the beneficiaries were dead, and George III had not managed to sign a new one in 1810, before his illness had permanently seized hold of his mind. The new King was not named in the will and all that passed to him he therefore received in his capacity as King. However, George IV simply regarded it all as being his personally. The ministers were too timid to object (Philip Whitwell Wilson, ed., *The Greville Diary*, i (1927), pp. 107–8). The wills of subsequent monarchs seem not to have encountered any similar difficulties.

Private Estates Act established that where the King was clearly a private person, the logic of tax exemption did not apply, as in the case where he became a private landowner. However, the King still retained tax exemption on stocks and shares, for it could be argued that the minor income it brought in was an income to the Civil List.

Finally, in 1830, the new, reduced form of the Civil List was brought in for William IV. This no longer funded any of the expenses of government; just the King's 'dignity' and 'personal comfort'. Therefore, the logic of tax exemption abruptly ceased, not just on rents from any private landholdings, but on other forms of income. But what had also ceased was income tax itself, in 1816, after the end of the Napoleonic Wars. So the question of extending the King's income tax liability obviously never arose in 1830, nor when Victoria became Queen in 1837.

On the reintroduction of the tax by Sir Robert Peel in 1842, it was logical, given the post-1830 financial position of the monarch, for the Prime Minister to get Queen Victoria to pay the tax on her own income, which she did, including on the bulk of her £385,000 Civil List. Moreover, Peel used his announcement of Queen Victoria's 'volunteering' to pay like everyone else as a means of making the tax more palatable. The tax was of course not popular, especially in peace-time, even though it was supposed to be only temporary and only to affect the minority who had an assessed income of over £150 a year; even then, it was applied only to the extent of 7d in the pound, or 3 per cent. Her Majesty's resolve to set a good example withstood the temporary doubling of the rate, due to the Crimean War, in the next decade.

Albert Asks for More

In two long begging letters of December 1849 and January 1850 to Lord John Russell, the Prime Minister, Albert, the Prince Consort, had grumbled in passing about his and the Queen's tax payments.[11] Albert, it was understood by government ministers, very much spoke for the Queen, and was the dominant partner, politically, until his early death. His mention of their both paying tax involved no objection to the principle of paying tax. It was simply part of his general argument for an increase in his government annuity from £30,000 to £80,000. There are considerable difficulties in translating the value of such sums from the nineteenth (and early twentieth) century into contemporary figures.

The very approximate figures that are conventionally used suggest we should multiply 1850 amounts by fifty to arrive at the equivalent for 1991. Therefore we may say that in modern terms, Albert was asking for an increase from about £1.5 million to £4 million. It is also very important to bear in mind that Britain was an incomparably poorer society in the mid-nineteenth century than it is today. The sums he was asking for, *relative* to the level of income existing then, were far greater in value than £1.5 million and £4 million would be today.

Despite there being no quarrel over income tax, Lord John Russell did not relish the prospect of facing the House of Commons to argue for Albert's request and wisely advised him to be patient. Albert made the plea that he needed more money for 'the ordinary establishment and pursuits of an English gentleman'. These he listed as 'a Hunting Establishment, a pack of Hounds, a breeding Stud, Shooting establishment, a Moor or Forest in the Highlands of Scotland, a Farm etc. etc. etc.'. The archives of prime ministers and chancellors of the Exchequer contain many such piteous pleas from needy royals.

What had set in motion the Prince's pay request was the recent death of Queen Adelaide, William IV's widow. The government was now saved the £100,000 a year it had given her, but Albert was loath to see this money leave the royal sphere, even though he acknowledged that it would soon be wanted for another royal use – namely, annuities for his and Victoria's large brood, when they reached adulthood.

As the figures bear out, Victoria was saving money out of her Civil List, enabling her and Albert to acquire private properties with public money. Osborne, a sizeable home on the Isle of Wight, was the first of these, becoming a Crown Private Estate, as defined by the 1800 Act. It initially cost £45,000,[12] but its ultimate cost, including the building of Osborne House, 'designed at vast expense in Italian renaissance style', was £200,000.[13] In today's prices, this would be £10 million.

In discussing Queen Victoria's finances at some length, Albert wished to make it clear that her being able to afford Osborne should not be used to turn down his pay request. It 'ought rather to be gratefully recognized by the Country which might have been expected to *provide* and I am sure would not have wished to see the Sovereign of England *without* a Marine Residence'. Soon the Queen was not without a Highlands residence either, the royal couple evidently being well enough off to be able to find £31,500 (£1.5 million in today's money) for the freehold on Balmoral's

17,400 acres in June 1852, after having leased it for four years. Albert had previously bought the adjoining 6,000 acres.[14]

The Queen was also able to indulge her weakness for jewellery around this time. Six months before Albert's written request to Russell for more money, the Queen had paid £1,400 (about £70,000 in current prices) for a suite of diamonds and rubies. And, three months after his rather aggressive but unsuccessful demands, she had bought a large emerald brooch and matching earrings, followed soon after by a very fine suite of opals costing £1,056.[15]

Nevertheless, in 1850, there is no doubting Albert's sense of grievance. He recalled, in a rather pained fashion, to Lord John Russell how the latter had told the Queen, back in 1841, that grants to the royal family 'were particularly obnoxious to the People'. Having to struggle along with the existing sums of money was particularly galling to Albert because 'the Country takes from the Sovereign his [sic] hereditary Revenues and gives him no means to acquire a private fortune; till very recently he could make no will . . .'.

Albert's disgruntlement at not being given the means whereby he and the Queen could 'acquire a personal fortune' might seem strange. After all, thanks to the Civil List, they were probably the best-off people in the country, and lived accordingly. Traditionally, monarchs had not accumulated wealth in the same way as landowners, merchants and factory-owners did. The funds of kings had also been the funds of governments, which had many calls upon them – legitimate government expenses, but also many sinecures and pensions for favoured members of the aristocracy and gentry. Kings therefore tended to pile up debts, while some, like Victoria's uncle, George IV, who died in 1830, were profligacy itself. Albert seems to be envisaging, at least financially, a new type of monarchy, though when it came to the Queen's role in government, Victoria and Albert (even though he had no official constitutional position whatever) clung to an outmoded version of it. They wanted not just more money, but more power too.

Albert's desire for capital was soon answered, not by the government but by an eccentric miser, John Camden Neild, who died on 30 August 1852 and left the Queen practically all his fortune of half a million pounds – a very great sum in those days.[16] Thea Holme's book on Chelsea, where Neild lived, tells us that he inherited his father's fortune:

which included a number of properties in the Home Counties. He devoted the rest of his life to being a landlord and collecting his rents. He walked miles to save coach fares, carrying his luggage in a brown paper parcel, and expecting his tenants to give him bed and board for the night. At Cheyne Walk [Chelsea] he lived alone in the tall empty house with its dirty windows festooned with cobwebs . . .[17]

'Miser Neild', as he was known, passed away having repeatedly declined to call a doctor, presumably on the grounds of cost. Victoria was congratulated by her uncle, King Leopold of Belgium, on being left a 'great fortune . . . It gives the possibility of forming a private fortune for the Royal Family, the necessity of which no one can deny'.[18] The Belgian King's letter added, with a touch of envy, 'such things only still happen in England . . .'*

Most authors have suggested that Albert and Victoria could manage to buy Balmoral only because of the Neild windfall. But in fact it was bought two months before Neild died,[19] from the income that Albert had described as so inadequate to Lord John Russell.

Both Osborne and Balmoral were bought after a good deal of haggling over price, which was not unusual in property transactions. Albert was not shy about using the royal status in his bargaining, which gave him a distinct edge. He used two methods. First, he and the Queen took a leasehold on the property and moved in. He knew 'full well', as David Duff put it, 'that once the British Queen was installed, little short of dynamite could evict her'.[20] Thus the vendors could not really sell it to anyone else and had to settle for rather less than they otherwise might have got. Second, Albert could also involve senior government ministers in the negotiations, which must have been daunting to the vendors. After Albert's death in 1861, Sandringham was bought for the Prince of Wales, but without the Prince Consort's ability as a royal property dealer they paid over the odds for the estate.[21]

---

* Perhaps they are still happening. One recent case which came to light was that of a dockworker, Frederick Adams, who in 1984 left his life savings of about £10,000 to the Queen. The lonely bachelor's 'drab house', as the *Daily Telegraph* described it, was decorated with magazine and newspaper photos of the Queen and with National Front slogans. His aunt, who lived next door, and neighbours were reported as being appalled at his leaving his money to such 'a very rich lady'. The *Daily Telegraph* thought that Her Majesty would pass the money on to charity.

Balmoral was bought in Albert's name because the 1800 Crown Private Estates Act came to be inapplicable in Scotland, meaning that the Queen could not own private landed property there. As a result of some mishap in the drafting of an Act early in Victoria's reign, whatever she bought north of the border would simply become swallowed up by the government-controlled Crown Lands. This obstacle to the Queen's becoming a private landowner in Scotland was obligingly removed by an Act in 1862, soon after the Queen inherited the Balmoral estates back from Albert on his death. Similarly, a private Act of Parliament had to be passed to allow Albert to acquire the estate in the first place, and another to close two public roads that would bring travellers too close to the estate.[22] And in 1873 a further Crown Private Estates Act was needed to remove a difficulty in the wording of the original 1800 Act.

A good deal of senior Civil Service and other ministerial time was, and still is, spent on unravelling such problems for the royal family. Such high-quality advice was and is given free. The long march to the present monarch's privileged financial and tax status has required a lot of such help. This assistance has also drawn a shroud of secrecy over the monarch's affairs, the 1862 Act laying down that the monarch's will need not be published.

Some of Neild's money was spent on a new castle at Balmoral, though there was already a firm intention to go ahead on that project.[23] Albert complained that 'the workers who have to be brought here from a distance and to camp in wooden barracks, have already struck several times, which is now quite the fashion all over the country'.[24] Although President of the Society for Improving the Condition of the Labouring Classes, Albert did not appreciate it when they took matters into their own hands and delayed the building of his new castle.

As Albert saw it, one of the ways for the working classes to be rescued from poverty was for them to be encouraged in the virtues of thrift. Thus he greatly favoured trustee savings banks, which unlike the other banks encouraged small-scale savers to deposit their savings with them. He was personally connected with one of the largest of these, St Martin's Place Savings Bank.[25] Perhaps he saw the Queen's saving on her Civil List as just the sort of thriftiness that the working class should show in regard to their more modest incomes in order for them too to be able to solve their housing needs, if not quite on the scale of their royal mentor.

A smaller amount of Neild's bequest was spent at Osborne. There were also other items like jewellery, but the large bulk of it must have remained to form the basis for Victoria's personal capital. In 1862, just after Albert's death, the Queen's Keeper of the Privy Purse confirmed to the Chancellor of the Exchequer, W.E. Gladstone, 'The Queen has private means as you know.'[26] The monarchy had shed its public spending role in 1830 for one of private accumulation.

Thus in 1879 we can observe the Queen as a private person financially, represented by her own private solicitor (a Mr White of White and Broughton). The legal issue on this occasion concerned who was entitled to some shares in the Waterloo Bridge Company, originally held by George IV.[27] The Law Officers of the Crown (Attorney-General and Solicitor-General) are only nominally the legal advisers to the Queen and are really part of the government. Hence her and subsequent monarchs' need for their own private solicitors. The Law Officers have been involved in the matter of royal finances, but in the role of interpreting relevant matters of law for the Treasury. They may not have been representing the royals, but this has not stopped them being highly sympathetic to royal needs, especially in taxation matters.

Dilke's Accusation

In 1871, at the height of republican feeling in Britain, the Queen's finances were a major political issue. Her unending widowed seclusion led to the question, widely asked, of what she needed all the Civil List money for. If the Queen was not participating in the pomp of monarchy, she was not paying for it either. Repeated approaches to Parliament to provide for her nine children brought further unpopularity. Two such requests were made in 1871. The occasion of Princess Louise's marriage meant a dowry of £30,000 (£1.5 million in today's prices) and an annuity of £6,000 a year.[28] In the summer, fifty-four MPs voted to reduce the £15,000 a year which Gladstone proposed when Prince Arthur came of age.[29] Later in her reign, after prolonged royal pressure, the government gave £36,000 a year to the Prince of Wales for maintaining his adult children.[30] Criticism of these grants focused on the fact that the Queen had enough money of her own with which to look after the royal family, without the public having to foot the bill.

The bulk of Victoria's Civil List was earmarked by Parliament for the expenses and the wages/salaries of the Royal Household. But because

Victoria did not spend all this money for these purposes she had by 1871 saved £509,000 (£22 million at 1991 prices). The fact that she transferred this sum to her Privy Purse,[31] a fund for her personal use, made Gladstone most anxious to conceal the matter.

As it was, the government openly and directly gave £60,000 a year to the Privy Purse*; and payments from the Duchy of Lancaster profits, which rose sharply towards the end of her reign, also funded it. Together with what was left from the Neild windfall, Victoria used such sums to build up her private fortune.

The radical MP Sir Charles Dilke joined in the republican agitation over the Queen's misuse of public money. And, also in November 1871, he accused Queen Victoria, on the basis of inadequate evidence, of not keeping to her 1842 commitment to pay income tax.[32] It was an understandable mistake, given the secrecy and deliberate evasions that surrounded the royal finances, though clearly he should have been more careful when it came to public criticism.†

How to counter Dilke most effectively became for about ten days a major concern for the ever-loyal Gladstone. The latter felt that the Queen's tax-paying, like her Civil List savings, would not stand up to too much inspection, for Victoria did not pay tax on Class II of the Civil List, from which the wages and salaries of the Household were paid, though the employees were taxed in the normal way. Gladstone thought the 1842 commitment to be taxed should include Class II.[33]

Robert Lowe, the Chancellor of the Exchequer, felt less apologetic than Gladstone, arguing, in a letter quoted here for the first time, that the details should be laid before the public. These included, as he pointed out to the Prime Minister, that the Queen also paid tax 'on her money in the funds' (i.e. her private investment in stocks and shares). As with everyone else, the tax was deducted at source and the dividends paid over net of tax. She paid also on the Duchy of Lancaster profits, as well as on rents received at Balmoral and on two-thirds of the Civil List.[34] The Queen

---

* Strictly speaking, this payment was part of the Civil List. But when referring to money saved on the Civil List, I do not include the money the monarch saved on this allowance, but only the money saved on the *other* parts of the Civil List, which were meant to cover wages/salaries and the expenses of the Royal Household.

† Not wishing to make the same mistake with regard to the present Queen, I checked with the Queen's press secretary in July 1990. Elizabeth II pays no income tax, nor does she make any voluntary contribution in lieu of tax.

was clearly a tax-paying individual, Lowe asserted: 'I see nothing that the Queen had done wrong and I should extremely regret to confine myself to general remarks which would certainly lead to the belief that there was something behind that would not bear daylight.' The Queen had, in her usual emphatic fashion, asked for a public defence of her reputation from the government, and was, understandably, extremely angry that she had been accused of not paying income tax. It was a 'deliberate falsehood' she told Gladstone.[35]

In the end, Lowe's speech, delivered at Halifax, was closer to Gladstone's desire for reticence than Lowe's enthusiasm for disclosure. He mentioned in very general fashion that the Queen had paid 'hundreds of thousands of pounds' in tax over the years.[36] The Queen at any rate was 'certainly pleased' with the speech.[37] Subsequently, Dilke was informed privately by a friend at the Treasury (early in 1872) that the Queen did pay income tax on her private investments and he duly apologized for this error,[38] even though this still left many criticisms of the Civil List arrangements for which he had no need to repent. He tried to obtain and was promised some formal clarification, from the Permanent Secretary to the Treasury, which would give the facts of what the Queen paid tax on and what she did not. However, Gladstone himself blocked the release of the information.

Nevertheless, Victoria paid income tax on nearly all her income. She did so despite never filling in the normal tax assessment form from the Inland Revenue. She was considered exempt from this particular requirement, on account of what was known as 'Crown immunity'.[39]

Royal Prerogative/Crown Immunity

Crown immunity in general, and Crown immunity from taxation in particular, needs some explanation, for during the twentieth century the latter has been invoked within government and by the monarch, but rarely publicly, to justify the moves from a tax-paying monarchy to a tax-exempt one.

Crown immunity was originally part of the whole panoply of powers exercised by the monarch and summed up in the notion of the 'Royal Prerogative'.[40] For centuries it has been accepted in law that the Crown is not usually bound by any particular Act of Parliament, unless it is specifically named in it.[41] Under monarchical government this was the harsh reality of rule by a king – laws generally were made for subjects, not for kings.

As discussed earlier, one law in 1800 did specifically mention the King. The Crown Private Estates Act gave George III what he wanted – the ability to own private landed property and to make a will. In return, William Pitt's government exacted the concession that the King's private estates should be taxed as if they 'had been the property of any subject of this Realm'. The Act specified *landed* private property because in practice, at the time, that was the only type of property that could be distinguished as wholly and indisputably in the private ownership of the King.

Within the Treasury, Crown immunity has increasingly been invoked in this century to argue that, because only landed property is specified, other forms of private income and Civil List income are exempt. But the mystical references to Crown immunity and the monarchy in a twentieth-century context are confused and fallacious. Crown immunity has always referred to the entity of government.

When there had been monarchical government, there was no point in a king's taxing himself, in the same way as it is a futile exercise for a modern government to tax itself. In neither case is any revenue actually raised. However, after 1830 government finance is organized quite separately from the monarch, and the rationale for the monarch's tax exemption ceases. This is especially true as regards purely private investment income.

With the growth of constitutional monarchy, the powers of the Royal Prerogative, such as Crown immunity, have effectively been appropriated by government departments etc., which are said to exercise power on behalf of the Crown. They have used it to escape the pointless exercise of paying tax, and for other purposes – for instance, to evade their responsibilities in matters of health and safety, much legislation on these matters, because of Crown immunity, not being applicable to hospitals or to the armed forces until recently. The prisons are still not covered by a good deal of health and safety law. One certainly does not applaud this use of Crown immunity. Rather, it is merely noted that the Crown, in relation to these powers of government, has in a functional and practical sense come to mean the state machine.

The increased reference to an impersonal 'Crown' and its powers from the early nineteenth century onwards reveals this fact. Formerly, there had been less need for such a disembodied term and it had been appropriate to talk of the power of 'the King' or 'the Queen'.[42] The growing use of the term 'Crown' during the nineteenth century, noted by the legal historian F.W. Maitland, was thus a means of recognizing the relative powerlessness of the monarch, yet maintaining her as a symbol of the state. And even then, judges, politicians and others, when desiring to express themselves more clearly, easily slipped into using the terms 'the government' or 'the public' instead.[43] In fact, one Law Lord in 1977 argued that:

> to continue nowadays to speak of 'the Crown' as doing legislative or executive acts of government, which, in reality as distinct from legal fiction, are decided on and done by human beings other than the Queen herself, involves risk of confusion.[44]

In other contexts, it would be important to highlight the residual political powers of the monarch and how they might be brought back to life if, for instance, there were a 'hung' Parliament. Yet no matter how one might envisage the resurrection of royal power, one would hardly argue that government finance, wholly or partly, would once again be channelled through the Civil List and the monarch's money once more become indistinguishable from the government's. The basis of the monarch's Crown immunity from taxation has therefore long since vanished. This is why on its few public outings the argument for it is merely stated, without elaboration or explanation.

For instance, the Treasury evidence to the 1971 Select Committee on the Civil List states baldly that, 'as part of the Royal Prerogative, the Queen is not liable to pay tax unless Parliament says so explicitly or by inevitable inference'.[45] But the assertion that this is absolute and unquestionable, unless legislation changes it, is false. This is not a purely theoretical argument, as was shown in 1901, when the Conservative government, for its own reasons, did not accept that Edward VII could claim Crown immunity from taxation.

2

Edward VII, 1901–10:

Precedent and Government 'Advice'

Official papers show that government ministers and civil servants were careful in their dealings, most of the time, to observe that Victoria's income-tax payments were voluntary (except on her private estates). As the Comptroller of the Exchequer, Lord Monteagle, put it in 1856, 'Her Majesty's contribution' should be seen 'as an act of grace and patriotism on the part of the Queen' and not as a legal obligation.[1] Like most people, the Queen may not have been quite so enthusiastic about paying as the above official suggested. Her reluctance took a royal form – she told Lord Rosebery towards the end of her reign that she felt it 'rather derogatory to her dignity' to pay the tax.[2] Since the sum in question still represented only 5 per cent in the last year of her reign, the damage to her dignity was relatively limited.

By the time Victoria died, she had been paying tax for nearly sixty years, which raises the question of whether a constitutional convention had thereby been established. With an unwritten constitution, the workings of the monarchy are governed in large measure by conventions, which are rules based on established practice, not contained in statutes or in the common law. In this imprecise area, it seems as good an argument as any to say that nearly sixty years of conformity to a particular practice would establish a convention. Indeed, Lord Melbourne, after his spell as Victoria's first Prime Minister, warned her of this at the outset, in 1842. He said her 'determination' to pay tax 'was right', but 'at the same time it is *giving up* a principle of the Constitution, which has hitherto exempted the Sovereign'[3] (my emphasis). Clearly, Melbourne was aware that in constitutional matters affecting the monarch certain decisions taken, which then became settled practices, might very well become conventions.[4]

Moreover, those powers of the Royal Prerogative which could supposedly allow the monarch to escape taxation no longer belonged to the monarch. As in nearly all other matters, such powers had effectively passed to government ministers. At the end of the day, if the government tells (or, to use the conventionally euphemistic term, 'advises') the King or Queen to pay tax, then pay they will. So it was with a Conservative government in 1901.

In that year Edward VII at last became King, after decades of ceaseless extravagance. It will be recalled that, since the 1800 Act, the monarch was free to dispose of his or her personal wealth. Victoria left her private fortune, described as 'considerable' in another Treasury memorandum,[5] not to her successor but to her surviving younger children,[6] though she did leave Edward her private estates, Balmoral and Osborne.

At the beginning of each reign, a fixed annual sum for the Civil List was worked out for the life of the sovereign. (Only in the last twenty years has it been increased during a reign.) Exactly how much money is needed for 'the support of the dignity of the Crown' is a matter for hard bargaining, particularly on the royal side. Conservative governments had traditionally tended to be rather more generous to the royals than Liberal ones; and the Conservatives were very generous to Edward VII in 1901. However, even Conservative chancellors of the Exchequer often find themselves resisting royal demands – if only to protect the royals themselves from parliamentary scrutiny and criticism when Civil List measures have to be approved by the House of Commons. One demand they were unable to resist was that of Queen Alexandra, Edward VII's wife. She rejected point blank the offer of £60,000 a year as her dower, the pension she would receive should she outlive her husband (which she did). She held out for, and got, £70,000 a year[7] – worth about £3.8 million in current prices. A subsequent royal demand, revealed here for the first time, involved the new King's unsuccessful attempt to escape income tax on his Civil List.

During the general bargaining process Edward certainly had an ally at the Treasury in Sir Edward Hamilton, joint permanent secretary and, as Auditor of the Civil List, responsible for overseeing royal finances. Hamilton had been appointed as an informal tutor in 1894 to help Edward's eldest son learn something about the Constitution,[8] a task he found rather daunting in its difficulty. He seemed to know everyone who was anyone, having been to Eton and been private secretary to two prime ministers (Gladstone and Rosebery). He had also been invited on a number of occasions to Edward's country home at Sandringham.

Hamilton noted that there was considerable 'waste and extravagance' in the way the Civil List had been spent.[9] Instead of advocating strict economy in the Treasury tradition, he argued for more funds to be devoted to the Civil List. It might have been difficult to advocate to his new King, at a meeting which started with the royal Auditor going down on one knee to 'kiss hands',[10] that he should economize. Rather, Hamilton favoured the strategy of disguising the increased money to be given to the King, so the increase would not be noticed. This plan was implemented in part by the government's meeting the bill for certain Royal Household items like pensions and postage, which hitherto had been paid from the Civil List. As part of the same process, he wanted the King to be relieved of income tax.

As indicated in the introduction, and as we shall see further, top Treasury officials have tended to be very sympathetic to the royal point of view. Hamilton himself came to develop 'a profound feeling for the King'.[11] Before the Cabinet committee met to determine the Civil List, he worried over their 'timidity',[12] in face of anticipated Commons criticism of giving too much to the King.

The Cabinet committee of Lord Salisbury's Conservative government, which considered the whole question of the Civil List, decided on 13 February 1901 to maintain the practice of deducting income tax from it.[13] It would look extremely bad, at a time when the government was planning to increase income tax to meet the costs of the Boer War, for the symbolic head of the British Empire, in whose name the war was being fought, to stop paying income tax. The question of Crown immunity does not seem even to have been considered by the government, or by Hamilton.

Thus, a few days after this Cabinet decision, the Chancellor of the Exchequer, Hicks-Beach, wrote to the King employing the form of language required for such communications: 'Sir Michael Hicks-Beach understands that Your Majesty is graciously pleased to continue the declaration made by Her late Majesty that Income Tax should be paid on the amounts assigned in the Civil List . . .'[14] The reply came back from the King's private secretary confirming that the King entirely agreed with the Chancellor's various proposals for the Civil List, which of course included the continuation of income tax.[15] However, by May the King had either changed his mind or, as he claimed, he had consented earlier solely because 'he had only just succeeded to an entirely new position and had little knowledge of the matter. He would have agreed to anything and trusted the minister.'[16]

Hicks-Beach, though, had little alternative in the end but to hold the King to his February commitment. It was a question of saving the monarchy from its own greed. The problem for the reluctant royal tax-payer was the attitude of Sir William Harcourt, a leading veteran of the Liberal Opposition and himself a former Chancellor of the Exchequer. He had indicated that he would bring the matter up in the House of Commons, should the government decide to remove the income tax, even on part of the King's Civil List. Hicks-Beach had gone to see Harcourt and tried his best for the King, but found him 'unpersuadable'.[17] If the matter came to a vote, Harcourt would lose, but it would still have been a public-relations disaster for the monarchy, and not only because of the war that was being fought amidst such nationalistic fervour and talk of the nation pulling together. The King's popularity was already far from certain, partly due to a number of scandals which had become public (leaving many more which had been kept out of the press). In the supercharged patriotic atmosphere, it would be asked how he of all people could find his taxes a burden. Others far less wealthy had no choice but to pay, and many young men were doing so with their lives.

However, the new King, amazingly, could not see the point. According to Sir Francis Knollys, his private secretary, he thought that 'the views of Sir William [Harcourt] who is not one of the official leaders of the Opposition, ought not to be allowed to prevail with the Government against those of the responsible Leaders of the Liberal Party'. He insisted that the Cabinet reconsider and asked Lord Salisbury to come and see him.[18] All to no avail. The Cabinet in June reaffirmed that the King had to pay tax.[19] As has so often been the case with royal finances, government ministers much prefer to give the royals more money when they do not have to face the House of Commons, or when the Commons can be successfully deceived. They seek to save the monarch from adverse publicity, which would result from having their demands met by the otherwise willing Treasury. Ministers, it should be noted, are not generally thanked for this service. Lord Salisbury found, in July, that the King was still 'very sore' about the matter.[20] By now Edward at least seemed to have recognized the need for secrecy, but he maintained that if the government had pressed Harcourt, then the Liberal ex-Chancellor would silently have swallowed his objections. It is possible the King had decided to tackle Harcourt himself, because on 18 July, unusually, his private secretary wrote to Harcourt asking if the King could make an arrangement to see him and have a chat 'as an old friend'.[21]

But matters had been sealed, at least for the time being, by the Cabinet decision of mid-June. The King acknowledged that 'he must necessarily yield to the advice of his ministers', albeit 'under protest'.[22] Hicks-Beach's announcement in the House of Commons on 18 June put matters bluntly. When asked whether the King would continue to honour Queen Victoria's pledge to pay income tax, the Chancellor stated that, 'we have advised that a similar course should be taken now and that course will be followed'. The wording of the Chancellor's answer is important in the history of the royal tax situation. Hicks-Beach's statement avoided any of the usual courtly language about 'His Majesty graciously consenting' etc. By saying that the government had 'advised' the King, Hicks-Beach was declaring that it was a government decision and the King had no option but to go along with it. This the King specifically acknowledged in the letter already quoted.

In other words, it is no argument to say that the monarch does not have to pay tax because of the Crown immunity which attaches to the Royal Prerogative. As far as all the relevant factors were concerned in 1901, effective power had passed to the government and the monarch had to do as he was told. Much as the King raged against the decision, he did not try to invoke the Royal Prerogative to claim that the government had no right to tax him.

What this means is that any modern government could equally 'advise' the present Queen that she should pay tax on at least her private investment income, and also her Civil List (wholly or in part) if the government so desired.

We know for sure that Edward VII paid tax on the bulk of his Civil List and on any rental income from his private estates, Sandringham and Balmoral. Moreover, he paid tax on his income from private investments such as stocks and shares, as had Queen Victoria. The tax was simply deducted at source and not refunded. (This is revealed from much later evidence; see Chapter 5.) Taxation on personal investments was not discussed in 1901 or in 1904 because it was not a pressing problem for the

King. Edward would have received little in the way of investment income then, because his extravagance kept him in debt until 1907. Perhaps the matter was raised thereafter. Sir George Murray of the Treasury noted just after Edward's death that, as regards paying income tax generally, the late King had 'never ceased to protest against it'.[23]

The King, it has to be said, did not quite appreciate the investigative function of the parliamentary Select Committee set up to recommend the arrangements for the Civil List. At an earlier stage, he wrote to Hicks-Beach thanking 'the Chancellor of the Exchequer for the tact he has shown in dealing with the committee, a difficult body to manage he fears'.[24] The new King acknowledged the terrific waste that went on in the royal household and promised to make economies, but 'regrets and is surprised that in a country like England, so devoted to sport, the committee should have struck out from . . . the Civil List the Salary and Wages of the Master of the Buckhounds and the Hunt Servants together with the expenses of the Hunt . . . and have thrown the whole onus of their cost on the King'.

Nevertheless, in spite of this unsporting gesture, Sir Edward Hamilton at the Treasury predicted that the King would be appreciably better off than Victoria had been with her Civil List.[25] Hamilton was right, and the King was able to save money for himself from funds that Parliament had allocated, predominantly, for salaries and expenses of the Royal Household. This occurred despite assurances to the House made by the Chancellor of the Exchequer in 1901, that the King's Civil List was not so large as to allow 'accumulation of savings after the duties of the Crown had been adequately performed'.[26]

Still, this did not stop a further royal request, in 1904, for the release of the King from his reluctant undertaking to pay income tax.[27] Later in 1904 came further complaints about the King's money problems which, it was claimed, necessitated the removal of income tax or a general increase in the Civil List.[28] Yet in 1904 alone, Edward diverted £32,511 (at 1991 prices, £1.7 million) from the Civil List to his own pocket.* As Hamilton realized, the extra money obviously could not be needed to meet the expenses of the monarchy, but to further finance Edward's

---

* During his short reign, Edward VII was able to siphon off for himself £261,592 (at 1991 prices, over £13 million) from the Civil List from funds predominantly earmarked for salaries and expenses of the Household (Report from Select Committee on Civil List, 1910, p. xiii).

lavish lifestyle. As the King's Keeper of the Privy Purse bemoaned, 'the King has no idea of the value of money, and consequently gives orders wholly irrespective of expense which it is difficult to avoid executing'.[29]

The Treasury report which reviewed Edward's 1904 pay request is at the Public Record Office,[30] but it remains, eighty-seven years later, closed to public inspection. The monarch's profligacy is still supposed to remain a secret. Within less than a year came another royal demand, for a special grant from Parliament for repairs to the royal palaces in 1905. However, the Prime Minister, A.J. Balfour (who had in regal style succeeded his uncle, Lord Salisbury), refused, because when it was put to the Commons, as it would have to be, the Opposition would demand a parliamentary inquiry.[31] This would of course find that Edward was already receiving more than enough money from the Civil List, letting the King in for some barbed comments. So naturally the Prime Minister and Chancellor politely turned down Edward's repeated requests during 1904–5, just as Lord John Russell had been unwilling to face the Commons with Prince Albert's case fifty years earlier.

Hamilton thought there was more to the King's financial situation than met the eye and that he was in debt to someone or some people.[32] However, the royal financial crisis failed to materialize and by 1907, as Edward's official biographer tells us, he was at last out of debt. Edward's banker friends had helped him 'make handsome profits out of judicious investment'.[33] In the meantime, he had found another way of making money.

Arise, Sir Alfred Harmsworth, Baron Northcliffe

Edward's royal prerogative was no protection against paying tax on his Civil List. However, part of his prerogative consisted of his formal role as 'the fount of honours'. All honours, such as peerages and baronetcies, are supposed to derive from the King. For Edward, the point seems to have been the conversion of this status into hard cash. Perhaps he desired to emulate his illustrious ancestors. James I had created the rank of baronet in pre-Civil War England precisely for the purpose of selling it off. It was midway between the lowest rank of the peerage (baron) and a knighthood. As with a knighthood, its holder was to be called 'Sir' before his Christian name. It was more valuable than a knighthood, because it was hereditary, but it ranked below a peerage because it did not carry a place in the House of Lords.

However, the vast bulk of honours had long since been decided by the Prime Minister, such corruption as there was benefiting the party in office. The Prime Minister would send his lists of those to be given honours to the monarch, who might protest at this or that name or at the 'fount of honour' being pumped too much for the provision of honours. But at the end of the day, the monarch could seldom resist the 'advice' of the Prime Minister. Suggestions from the monarch on honours could be indulged as regards top courtiers, but very rarely otherwise. However, Edward showed that when he employed great persistence, over a period of time, the government could be persuaded occasionally to humour him by agreeing to his nominations for honours. After all, it was an area where considerations of policy were not necessarily involved.

1904 and 1905 were the years when Edward was pressing the government unsuccessfully for his Civil List to be increased. This was also the time when he pressed for honours for Alfred Harmsworth, the extremely wealthy proprietor of the *Daily Mail*. Although Harmsworth was neither a friend nor a courtier, the King obtained for him first a baronetcy in 1904,[34] then, in 1905, a peerage, making him Baron Northcliffe.

In his book *The House of Northcliffe*, Paul Ferris is sceptical about the suggestion that Harmsworth bribed the King. Though he mentions a family story about how Harmsworth obtained his peerage in 1905, which describes how Mrs George Keppel, the King's girlfriend, 'was involved on Alfred Harmsworth's behalf and that a hundred thousand pounds changed hands [over £5 million at 1991 prices] . . .' Ferris then goes on to say that 'one of Alfred's mistresses, a mysterious woman with aristocratic connections, could have played some part. But Alfred's tracks are well covered.'[35]

Ferris's comments did nothing to kill off the story in the Harmsworth family. Three years after his book came out, Cecil King, a nephew of Alfred Harmsworth, was having lunch with another of Alfred's nephews, Sir Geoffrey Harmsworth:

He confirmed the suspicion that Northcliffe bought his peerage from Edward VII for a hundred £1,000 notes. The money was needed for Mrs Keppel. Geoffrey said that Stern's barony of Michelham was bought at the same time. What is known is that Northcliffe's peerage was pressed on Balfour by Edward.[36]

This is interesting, because it was the same Geoffrey Harmsworth who had jointly written a long detailed biography of Northcliffe, which reached the conclusion that there was no evidence for thinking that the latter bought his title. The book had only considered Balfour and the Conservative Party as the possible vendor, not the King.[37]

The King Edward connection is revealed in the Balfour Papers in the British Library, which show that earlier, starting in December 1903, the King had strongly recommended Alfred Harmsworth for a baronetcy.[38] It was extremely unusual to move up from a baronet to a baron, as Harmsworth did, with the King's help, in only eighteen months. A multi-millionaire banker, Herbert de Stern, was recommended by Edward for a peerage at the same time.[39] Having been made a baronet on 30 June 1905, he had had to wait only five months for promotion to his barony of Michelham, 'bought at the same time'. Five months is the absolute record and, by itself, makes the whole affair look very fishy. (Michelham just pips Lord Beaverbrook, who with Lloyd George as Prime Minister went from baronet to baron in six months.)

The official history of *The Times* (of which Harmsworth was proprietor from 1908 to 1922) records that his Northcliffe peerage was bought and quotes an earlier remark of Harmsworth's: 'When I want a peerage I will pay for it like an honest man.' It is clear from the King's and other letters that if anyone was paid off it was the King, not Balfour or the Conservative Party.

An extra piece of evidence, not produced by Ferris or anyone else, is that Sir Edward Hamilton of the Treasury was informed by the Prime Minister's private secretary, J.S. Sandars, that the King had gone all out to get Harmsworth his earlier baronetcy; so much so that 'Balfour feels it almost impossible to decline'. Hamilton asked the same question: 'what does it mean? Evidently it must be on account of some service rendered to a lady.' Sandars handled a lot of the details of honours for the Prime Minister, and Hamilton learnt from Sandars 'that the baronetcy for Harmsworth which was so tremendously pressed by the King was as I imagined done at the instance of someone else for a very valuable consideration'.[40] The 'someone else' and 'a lady' involved in the purchase of the baronetcy could have been equally involved with the subsequent acquisition of the peerage. Both fit Mrs Keppel of the Harmsworth family story.

The idea that the money was for her is strengthened by the fact that the Keppels were short of money, their problems having been caused precisely by the 'elevation' of the wife to the part of royal mistress. Especially when Edward became King, she and her husband had to live in greater style than hitherto.[41] The King would have felt constrained to help out, but lacked the wherewithal from his own resources.

Moreover, if we examine Edward's reaction to a peerage for the previous newspaper proprietor to be ennobled, we can see how far he went to accommodate Harmsworth. In 1903 Sir Edward Levy-Lawson, a friend of the King's, became only the second newspaper peer. The King specifically asked Balfour to obtain an undertaking from Levy-Lawson, who was then 70 years old, that he take no further active part in the management of his paper, the *Daily Telegraph*.[42] The assumption seems to have been that it was not compatible to manage a newspaper and to be a peer. Such rigid standards were waived by Edward when he pressed the case of Harmsworth, just two years later.

Several writers have suggested that the immense power of the North-cliffe press would inevitably mean that governments would seek to gain his support by supplying honours to him free of charge. However, at the time this practice had yet to be established, there being only two press peers, from amongst a far greater number of newspaper proprietors than exist today. Secondly, Harmsworth was yet to attain the pinnacle of his power – he had not yet purchased *The Times*. Thirdly, and most important, he was a Tory. It was for inclusion in the Tory government's resignation honours list that the King pressed Harmsworth's name for a peerage. The proprietor of the *Daily Mail* could have had little hope of obtaining such an honour from the incoming Liberal government, which soon achieved its expected landslide victory at the polls.*

Hamilton was a long-time friend of the King's, generally approved of His Majesty and enjoyed his many visits to Sandringham and Balmoral. But he had suspected him, when he was Prince of Wales, of suggesting honours to the Prime Minister for material gain. For instance, in 1881

---

* In fact, the Liberal government did extend honours to some Tory press proprietors, including a baronetcy to Harmsworth's brother in 1910 and two others made peers in 1911. But this non-party generosity could not have been anticipated in 1905.

he confided to his diary, 'The Prince of Wales has recommended for baronetcies 4 men ... it is perhaps hardly fair to say so, but these recommendations have rather an ugly look about them.'[43]

There were other ways for Edward VII to exploit his status, other than selling titles. His friendship was socially valuable. Those who had the money but not social recognition found Edward, especially when he was Prince of Wales, quite accommodating. But they had to entertain him and his cronies lavishly, provide investment advice and help his more impecunious friends. One seeker of social acceptance in the highest circles was the Hungarian Jewish banker Baron Hirsch. He simply purchased an introduction to Edward in 1890, from Crown Prince Rudolf of Austria. Almost immediately he became Edward's 'unofficial adviser and confidant'. When he died in 1896, this position was passed on to his executor, another Jewish banker, Ernest Cassel (who converted to Catholicism). These relationships seem to have been hard-headed and unsentimental, based on what each could do for the other. Hirsch and Cassel could provide money in one form or another. In return, Edward drew them into his circle, thus giving them lightning social promotion which, especially for Hirsch, was gratifying in itself and also provided the kind of contacts which offered even better chances for the financiers to make money.

The Rothschilds and the Sassoons, also Jewish bankers, were also friendly with Edward. Sir Philip Magnus, Edward VII's official biographer, has thus spoken of the King's 'philo-semitism'.[44] It is true that on occasion 'Society', which took anti-semitism and many other prejudices pretty much for granted, was often dumbfounded by Edward's consorting with Jews. But when it came to a Royal Commission's proposals to impose 'stringent' control on Jewish immigration, Edward was enthusiastically in favour.[45] This was so despite a minority dissenting report, written by his friend Lord Rothschild and the Permanent Secretary of the Home Office, which rejected the case for controls.[46] Moreover, the general findings of the majority Commission's report refuted the anti-alien propaganda of the yellow press and the Conservative right-wing.[47] In examining Edward's social attitudes, it is more correct to speak of Edward's 'philo-bankerism'.

Magnus is closer to the truth in saying that Edward 'regarded money as the most practical and convenient social yardstick'.[48] He did not want to pull down the caste barriers of royalty and aristocracy, because his own pre-eminent social position was not primarily based on money but was inherited. Instead, what he did was to use his position as 'social gatekeeper' selectively to admit certain of the *nouveaux riches* into his social circle, and thus the upper realms of 'Society' generally, providing he was amply rewarded. He had a vested interest in the old caste barriers, if only to ensure that the socially insecure possessors of new wealth would seek his favour.

Another banker friend was Horace Farquhar of Parr's Bank, a founder of the British South Africa Company. His position at King Edward's Court did not, it seems, stop him, and in fact in 1907 assisted him, from making some money via dubious speculation. This concerned the shares of a gold-mining company, Siberian Proprietary Mines Ltd, and some linked companies. *The Times* describes the method employed:

> The whole affair has been very cleverly worked; statements were published heralding the appearance of the companies, but offering no shares for subscription, so that no legal liability under the Companies Act was involved, and the public, if it wanted shares, could only obtain them at the prices put on them by those who were arranging the drama. An attractive rise in prices was thus easily secured, and the movement was assisted by the appearance of prominent West End names on the boards of the various companies, one of the directors of the Siberian Proprietary Co. being closely connected with the Court [this was Knollys, the King's private secretary, whom *The Times* was too delicate to mention by name]. 'Tips' circulated at bridge parties, and elsewhere did the rest.[49]

Lord Carington, an old friend of King Edward's, observed that after the shares had been pushed up to an inflated price (£16) by the methods outlined above, 'they have fallen to under [£]7 and it is supposed Horace Farquhar has been at the bottom of it – It is deplorable that the King's private secretary and the Queen's Lord Chamberlain should have been "let in" and mixed up in an affair like this.'[50]

One wonders if Farquhar let the King in on the deal, for, as Magnus notes, he and Cassel helped Edward make 'handsome profits out of judicious investments'.[51] It is precisely the inside knowledge of well-placed financiers that yields the handsome profits. And indeed, Edward as King had privileged knowledge of his own to convey to financiers. Another biographer of Edward, Gordon Brook-Shepherd, mentions an instruction from the King to Cassel that he wished to receive the proceeds of a successful investment in cash. But Brook-Shepherd maintains that the papers of Sir Ernest Cassel reveal nothing untoward about Edward's financial dealings with Cassel;[52] he does not mention that Cassel's papers have been thoroughly 'weeded'.[53]

Edward, on his death in 1910, left, it is said, about £2 million[54] (at 1991 prices, £100 million). This is the figure given, at the time of controversy over the Queen's wealth in 1971, by John Colville (later Sir John Colville). He had been the Queen's private secretary when she was Princess Elizabeth, and his mother had been a long-serving courtier to Queen Mary. Colville stated that his information about the whole question of royal wealth came from a member of the royal family, though he declined to say which one. From the context, it is clear that Colville was talking only about investments, and was excluding the art treasures, jewellery etc. and also Balmoral and Sandringham from the figure. If £2 million is correct, this sum alone, relative to the amounts that the wealthiest were worth, would have put Edward VII close to the very top. And Magnus states that the King got out of debt only in 1907. At that time, £2 million was a gigantic sum to accumulate, whether honestly or dishonestly, in just three years.

We have two indications of where the money went or where it did not. George V's private secretary says in his diaries many years later, 'Edward VII never left his eldest son [George V] any money.'[55] There is a reference elsewhere to Edward's widow being left £200,000.[56] Edward had three daughters, plus of course his girlfriend, Mrs Keppel, who were likely beneficiaries. The new King received all the fabulous art treasures, jewellery and so on that traditionally were passed from one monarch to the next, plus Balmoral and Sandringham. Also, some of the money left, for example, to Edward's widow, Alexandra, may have reverted to the monarchy on her death. In any case, as we shall see, George V had other sources from which he could and did accumulate a private fortune of his own.

3

George V, 1910–36

The Royal Prerogative did not shift the monarch's obligation to pay tax on the Civil List. It was the Permanent Secretary to the Treasury, together with Lloyd George, Chancellor of the Exchequer in the Liberal government, who managed this at the beginning of the next reign, in 1910. George V's Civil List was fixed as follows:[1]

		£
Class I	Their Majesties' Privy Purse	110,000
	(£77,000 to the King, £33,000 to the Queen)	
Class II	Salaries of His Majesty's	
	Household and Retired Allowances	125,800
Class III	Expenses of His Majesty's Household	193,000
Class IV	Works (i.e. internal maintenance to Palaces)	20,000
Class V	Royal Bounty, Alms and Special Services	13,200
Class VI	Unappropriated	8,000
		470,000

Another £146,000 was paid in annuities to other royals. Also, the government paid out certain other money for the royals, including the upkeep of the royal yachts and the external maintenance of the Palaces. The total the royals received from the state was over £800,000. In today's terms £800,000 may not, of course, seem a great deal. The same might still be said if we add the money withdrawn from the Duchies of Cornwall and Lancaster for royal use, £92,085 and £64,000 respectively.[2] This would bring the total received by the royals to about £1 million, without including the unknown sum of what the King received by way of private income.

It is difficult to be precise in gauging what the equivalent sum would be eighty years later. The system generally used suggests that we should multiply 1910 prices by fifty, making the £800,000 provided by the state worth £40 million today. A more illuminating comparison can be made by looking at other forms of government expenditure. For instance, in 1910 the government paid out £8 million in old-age pensions to about 650,000 applicants.[3] Thus the £800,000 spent on the royals was about 10 per cent of the total pension bill. The money going to the royals can also be placed alongside general earnings at the time. A skilled manual worker, working for at least forty-eight hours a week, earned about £100 a year, without overtime. An agricultural labourer on the King's estate at Sandringham earned £42 a year.[4]

From the reintroduction of the tax in 1842 until 1910, income tax had been paid on Classes I and III of the Civil List. As regards Class II, only savings on this class (wages/salaries), which were transferred to the Privy Purse, were taxed. Total tax on the Civil List had cost Edward VII about £18,000 a year.[5]

Lloyd George, despite being feared by the royals as the incarnation of all things radical, was about to render the service of removing this charge on the Civil List. What would have been uppermost in the Chancellor's mind was that there were important constitutional issues facing the Liberal government, namely, the reform of the House of Lords and Irish Home Rule. The former was very much the issue of the year, and two elections were fought in 1910 about it. The King's role was of great importance. It may have been considered worthwhile to humour him by removing Civil List taxation, and the usually obliging Treasury had at the outset proposed the measure.[6] In accomplishing this task, the famed Lloyd George dexterity was much in evidence.

He described the sovereign's payment of income tax as 'purely voluntary'.[7] This may have been true of Victoria, but not, as we have seen, in the more recent, and thus more relevant, case of Edward VII. In the same Civil List debates, another minister concerned with royal financial matters, the Chancellor of the Duchy of Lancaster, said that Edward VII and Victoria had paid tax as 'an act of grace'. Yet nothing could have been less gracious than Edward VII's income-tax payments.

Lloyd George presented a new reason to persuade the Commons that it was absurd for the state to tax the Civil List allowance 'made to the Sovereign towards the maintenance of the dignity of the Crown. It is either adequate or it is not adequate for that purpose. If you deduct the sum of the Income Tax it seems to be giving with one hand and taking away with the other.'* An 1897 Treasury report on royal finances had likewise referred to the 'clumsiness' of such an arrangement, but then went on to ask whether others who worked for central government might not avail themselves of the same argument, as regards *their* taxation.[8] Moreover, whatever the general merits of this viewpoint, it would not be possible to apply Lloyd George's argument to Class I of the Civil List. This consisted of payments for the King and Queen's Privy Purse, which was almost exclusively for their personal expenditure and amounted to £110,000 out of the £470,000 for the Civil List as a whole. In 1901, even the Treasury in the form of Sir Edward Hamilton had described Class I as 'much more *bona fide* "income" than other parts' of the Civil List.[9] The other two main classes were specifically earmarked for wages/salaries and expenses of the Household.

The Chancellor also argued that there would be an exchange. The King, in return for not being taxed on the Civil List, would foot the bill for the costs of visiting heads of state and of return visits by the British King. Lloyd George claimed that this would be a more or less equal exchange. This, however, was simply not true, as even Sir George Murray's earlier Treasury memorandum, which proposed the exchange, had admitted. It was drawn up only two days after Edward VII's death, and bears the hallmark of a deal struck between Murray and Knollys, acting for the new King, as he had for his father. Knollys will have learnt from the failure in 1901 to get the tax removed the importance of acting quickly to take the initiative. Murray commended the trade-off to Asquith, the Prime Minister, 'in the interests of peace' between the Treasury and the Court.[10]

Just before George V became King, the House of Lords finally agreed to pass Lloyd George's 'People's Budget'. The Tory-dominated Lords had done so only after the first 1910 General Election had been fought

---

* Isaacs, the Solicitor-General, had drawn up a legal opinion for the government concerning whether the King was taxable, employing the argument of Crown immunity. Lloyd George, a lawyer himself, seems not to have thought this argument convincing, for he did not use it in the Commons debate.

on the issue, and the Tories had lost. This budget included extra taxes to finance rearmament, particularly to provide more dreadnoughts, and also for the old-age pensions initiated in 1908. Lloyd George's budget was something of a watershed in ushering in the modern era of much higher taxation[11] (which still applies, even if since 1979 much of the tax burden has been shifted from income tax to VAT and National Insurance). Apart from a new tax on increased land values, a super-tax on extremely high incomes was introduced. If George V was still paying income tax, the government would have thought it only logical to 'advise' him to pay the new tax as well, which would have increased the total amount of tax paid on the Civil List by 40 per cent, to about £25,000. Not as much documentation is available (though it must exist in the Royal Archives) as for the negotiations in 1901. But the prospect of a higher Civil List tax bill could not have pleased the King and his advisers.

This 1910 swap arrangement concerning income tax is certainly not one of the exchanges, unlike that of 1760 (see Chapter 6), that monarchists grumble about. In fact, they don't mention it. Moreover, along with so many other charges, the costs of visits of heads of state to Britain and of return visits are no longer borne by the monarch's Civil List but by a government department, in this case the Foreign Office. Up until 1972, a small portion of the costs of such visits was contributed from the Civil List as part of the 1910 swap, but even this was swept away in a bland announcement of the Select Committee Report of 1971. This change might have been less straightforward had the Labour members of that Committee been aware of the connection with the tax issue.

The Civil List during the First World War

Income and super-tax (initially paid on incomes above £5,000 a year, and subsequently on rather lower incomes) increased rapidly during the war. If the King had still been paying tax on the Civil List, it would have cost him a total of £478,000 for the war years. Moreover, the King was enabled to make an actual cash saving on account of the war, because he incurred far fewer expenses (no visits from heads of state, fewer Court functions and generally less entertaining). The King in early 1916 wished to hand back the savings thus accumulated during the war. He and his advisers would have been aware that Victoria had incurred great unpopularity when, because of her seclusion, she was judged to be hoarding money; and there had already been press comment on the fact that George III had given back to government part of his Civil List during the Napoleonic Wars. In fact he had pledged to hand back £20,000 in 1798. Sir Frederick Ponsonby, the Keeper of the King's Privy Purse, looked into this and told the Chancellor of the Exchequer, now Reginald McKenna, that it could not have been a genuine sacrifice by George III, but 'was done by jugglery with figures in some way'.[12] Thus did that King set a precedent for other such gestures.

George V, thinking the public would want to know what happened to the savings he had made since the war began, planned to make a public statement that such savings (without specifying the amount) would be returned to the Exchequer. On the surface, this seemed a perfectly commendable action, but Asquith and McKenna were less than impressed. They perceived that the whole question of income tax could be revived, especially with the mounting tax burden on the population. They thought that after the eulogies in the press on the King's repayment to the Exchequer, other wealthy people including Members of Parliament would be exhorted to follow suit. Such pressure would be resented by many of the latter, whose reply in Parliament and the press would be 'that the King did not pay income tax and that he would not even now be paying what might fairly be expected of him'.[13] Also, even had they considered the King's gesture genuine, encouraging them to give their money away was not one of the roles this class of people wanted the monarchy to play.

Asquith and McKenna at first recommended that the King should relatively quietly give the Civil List savings away to a charity like the Naval and Military Pension Fund.[14] But on the whole it was the King's view which prevailed. After a meeting between the King and Asquith, it was decided publicly to announce that a sum of money would be repaid to the government. Sir Frederick Ponsonby, representing the King, had originally suggested the figure of £50,000. But the Prime Minister and Chancellor managed to extract £100,000. The King had not liked the charity option because he felt that 'any subscription . . . to some particular charity would not have the desired effect upon the public, who might be suspicious and imagine that this did not represent the total savings on the Civil List'. However, this was precisely the state of affairs with the savings in the Civil List made *after* he paid over the agreed £100,000, in April 1916.

Thereafter, George V made further savings of £155,000 on wages and expenses of the Royal Household.[15] During the whole of the period 1914–18, £77,000 (according to George V's biographer, Kenneth Rose) was donated to charities. This therefore left a surplus for the King of £78,000 from the £155,000 savings of 1916–18, which were not returned to the Exchequer. This figure of £78,000 can be compared to the amount paid to an ordinary soldier for the duration of the war – £78.

As for the donation of £100,000, the King was right. It did not lead, as Asquith and McKenna had at first feared, to a bout of mutual recrimination within the upper classes, cheered on by socialists and pacifists, about who was supposedly sacrificing the most. But we can perceive the way that government, understandably, saw the royal tax issue in war-time as highly sensitive, as had Hicks-Beach and the Tory Cabinet during the Boer War.

During the war the King was able to buy more valuable stamps to add to his vast collection. In his book on the subject, Sir John Wilson, the Keeper of the Royal Philatelic Collections, records that during this time the King bought at least ten whole collections from various people and had his pick of many other collections that had come up for sale.[16]

Shall the King go to Open Parliament in a Taxi-cab?

In 1920, after the war was over, there was, according to the version provided by Sir Frederick Ponsonby, a financial crisis in the Civil List. On behalf of the King, Sir Frederick asked as a matter of urgency for a large increase. The King had had to concede wage increases; similarly, price rises had hit the various expenses of the Household, and there was also the expense of internal repairs and maintenance to the Palaces that had been delayed during the war. The combined deficit on the Civil List for 1919 and 1920 was anticipated to be about £60,000. Ponsonby stated that the King could meet this figure, but after that it was a question of 'vast' cuts, including disposing of the royal horses, carriages and cars.

In reality there was no financial crisis because the Civil List savings for 1910–18, even after the refund to the Treasury and donations to war-time charities, provided a very adequate cushion of over £220,000. The real problem was that most of this sum seems to have gone into George V's private pocket. Ponsonby's letter to the Treasury did not acknowledge the savings made from 1910 to 1914, only those made during the war. And as regards these, although Ponsonby insisted that 'the King decided to give away all the savings on the Civil List', he immediately qualified this picture of royal unselfishness. It was a case of the King 'merely keeping the normal balance which it has been customary from time immemorial for the Sovereign to put by to meet abnormal expenditure and eventually to form a sum which could be left to his grandchildren, who will receive no grant from Parliament'.[17] Never had such an argument been put in public regarding any portion of the Civil List. It might be thought that only Class I of the Civil List plus the Duchy of Lancaster revenues, which also went to the Privy Purse, would be used for the problematic grandchildren. However, money also came from Class II, earmarked for wages and salaries, and Class III, provided for expenditure of the Household on food, transport etc.

Moreover, George V did not yet have any grandchildren. Of the nine he did eventually have, there would appear to have been little cause for alarm.* Also, this less than urgent need to accumulate had probably been accomplished before George even became King.

As Prince of Wales (1901–10), George received a government annuity together with the revenues of the Duchy of Cornwall, which largely consisted of property in the West Country and south London. According to the Treasury officials who handled royal finances on behalf of the government, he had been given so much that 'he will hardly know what to do with his money'.[18] This is confirmed by another Treasury man, Sir George Murray, who in 1910, when the details of George V's Civil List were being put together, commented that, 'It should perhaps be mentioned that the present King, who is a very careful person in money matters, has saved a considerable sum during the last reign.' Thus George V did not really suffer that much as a result of his father not leaving any of his investment fortune to him.

George V was a long way from being in financial trouble in 1920.

---

* The present Queen and Princess Margaret have received money from the state. The Duke of Kent, Princess Alexandra and the Duke of Gloucester receive money from the Duchy of Lancaster. Lord Harewood and his brother, the Honourable Gerald Lascelles, will have inherited money from their father, who himself inherited nearly £2.5 million in 1917. Prince Michael has inherited money from Queen Mary, and receives money as a company director, as does Lascelles and as did Harewood. Prince William of Gloucester also inherited significant wealth before his death.

Rather, he was concerned that he might not be able to continue his practice, and that of his predecessors, of using Civil List money for private purposes. Edward VII and, for most of her reign, Queen Victoria were used to transferring money allotted for running the Household to their Privy Purse. In Victoria's case, it went towards the accumulation of her fortune. In Edward's, it mostly went in extravagance. By the time we get to George V, it is back to accumulation. As Ponsonby indicated, concerning the yet-to-be-born grandchildren, the First World War was not to stand too much in the way of personal enrichment. The reference to grandchildren is merely a euphemism for the policy of adding to a considerable private fortune, at the expense of the tax-payer.

The verdict of Sir George Murray in 1910, that George V was 'a very careful person in money matters', is correct only if one uses royal criteria. Compared to his father he spent less. But six years before Murray's assessment, he paid £1,450 (at 1991 prices, £72,500) for a stamp, then a record price.[19] He also resembled his father in the way he spent money to keep up Sandringham. However, such was the level of provision from the state to the King that he could accumulate from the Civil List. This process of acquisition is not related in the official biographies of George V or in other writings on the monarchy, except in one extremely brief reference.[20] The mundane desire to accumulate money does not fit with the conventional image of majesty. These savings have a modern significance also. This money, together with the earlier savings from the Duchy of Cornwall and, during the reign, savings from the Duchy of Lancaster profits and Class I of the Civil List, went to form the beginnings of the present monarch's private fortune.

In the whole reign, net savings on the Civil List averaged nearly £22,000 a year; in the war years this figure dropped, but only to just over £17,000. These transfers to the Privy Purse had to be approved by the Treasury, who saw nothing wrong in them. Never did they ask for the money back, when it was not to be used for the purposes for which it was intended. Nor is it likely that they even thought of the other alternative, of raising the far from generous rates of pay to those who worked 'below stairs'. It was only after the First World War that the King loosened the purse strings, the pay increases he conceded then being patriotically known as 'war bonuses'. They did not all go to the lowest paid groups. For instance, the Deputy Ranger of Windsor Park, who was the son of the 8th Baron Middleton, received £1,042 in 1919 and £1,168 in 1920 in war bonuses, many times what any of the staff earned in total.[21]

Ponsonby also mentioned as regards the Civil List that 'it is often argued that the King should pay taxes like his subjects, but this merely means a . . . reduction in the ceremonies . . . Cutting down on Beefeaters, footmen or grooms . . .' Ponsonby asked for the Civil List, fixed at £470,000 in 1910, to be increased by at least an extra £103,000. This, he argued, should include at least £10,000 for the Privy Purse, a figure he changed immediately after to an extra £25,000 for the Privy Purse.[22]

Not surprisingly, just after the war, the government avoided the option of asking Parliament for public money. The request from the Palace arrived in late November 1920, precisely at a time of very sharply increasing unemployment as the post-war boom abruptly ended, creating two million unemployed, many of them ex-servicemen. For Their Majesties, on the other hand, the situation could not have been too dire: in 1921 Queen Mary paid out a sizeable sum for the jewellery which belonged to the Grand Duchess Vladimir of the deposed Russian Imperial Family.[23]

Ponsonby, in arguing for a permanent increase in the Civil List, had held out the appalling prospect of royal penury, with 'the King going to open Parliament in a taxi-cab'. However, this was not a boast any London cab-drivers, famous for recalling famous passengers, could make.

On royal finances, the government took action in three ways. Firstly, it remembered that the King had lots of money tied up in his Duchy of Lancaster, which like the Duchy of Cornwall was mainly a collection of landed property. The government arranged a one-off transfer of £100,000 to the King's Privy Purse. Secondly, the royal image was protected. The Chancellor of the Exchequer was economical with the truth by stating that 'His Majesty, having in mind the serious state of the national finances at the present time, and showing thereby his public spirit in this as in all matters, is not prepared to assent to any action being taken by the government which will involve any additional charge upon public funds'.[24] Perhaps the Chancellor, Austen Chamberlain, or Lloyd George himself had persuaded him to this point of view, for the good of his reputation, but it was the opposite of his original stance. Thirdly, the Treasury initiated a study of the expenditure of the Royal Household.

The committee which undertook this task consisted of the Permanent Secretary, Sir Warren Fisher; Ralph Harwood, also of the Treasury; Sir

Frederick Ponsonby; and an accountant who had sat on a number of government inquiries. They produced a report,[25] not previously consulted by writers on the royals, which was submitted to George V in December 1921. It recommended economies, which were implemented and saved about £40,000 a year. The report noted that the scheme of wage and salary increases, still described as a 'war bonus' and adapted from that which had been applied in the Civil Service, had been very costly:

> Though we find [in Britain generally] . . . that there has been a small increase in wages of domestic and other servants who are boarded and lodged at their employer's expense, the percentage increase is not comparable with that which has been given to Your Majesty's servants in the form of war bonus.

The cuts recommended for the domestic staff 'are not very great, and they still leave the total cash remuneration in excess of comparable rates outside the Household', in addition to the several significant non-cash benefits.

The cuts for the controlling and secretarial staff were to be greater for those who lived in, but the majority who lived out were hardly to be affected. The largest cuts were to be on the women servants who lived in, but His Majesty was assured that 'emoluments in this class will still be much superior to those given to the best classes of domestic servants in private service'.

The recommended cuts in wages and salaries were implemented, and amounted to just over 7 per cent of the relevant wages and salaries bill. But the idea was to provide for further reductions, as now, after a period of rapid price inflation during and just after the war, prices were falling steadily. Much larger savings were anticipated and in fact were made. Also, twenty-two staff were made redundant from the Royal Mews, fewer staff being needed there, with the greater importance of cars after the war, to look after the horses.[26] By the standards of the day the redundancy terms were generous, but nevertheless the Mews staff were made unemployed at a time of mounting unemployment, with their type of skills no longer in demand.

The greatest savings that the report pinpointed were, however, in the food bill, which was to be cut by no less than 60 per cent, from £50,000 to £20,000. Prince Albert back in 1854 had discovered a 'peculation' amounting to a huge £15,000,[27] and it seems that some of His Majesty's loyal servants in 1921 were on to a 'nice little earner'. On a conservative estimate, the average cost for food per day for the King's staff was 12 shillings and 5 pence (in presentday terms, £14) before any costs for cooking and serving. This was three times the cost of food for army officers and the report noted that most of those consuming the food were mere domestic servants.

Because the report was to be submitted to His Majesty, it was not deemed proper to be too forthright in identifying a large-scale fiddle. It was described as 'bad buying'. Instead of paying wholesale prices for truly wholesale purchases, retail prices were paid – in fact, 'excessively high retail prices'. At least 40 per cent too much was paid for meat, up to 84 per cent for margarine and 100 per cent for certain fruits:

> A single official, a comparatively subordinate one at that, combines the duties of fixing prices with the tradesmen (by *verbal* negotiations) and the placing of all the orders with them, and the receipt of the goods and certification of the accuracy of the bills.

The committee submitting the report also felt that the quantities ordered could not possibly have been consumed, for on average the meat, poultry and fish ordered was two and a half pounds (1.13 kilos) per person, every day. Therefore, 'we are forced to the conclusion that there is a leakage'. Either food which had been paid for was not delivered, or once delivered it was smuggled out, or a combination of both. Such peculation was common in hotels and restaurants and was the source of conflict between management and the chef, or whoever certified the delivery of the food. It was all too easy for the latter to come to a cosy arrangement with the supplier, who would provide a kickback to the chef. But nothing on this scale.

The Master of the Household was the member of the King's Household responsible for its running. After criticizing his lax attitude, the report states that 'the holder of that appointment would rarely be equipped' to be proficient in matters of business, 'being selected as he generally is, and probably must be, for his qualifications to carry out the social and ceremonial duties appertaining to his Office'. This is a nice way of saying that he received a large salary for being a titled nonentity. The Master of the Household was in fact the son of the 7th Earl of

Albemarle, the Honourable Sir Derek Keppel. Whereas getting rid of some of the Mews staff was possible, sacking the son of an Earl was not quite the done thing. Moreover, he was the brother of the Honourable George Keppel, who had rendered the service of 'mari complaisant' to Edward VII. Instead, to introduce some financial control into the Royal Household, the Treasury obligingly supplied Ralph Harwood, one of the four-person economy committee, to be Ponsonby's deputy at the Palace.

What caused real horror in the report was the way that 'the servants have been pampered'. And indeed, as regards food they were. Only Scotch beef would do and all bacon had to be Irish: 'Royal servants are affecting to despise meat of quality which the ordinary professional and middle class members of the community, with incomes of £1,000 to £2,000, cannot afford to buy.' Similarly, Gabriel Tschumi, who was a chef at Buckingham Palace from 1898 to 1932, described how many of the servants, particularly from Edward VII's era, had also developed a very discerning palate for fine wines, which were supplied with meals.[28]

Apart from the cost, one can see the outrage at the blurring of class divisions in the consumption of food at the Palace. The monarchy does not exist to fulfil this function. Very little of the cutbacks were going to affect the smaller number of top 'Household' staff. In fact, against all the logic applied to the lower orders in the employ of the King, whose pay was being cut, Ponsonby was to have his salary increased from £2,500 to £3,000 a year,[29] while Harwood, coming into the Household to fill the new post of Deputy Treasurer to the King, would receive a salary of £2,200 plus a free London home. At the Treasury he had been on a pay scale ranging from £1,000 to £1,200, and had been one of those ordinary middle-class members who could not afford the high quality meat given to the servants. Generally, though, the main beneficiary of the shake-up in the Household was His Majesty. The economies made in food as well as in wages allowed the only leakage from the Civil List to be to his Privy Purse.

The dangerous prospect of royal poverty anticipated by Ponsonby, unless the government increased the Civil List, was averted without any such increase. And with falling prices during the latter part of his reign, George V was able to save a net total of £487,000 from his Civil List during his twenty-five years as King.* This sum, worth over £16 million in current prices, was in addition to his earlier accumulations as Prince of Wales.

Further savings, probably also totalling about half a million pounds for the reign, occurred on the other sources of Privy Purse funding.[30] Firstly, there was Class I of the Civil List which, unlike the Civil List savings, was paid *directly* by the government to the Privy Purse (£77,000 for the King and £33,000 for the Queen). Secondly, there was the money from the Duchy of Lancaster profits, from which George V withdrew an average of £64,000 a year throughout his reign. Virtually all such income was purely at the King's disposal for his own purposes. What did he do with it all?

We have an indication from 1925, on an occasion when the King was giving his views on investment to Walter Guinness, a minister in the Conservative Cabinet. 'To my surprise,' recalled Guinness, 'he agreed that government funds were a much safer form of investment and said that he always put his own savings into such securities.'[31] Thus the tax-payer was able to pay further sums to His Majesty in the form of dividends on government stock.

Apart from such private investment income, on government stock, company shares and interest, £185,341 in 1925 (at 1991 prices, over £5 million) accrued to the Privy Purse.† However, the King did not save all this money. There was one item which, following his father, Edward VII, involved the massive 'waste and extravagance' that had horrified Sir Edward Hamilton at the Treasury[32] and later was to horrify his son, who wanted the money for other purposes. This item was the upkeep of Sandringham in Norfolk, which in 1913 cost George V £50,000 a year (at 1991 prices, £2.4 million); maintaining Balmoral cost another £20,000 (at 1991 prices, £0.95 million).‡

---

* Civil List savings during his reign were £664,000, less £100,000 returned to the government in 1916 and £77,000 to charity during the war.
† This was made up of £77,000 from the government for his personal use, £38,341 saved from the Civil List and £70,000 from the Duchy of Lancaster profits.
‡ Having Sandringham already, together with its running costs, meant that Edward did not need nor could he afford to maintain both Balmoral and Osborne, which he inherited from his mother in 1901. He thus gave Osborne to the nation, much to the consternation of many of his brothers and sisters, who still hoped to use it. Victoria had tried unsuccessfully to get Balmoral and Osborne designated official residences, so that the government would foot the bills.

Sandringham

Edward VII, on several occasions, publicly boasted how well the labourers at Sandringham were housed. In 1884, whilst still Prince of Wales, he told the House of Lords that, 'I have been much occupied in building fresh dwellings for the poor and the working classes ... I hope that now there is hardly one person on the estate who can complain of not being adequately housed.'[33] A few months later, his agent, Mr Edmund Beck, echoed the Prince when giving evidence to a Royal Commission on Housing, of which the Prince was a member. But he also suggested that, twenty-two years after the estate came into royal ownership, during which time seventy cottages had been newly constructed or restored out of the total of 300, there were some who might complainn of not being properly housed. Beck stated that there were still some 'very bad' cottages, but 'that the bulk of those places that are nothing better than filthy hovels, are rapidly going away'.[34] Eventually, it seems they were indeed removed.

But had there been no 'filthy hovels' remaining, there was still the problem that the Prince did not provide enough cottages for all the labourers he employed on his own farm. Thus many of Sandringham's labourers had to live in nearby Dersingham, where they often could not afford a decent cottage because they were more expensive than those rented from the Prince. Beck records that such labourers would dearly have loved to move to Sandringham, had there been sufficient cottages.

Looking at the estate thirty years later, we see that, as at Balmoral, the initial estate was greatly added to by purchases of further land, expanding from about 8,000 to 15,000 acres, by the addition of Anmer in about 1890 and Flitcham in about 1910.

In 1884 Beck had mentioned that the wages paid by the Prince on the 1,000 acres he farmed were about 10 per cent higher than those paid by his tenant-farmers. This differential seems to have disappeared thirty years later, by 1913, and wages were lower than those described by Beck, even though prices were higher. Thus, three years after Edward's death, his long-time friend, Lord Lincolnshire, noted that the low wages paid at Sandringham to the sixty or so labourers on George V's farms were much talked about in Norfolk.[35]

Lord Lincolnshire's brother, Sir William Carington, was 'Fritz' Ponsonby's predecessor as Keeper of the King's Privy Purse, and he kept Lincolnshire informed about the estate:

> It consists of a tract of country 9 miles long by 5 miles wide – all under game [for shoot]. Two-thirds of the property is let to 15 tenant farmers who occupy farms of over 600 acres each, at a low rent: there are only 3 small holders.* Nearly £200,000 has been spent in repairs and new buildings since 1865; last year over £8,000 on this item alone: and yet the gross rent is only £6,000 a year. In the face of all this extravagance some of the labourers on the Royal farm only get (including harvest money) 16s a week: and as they pay 1s 8d for a cottage, it brings the total cash down to 14s a week. There will be a terrific scandal if this comes out, and I have persuaded Bill [Lincolnshire's brother] to ask the King to grant at once a minimum wage of £1 a week, and a Saturday half holiday as well.[36]

Kenneth Rose, the latest biographer of George V, argues that the latter had simply inherited the Sandringham régime from his father in 1910, and knew nothing of how the farms were run. If this was so, it says much about the King's general outlook: he had spent much time there, throughout most of his life, and he was, after all, 48 years old. Also, it took three and a half years, after Edward VII's death, plus Lord Lincolnshire's intervention via his brother, to change matters.

The King saw the wage rise as a heavy burden but agreed to it, though it was not to be extended to 'a few not able-bodied men who are employed out of compassion'.[37] His Majesty also cut Lincolnshire's proposed £1 a week to 19 shillings, including harvest money, further easing the heavy burden. This new rate still fell below the minimum wage calculated at the time, of £1.025 necessary for a couple with three children to live in the countryside. The £1.025 was a minimal figure which included no allowance for expenditure on children's toys, beer, tobacco, fares, postage, newspapers or amusements.[38]

---

* Lord Lincolnshire was himself a large landowner and had been the Liberal Agricultural Minister from 1905 to 1911. His comment on the lack of smallholders implied a criticism, as he promoted such on his own lands. Before becoming the Marquess of Lincolnshire, he was known as Lord Carington. As Carington he was quoted in Chapter 2, concerning the involvement of Edward VII's courtiers in a City scandal.

Even if the rise had covered all sixty labourers, the cost to His Majesty would have been only £624; by shaving off a shilling from the £1 that Lincolnshire recommended, the maximum cost of the increase was kept down to £468. This was considered a great sacrifice to someone spending £50,000 a year on keeping about thirty-five square miles stocked adequately with game birds, and who saved over £25,000 from his Civil List in 1913. It was not only a question of saving money on wages. Even if he did not perceive it, the King could afford the wage increase and much more. Had he considered being more generous than the 19 shillings, his tenant farmers would have accused him of putting them in difficulty by driving up the local wage rate too much. That would have endangered their ability to pay him rent and also have been a breach in class solidarity. As it was, local farmers felt he had broken ranks, enabling the union to campaign for 'the King's wages and the King's conditions'.[39]

Without including income derived from his private fortune, the King's income, purely for his personal use, was in 1913 £163,667 (at 1991 prices, £7.9 million). This sum was not needed to meet the expenses of the monarchy – salaries, expenses of the Household, upkeep of the Palaces etc. – for which the government provided Classes II and III of the Civil List. The above figure was 3,313 times greater than the annual pay of a labourer at Sandringham, even at the increased rate of 19 shillings.

There is a somewhat different version of how the King's attention was distracted from shooting countless pheasants, partridges and the like and made to focus on the matter of his labourers' pay. It is featured in the official history of the National Union of Agricultural Workers, written in 1947 by Reg Groves. 'A number of the farm workers [employed by the King at Sandringham] were members of the union, and on their behalf R.B. Walker [General Secretary of the union] met the King's agent, Captain Beck, and put forward the case for higher wages and the half-holiday.'[40] It may also have been the activities of the union which prompted Lord Lincolnshire to intervene through his brother, for the union was gathering strength through 1913.

In any case, the strike that hit the farms of the King's tenants in Sandringham in February 1914 was avoided on his own farms, as the King had already granted what the union was asking for. Lincolnshire noted that the pay increase and half-holiday had been carried out only just in time to save His Majesty from the embarrassment of facing a strike in his own back yard.[41] His tenants, however, tried to beat off the union, by bringing in blackleg labour, paid at rates much above what the union were asking. The King could have discouraged this practice on his estate, but apparently did not. Such methods did not succeed and the union was by and large victorious.

There are indications that, by this time, labourers' cottages were better than those in many 'open' villages. This would not have been difficult. The *Norwich Mercury* carried a long article in 1919 entitled 'Housing Scandal – Indescribable Condition of Norfolk Villages'.[42]

Sandringham Labourers After the First World War

There seems to have been little change in the running of Sandringham and the extravagance that had so shocked Sir Edward Hamilton and the Marquess of Lincolnshire. George V's eldest son, the Duke of Windsor, described matters in *A King's Story*, published some fifteen years after his abdication. George V had spent money on Sandringham 'with a prodigality that was the wonder of my father's neighbours', while 'game birds for the King and his guests to shoot were still being raised' on an incredible scale.[43]

During and just after the war, agricultural labourers had benefited from the setting up of wages boards which had fixed wage levels in each county. However, this system was scrapped by the government in September 1921 and wages were cut. Though the general price level was falling, the cuts in the wages were much greater still. By the end of 1923, real wages had been driven back to the pre-war levels that had sparked the strikes in Norfolk in 1914.

Wages were 46 shillings a week in September 1921, but at the beginning of 1923, 25 shillings was the general wage in Norfolk.[44] Even the arch-Tory paper the *Morning Post* felt moved to write about the distress amongst agricultural workers in Norfolk.[45] A few farmers, such as the Earl of Kimberley (a Labour peer), paid as much as 30 shillings,[46] but the King was not amongst these. He had cut wages along with other farmers and was paying 25 shillings, doing with his sixty workers at Sandringham only what he had done, through the economy plan outlined above, with his staff at Buckingham Palace and Windsor. But he wisely did not cut wages further, nor did he increase hours, as did most other Norfolk farmers.[47] At least, he did not do so before or during the month-long 1923 strike which affected much of Norfolk, including eight of his tenant-farmers. Another factor inhibiting strike action, as the local paper hinted, was the fact that His Majesty's older labourers were worried at the risk of losing their pension, to which they were entitled on reaching the age of 70.[48] Thus, as in 1914, he avoided an embarrassing strike. A compromise in the dispute was reached with the intervention of the Labour party leader, Ramsay MacDonald. But many farmers refused to re-employ those workers who had been active in the strike.[49]

During the strike, in April, the Conservative Minister of Agriculture 'met the King at lunch ... The King got me to sit next [to] him after lunch; talked a lot about agriculture in a most Tory vein; all against a wages board.'[50] The Prime Minister, Bonar Law, was initially for such a board after having read a report by certain agricultural economists. But wages boards would increase wages, and thus the Agriculture Minister, Sir Robert Sanders, and the farmers' representatives, with the outspoken approval of the King, dissuaded Bonar Law. Yet in the following year, 1924, wages boards were reintroduced by the first Labour government in a muted form, and they increased wages everywhere.[51] His Majesty would have been further displeased when the adjoining constituency of North Norfolk got its first Labour MP, in the election which returned the minority Labour government. Noel Buxton, previously a Liberal MP, became the new Minister of Agriculture and was responsible for reintroducing the boards.

William Burkitt wrote an article in 1931 on the King in his role as farmer. Discussing Sandringham, he praised the housing provided for the estate employees. Burkitt was equally impressed with another piece of evidence of the squire's concern for those in his care. He referred to 'the absence of inns or public-houses on the estate, H.M. the King having abolished these and provided village clubs in no less than five parishes'. Not only were these clubs comfortable, but 'there are rooms for Women's Institute meetings, concerts, dances and other events. The clubs are equipped with good billiards-rooms, and the sale of beer is permitted but no other intoxicants.'[52] Some of these clubs probably date back to the last century. The Prince of Wales's agent, in his evidence to the Royal Commission, described how the Prince was building one at that time. He was consulting with the local clergy on what rules should be applied to members.

The same restrictions on alcohol were not imposed on George V and his Household. The King, though not a heavy drinker by any means, was partial to wine, sherry and some spirits. There had been a period during the First World War when he had been pressured by Lloyd George to set a good example and give up drink for the duration of hostilities, but he never ceased to complain about it, because his example was not followed by Lloyd George or the government of which he was a member. His Majesty was sensitive to this double standard of alcohol consumption, but applied one of his own at Sandringham.

4

From Tax-payers to Tax-avoiders

Queen Victoria's Children

The removal of income tax on the Civil List in 1910 became a prelude to further changes. In George V's reign the move to a non-tax-paying royal family began in earnest. In 1913, a legal opinion was obtained from within Whitehall, from the Law Officers, which said that the Acts which granted Queen Victoria's children annuities had not really intended that they pay tax.[1] Up until then, some or all of them had been paying. In 1871, the Chancellor of the Exchequer, Robert Lowe, had mentioned Victoria's eldest daughter paying her tax through Coutts Bank. Another daughter, Alice, is mentioned in an old Treasury file as also having paid.[2]

Queen Alexandra and the Younger Children of George V

After the First World War, taxation rates continued to rise, giving a further impetus for royals to demand relief from spiralling tax bills. In 1920, as well as Ponsonby's 'taxi-cab' letter about the King's money problems, there came a piteous plea from Edward VII's widow, Alexandra,[3] who had successfully held out for the £70,000 dower. She was now receiving this, but paying £41,600 in income tax and super-tax, whereas in 1911 she had paid only £5,833[4] (even then she had tried to get out of paying these taxes). She had also been left the use of £200,000 in capital by the late King.[5] Alexandra was extremely rash with money. Rather like her late husband, she realized that she would always be bailed out financially. When asked to think in terms of economy, she said, 'I don't care, I shall do as I please; if I get into debt *they* can pay.'[6] By 'they', she meant the government. Now Alexandra was nearing 80, and in July 1920 the Treasury, realizing it was rather difficult to change the habits of a lifetime, exempted the first £50,000 of her annuity from tax. This did not prove to be enough, and in March 1921 the figure was increased to £64,000. Kenneth Rose concluded that 'for once the Treasury behaved indulgently', but Treasury indulgence towards royalty was much less rare than Mr Rose believes.

A year later, a similar concession was made to the four grown-up children of the King, who were also receiving annuities from the government. In 1922, 80 per cent of their annuities were relieved from taxation by the Treasury, as 'representing in their opinion a fair equivalent of the average annual amount expended wholly, exclusively and necessarily by the aforesaid children [of George V] in the performance of the duties in respect of which the annuities are payable'.[7] Thus 80 per cent of the Duke of York's £25,000 a year came to be viewed as tax-deductible expenses. Of course, the royals have to pay people like private secretaries, who are 'wholly, exclusively and necessarily' employed in the day-to-day workings of royalty. But 80 per cent seems a bit steep. At least this arrangement was later, in 1926, made public by the Prime Minister, when answering a question in the Commons. This was not the case with the arrangement made in 1921 by the remaining child of the King, the Prince of Wales (later Edward VIII and Duke of Windsor). As with the present Prince of Wales, he had no government annuity, but he did receive the revenues of the Duchy of Cornwall.

The Prince of Wales and the Duchy of Cornwall

From at least 1849 the Duchy of Cornwall, with its considerable estates, had paid the income tax to which landlords were liable – Schedule A.[8] In 1913 the Inland Revenue approached the Duchy about submitting valuations and paying a new landlord's tax, on income from mineral royalties, one of the taxes introduced in Lloyd George's recent 'People's Budget'. The Duchy complained that it did not have to pay and eventually the Law Officers of the Crown were brought in. Their opinion was that because of Crown immunity (see Chapter 1), the Duchy was not liable:

The same principles which render the provision of an Act of Parliament inapplicable to the Crown unless the Crown is expressly named, apply also to the Prince of Wales in his capacity as Duke of Cornwall. This result arises from the peculiar title of the Prince of Wales to the Duchy of Cornwall.[9]

This author has already registered his disagreement about Crown immunity from taxation being made to embrace the twentieth-century monarch, rather than just the state. But now 'the Crown' was to be even more elastic. The term was stretched to include 'the Prince of Wales in his capacity as Duke of Cornwall'. It is true that the Duchy legally reverts to the monarch if there is no Prince of Wales, so that the Duchy can then be said to be in the possession of the Crown. But even if one accepts the notion of Crown immunity for the monarch, one would think the immunity should apply only when the monarch possesses the Duchy. How, in 1913, when there was a Prince of Wales receiving the Duchy revenues, could he enjoy Crown immunity? No doubt it had something to do with his 'peculiar title', but the 1913 legal opinion steers clear of any explanation of what the peculiarity consists of.* It was this opinion which was quoted during the 1971 Parliamentary Select Committee, in order to justify the Duchy's present immunity from tax. The expert witness from the Inland Revenue quoted part of the 1913 opinion and added blankly, 'what the peculiar title is, I am afraid I cannot say'.[10]

However, the Law Officers in 1913 were not simply signposting another route to royal tax exemption. Aware that there were dangers along that particular road, they concluded cautiously that, though not liable to the tax, it may be that the royal owner of the Duchy:

> will not wish to insist upon his privilege of exemption . . . We would most strongly deprecate the bringing to an issue of questions such as those here set out. It is obvious that if such a matter were litigated the Duchy of Cornwall might find that even though they succeeded their success in the Courts did not conclude the matter.[11]

---

* In 1850 the Solicitor-General could not discern this peculiar title and its connection with Crown immunity. He declared that when there is a male heir to the throne who enjoys its revenues, as in 1913 and today, the Duchy 'was not connected with the Crown in any way'. (*Hansard*, 25 March 1850, col. 1375)

In other words, people who read about such a case might think that the Prince of Wales should pay, whatever his 'peculiar' title to the Duchy. The Law Officers' contention was that the Duchy should pay up, so that public opinion should not be troubled by such thoughts.

From the contents of a later Treasury memorandum we know that the Duchy did pay all the various taxes that any other estate owner would pay,[12] including super-tax. And Lloyd George as Chancellor may have recommended that the Duchy pay the mineral rights tax. But the latter was fairly minor compared to the income tax and super-tax paid on the rents gathered from the Duchy's landed property. In this case, it seemed that not even the magical Crown immunity could weave its spell and make the tax go away, for the immunity applies only where the Crown is not 'expressly named' in legislation. The problem was that Income Tax Acts did expressly mention that the Crown had to pay Schedule A income tax on its rents. Schedule A used to be (until 1963) collected at source – that is, the tenants deducted the tax from their rent and periodically paid it to the Inland Revenue. The 1918 Income Tax Act specifically stated that tenants of the Crown should do this, at the expense of the Crown as landlord.[13]

Of course, this is a case of the government taxing itself so as to pay itself and causing, it might seem, needless paperwork. But a property owned by the Crown Lands, or some other government landlord, might be sold to a private landlord who would be liable to the tax. Rather than have some lengthy transitional period, on change of ownership, during which the tax was not being collected, it was thought better to simply have all Crown tenants deduct the Schedule A, as did other tenants, thus preserving the 'machinery' of collection.

The Duchy paid tax in this way until 1921. A Treasury document from that year, which took me a great deal of searching to find, tells us what happened. Headed 'SECRET', it reveals how the Prince took the initiative in removing his tax liability. He successfully pleaded 'the higher cost of repairs and similar outgoings' and that 'the burden of taxation has enormously increased; whilst on the other hand, . . . having come of age', he was 'taking a much more active part in public affairs, which involves . . . greatly increased expenditure'. Moreover, the Law Officers in 1921 could 'see no reason to differ from the principles laid down in the opinion of the Law Officers of the Crown . . . [in] 1913'.[14] The Attorney-General and Solicitor-General, like their predecessors in

1913, did not manage to explain the nature of the 'peculiar title' to the Duchy.

Nevertheless, the 1921 Law Officers came to the conclusion that the Income Tax Act did not mean to tax the Duchy. So, after 1921, there was a very peculiar arrangement indeed. The Duchy tenants continued deducting the tax and dutifully paid it over to the Inland Revenue, who now refunded it to the Duchy, without the tenants or anyone else knowing.[15] The Prince also took the opportunity to claim back the tax he had paid to the Inland Revenue for the previous tax year, 1919–20.

The tax-exemption given to the Duchy did not let it off totally, however. The deal struck with the Treasury involved the Prince's making a 'voluntary contribution' to the government. He agreed to pay the Exchequer '£20,000 p.a., subject to variation (either upwards or downwards) as might seem desirable'.[16] This saved him about £15,000 in the first year and more in subsequent years. In fact, both the profits and the money extracted by His Royal Highness from the Treasury increased after 1921,[17] allowing him to accumulate an immense private fortune, by the standards of the day, without it ever seeming 'desirable' to increase his contribution to the Exchequer.[18] Taxes after the First World War were much higher than before the war, at over 50 per cent on his level of income. But by his special arrangement, the Prince was able to keep his payments to the Exchequer down to 22.4 per cent for 1921–35,[19] about the same proportion as his pre-war tax bills.

Relieving the Duchy from the obligation to pay tax was not, it should be stressed, a purely legal decision, for it could still be the case that the Prime Minister or Chancellor of the Exchequer could 'advise' that the tax be paid, in spite of any claims to Crown immunity. Quite simply, they could take the line, as was taken in 1901, that it would be detrimental to the reputation of the monarchy itself to cease paying tax. So any legal judgment about Crown immunity and royal taxation has to await confirmation or rejection by a political decision. In this case, government approval for substituting a lower voluntary payment was given – by the Chancellor of the Exchequer at the time, Sir Robert Horne (a Conservative in the Lloyd George coalition).[20]

It is unlikely that he would have given the go-ahead if he had felt obligated to make an announcement in the House of Commons. And indeed, the whole matter was, and still is, shrouded in secrecy. Up to

1921, the accounts of the Duchy of Cornwall (and Lancaster) had been published and were available through the government's Stationery Office. But in the first year of the Duchy's substituting the £20,000 payment, this ceased. The accounts were prepared in a form to be published with a price of 6d printed on the outside, but were not in fact so published.[21] Certain changes at this time were taking place in the publication of such material, but this was certainly a convenient moment to stop the accounts becoming publicly available and finding their way into various libraries. It made it less likely there would be awkward questions raised about the tax issue.

Advantage was taken of a nineteenth-century Act of Parliament[22] whereby publication was not required, only that the accounts be presented to Parliament. In practice, this meant one copy to the House of Commons library and one to the House of Lords Record Office. This was complied with, but the Duchy accounts were not to be published again until 1982. To make discovery of what happened even more unlikely, a straightforward piece of deception was employed in the accounts. The £20,000 voluntary contribution was included under the heading 'taxes and parish rates' in the accounts, to make it seem that the Duchy was still being taxed.[23] A curious piece of accounting practice for a body that claimed and got tax exemption.

Further deceptions have followed. As Andrew Duncan noted in his book *The Reality of Monarchy*, 'until the beginning of September 1969, Buckingham Palace authorities were underestimating the revenue from the Duchy, and claiming publicly that it was subject to tax'.[24] He also mentioned how a Central Office of Information booklet, *The Monarchy in Britain*, which was 'intended to be used for reference purposes', clearly suggested that Prince Charles paid income tax on all his income. Duncan discovered that this was not true and that the Prince on becoming 21 made a voluntary contribution of 50 per cent to the Treasury (25 per cent since 1981), in lieu of taxation, which at that time would have been over 80 per cent. The booklet stated that all royals except for the Queen were liable to death duties, but in fact the government did not hold the Duchy liable to this tax, or to capital gains tax.*

---

* One might give the benefit of the doubt to the Prince and Palace authorities, putting it down to confusion rather than conspiracy. Indeed the fact that Duncan was given the information in the first place about the voluntary contribution suggests an imperfect conspiracy. However, as is described in Chapter 7, misinformation was not just being spread about the Prince and the Duchy, but about the Queen herself.

In 1973, Willie Hamilton, the republican MP, sent a series of questions to Prince Charles's private secretary, Squadron Leader David Checketts, who replied promising answers as soon as he had 'an opportunity to consult with the Prince'. Hamilton was eventually told that a 'voluntary surrender' of a portion of the 'net revenue' of the Duchy 'follows a precedent set by the previous Prince of Wales'.[25] This conveniently omits the fact that this earlier Prince of Wales was *already* paying tax and wanted to reduce the amount paid to the government. The implication one would draw is that, previous to this apparently unprompted offer to the public purse, he paid no tax at all. When I first read this I thought here was someone whose large tax-free income was weighing on his conscience, and who had needed to unburden himself by making a regular donation to the government.

This practice of being 'economical with the truth' comes naturally to many leading civil servants. In regard to the Duchy's tax position, past and present, the evidence given by Mr J.P. Strudwick of the Inland Revenue to the Select Committee on the Civil List, in 1971, was a masterpiece of the genre, and there was no danger of the republican member of the committee, Willie Hamilton, picking up the scent. As with much else in this chapter, this is the first time that the facts of the Duchy's tax-paying history have been made public. If they had been made public back in 1921, the Duchy and the Prince of Wales would have attracted even more criticism for the extreme slowness in replacing worn-out housing stock on the Duchy's south London estate at Kennington.[26] Such new housing was needed to help deal with the considerable problem of overcrowding in the area. Nor would a Prince so eager to increase an already high income have fitted well with the public Prince, who was becoming famous for utterances of concern for the unemployed and homeless. In his memoirs, the Duke of Windsor said the Duchy revenues were for his expenses. In fact, like his father, he saved a very sizeable sum from his Duchy income (see next chapter), much of it due to the voluntary contribution arrangement.

If the tax privileges of the royals were and remain right and proper, then it is surprising that there should be all this concealment. The real reason must be that the stratagems used by earlier generations of royals to pay less tax are not consistent with the illustrious image of royalty, and that greater openness could lead to a number of better-informed questions about its existing tax position.

It should be said that taking action to avoid taxation at this time was not unique to the royal family. As Philip Knightley explains in his book on the Vesteys (Dewhurst the butchers etc.), 1921 was the year of another move to avoid taxation. They were able in that year to construct a legal means of avoiding British tax whilst still living in this country. Previous to this, in 1915, they had moved out of Britain in order to avoid tax. In 1922, Lloyd George proposed Sir William Vestey to the King for a peerage. The King felt their having avoided tax in the middle of the war was a highly unpatriotic act. He also felt that the selling of peerages, in the manner of Lloyd George, sullied the monarchy in its role as the 'fount of honour'. Knightley claims that Vestey paid £20,000 into Lloyd George's treasure chest to join the House of Lords. Knightley also says the King asked to see Vestey's evidence, given in 1919 to the Royal Commission on taxation, and was unimpressed. Vestey had told the Commission, 'the present state of affairs suits me admirably. I am abroad; I pay nothing [in tax].'

Thus, even without knowing of the ingenious 1921 scheme to permanently avoid tax, the King objected in the strongest terms to Vestey's becoming a Baron. As we shall see, the King himself was still paying some tax, even if he had escaped it on the Civil List, so he could be said to have some sort of justification for his feelings towards Vestey. Yet it was George V himself who was responsible for the penultimate royal offensive against the Inland Revenue. And by the 1970s, the royals and the Vesteys, with their similar attitude towards paying tax, met happily on the polo fields and racecourses of the Home Counties. In 1984 Lady Vestey, wife of the 3rd Baron Vestey, became a godparent to Charles and Diana's second son, Prince Harry.

Shoulder-to-shoulder with the Unemployed?

1931 is a very important date in the history of the monarchy. Ramsay MacDonald, at the King's request, split off from his Labour colleagues to head a 'National' Government, during the first of the currency crises which have beset Labour governments. The National Government was in fact a largely Conservative government, which implemented largely Conservative policies. Unemployment benefit was immediately reduced by 10 per cent, and soon after that the hated Means Test was introduced.

It was not war-time, but many, including the King, felt that it was just as much a national emergency. Therefore, at MacDonald's suggestion, he repeated his economic 'sacrifice' of the war years. It was announced that the King had voluntarily reduced his annual Civil List by £50,000, and that the Prince of Wales would pay as part of his contribution to 'National Economy' £10,000 a year.[27] The first the Prince knew about this was when his father telephoned him in Bayonne in the South of France. 'The prince was in a night haunt at the time and was furious: "The King and I are being had for a pair of mugs." '[28]

It seems that the King had considered promoting the idea amongst his staff that they should volunteer to have their wages reduced, and that the reductions could also be announced as a contribution towards national economy. However, the Prime Minister argued this 'would be most improper', since, as staff were paid from the King's Civil List, not by the Treasury, the saving would be not to the nation, but to the King himself.[29]

MacDonald's warning seems to have been effective, and the Civil List reduction does not seem to have been made from staff pay. The sums for staff pay from the Civil List decreased only slightly.[30] The real savings were made in the running of the Household, aside from salaries – so much so that there were still savings to be paid to His Majesty's Privy Purse, even after the £50,000 to be repaid to the government.[31]

Nevertheless, since 1931 it might have seemed, with a feat of imagination, that the King was standing shoulder-to-shoulder with the unemployed, similarly suffering a 10 per cent cut in his income from the government. But in 1932, 'it was represented to the Chancellor [of the Exchequer] that His Majesty would wish to be relieved of the charge of income tax from the Duchy [of Lancaster] revenues and the Chancellor concurred in this exercise of His Majesty's undoubted prerogative'.[32] Certainly the Chancellor of the Duchy of Lancaster, Sir John Davidson, had already been consulted. But it was not quite as simple as that. As Sir Ralph Harwood, Ponsonby's deputy at Buckingham Palace, wrote to Davidson, there was the question of 'whether it is politic for His Majesty to avail himself of this legal immunity'.[33]

This was the same Harwood who had been at the Treasury until he was drafted in to help give some financial control at the Palace. This was just after the 1921 committee, of which he had been a member, had uncovered the overeating and overcharging of food and had also recommended wage cuts. On this latest tax matter, Harwood had been able to get his old department on the royal side (which was not that difficult anyway) by writing to his erstwhile boss, still Permanent Secretary at the Treasury, Sir Warren Fisher, and in 1933 it was agreed that the King's request should be granted.

The King stood to gain over £20,000 a year (at 1991 prices, £600,000) from the lifting of income tax on the Duchy's rental income. This had not been judged politic in 1910, when earlier requests were made to relieve the Duchy of this tax.[34] During the Civil List debates of that year, Lloyd George, as Chancellor of the Exchequer, felt obliged to assure the Commons that the King would continue to pay tax on the Duchy. The 1936 Treasury report remarked that removing the tax would fly in the face of this assurance.[35] Once it had become a parliamentary matter, by Lloyd George's binding the King to pay, then there should have been some announcement to Parliament that he was ceasing to pay. But if the Chancellor of the Exchequer, Neville Chamberlain, had announced it in the Commons, there would have been comment that the King's gesture of sacrificing 10 per cent of his Civil List income was sham and hypocrisy.

Not having to pay tax, the King from now on extracted at least an extra £20,000 p.a. from the Duchy of Lancaster. His publicized way of saving the government money from 1931 until 1935, when the government restored the full Civil List, was significantly offset by his newly acquired tax exemption. Moreover, the latter was a permanent loss to the Exchequer and has therefore dwarfed the amounts returned to the government during 1931–5, the period of economic emergency. It was also a case of giving with one hand and taking back with the other, which Lloyd George so deplored in 1910.

Probably the experience of the Duchy of Cornwall led the King and his advisers, government ministers and Treasury officials to realize that it was possible to circumvent Parliament. Few people asked about these often complicated matters, especially since the publication of the accounts of the two Duchies had been stopped in 1921. So there was little risk of being found out, which in fact has not happened until now.

Unlike with the Duchy of Cornwall, the change was shown openly in the accounts. But the various Treasury reports and letters of the 1930s show that the King did not volunteer a contribution in lieu of taxation in the same fashion as his son's £20,000 from the other Duchy. Probably the Chancellor of the Duchy, Davidson, had contemplated this, but only as a fallback position. It seems likely that this is what Harwood had referred to in 1933 when he asked Davidson to keep strictly between themselves

Davidson's 'idea of a possible compromise ... unless we should fail to get the complete thing for which we are asking'[36] – which, of course, they did.

1933 was also the year that Queen Mary found it possible to pay over £60,000 (at 1991 prices, £1.9 million) for the jewels of the Empress Marie Feodorovna, mother of the last Russian Czar.[37]

5

George V to George VI:

Taxation on Private Investments

The royal income-tax burden was being lifted in successive stages. First, George V's Civil List was exempted in 1910. Likewise, from 1913, the annuities paid to Queen Victoria's remaining children were no longer taxed. Queen Alexandra's annuity in 1920 and 1921 was made virtually tax-free. In 1921, the Duchy of Cornwall ceased to pay tax, making a 'voluntary contribution' at a reduced figure instead. In 1922, George V's younger children had a minimum 80 per cent of their income automatically exempted from tax. And in 1933, the King's Duchy of Lancaster was made effectively tax-free. Of these seven changes in royal tax status, only two were made public at the time. And in one of these, George V's Civil List in 1910, though it was openly announced by Lloyd George, deception was employed to suggest the cost of removing the tax was less than it actually was. All in all, it was a long job reversing the precedent set by Queen Victoria in 1842.

What further progress could the House of Windsor make in ridding itself of the turbulent taxman? What other changes have been necessary before we reach the present tax-free position of Elizabeth II?

George V's Private Investments

The private income of the monarch was still taxed in various ways. Rents from the King's private landed estates were taxable under the 1800 and 1862 Acts, as described in Chapter 1. Crown immunity applied only if the Crown was not specifically mentioned, whereas these Acts were specifically about the monarch, who was stated to be liable to tax on her or his private estates. Sandringham, where there were a number of tenant-farmers, provided the bulk of such rents (£6,000 p.a. in 1913). But the extravagance with which Sandringham was run meant there were always heavy losses, so it is doubtful if there was ever very much tax to pay. Rental income from Balmoral was not very great as little land was suitable for farm letting. Just the same, in principle, rental income from these estates or any others could not escape liability to income tax, except by changing the law, which involved Parliament and publicity.

This leaves for consideration only George V's private investments. As described in Chapter 3, the tax-payer had subscribed a net sum of £487,000 (or £16 million at current prices), diverted from the Civil List to the King's Privy Purse. We also know that he saved money from funds which went to his Privy Purse in more orthodox fashion. These were the £77,000 from the government and the profits from the Duchy of Lancaster. Also, before he became King in 1910 we know he had amassed a considerable fortune. What do we know of the tax position on the investment income from his personal fortune?

A Treasury report, marked 'Secret', drawn up for the Conservative Chancellor of the Exchequer in 1936, gives us the answer.[1] A minority of all investment income at this time, such as interest on bank deposits,[2] was paid out gross, without income tax being deducted at source. But the most attractive investment which escaped deduction at source was War Loan, a type of government stock raised to help finance the First World War and which accounted for about a quarter of the National Debt.[3] War Loan's special tax status was a bait used to attract badly needed investment during the Great War, especially from the Empire, whose investors could escape being caught up in the British tax system.

Of those who were resident in Britain, everyone, except the King, was liable to pay tax on such income eventually, for they would have to declare it when they filled in their annual tax assessments. The King was not subject to this process, because the Inland Revenue did not ever require him to complete a tax assessment, on the grounds of his so-called Crown immunity. As the 1936 Treasury report put it, any of his investments, for instance, 'held in any Government Loan, the dividends of which are not subject to deduction of tax at the source, would not be taxed . . .' The Revenue, having missed the chance of deduction at source, did not get a second opportunity as far as the King was concerned.

This was the basis of the tactic employed by the Duchy of Lancaster after 1933, when it had succeeded in getting income tax lifted on its rental income, but had not been able to do the same for tax on the Duchy's much smaller investment income. The Duchy simply switched its holdings of government stock into 3.5 per cent War Loan.[4]

However, the monarch himself did make the type of investment where tax was deducted, and he did actually pay this tax. The secret report of 1936, and other evidence, tells us that 'income tax deducted at the source is not reclaimed by His Majesty'. The great majority of investment income in stocks and shares was paid after subtracting standard-rate income tax – 22.5 per cent in 1936. Dividends on all company shares and in government stock, other than War Loan from the First World War, were paid out net of tax. As is still the practice nowadays, the company sent the tax deducted in this fashion to the government on behalf of the shareholder (since 1973 it has been called Advanced Corporation Tax). And on most government stock, the government simply retained the tax. On such investment income, George V did not reclaim the tax he paid, though the report held that he could have done so because of Crown immunity to taxation. That is to say, George V did not stand on his legal rights, as interpreted by the Treasury, to claim back any tax paid in this way.[5] The Queen, however, does so today, and has been allowed to do so by government.

The King did not pay surtax, originally called super-tax, the additional tax on those with very high incomes.[6] To do so would have involved being assessed for tax, which the monarch would not be unless he volunteered. He never did.

We have the remark made by George V to Walter Guinness in 1925 about putting his 'savings' into government stock. But it seems clear that he also invested in the private sector. Firstly, this can be deduced by the way that any investment in government stock would most likely have gone into War Loan, because of the King's unique tax advantage. Therefore, the tax we know he paid, which was 'not reclaimed by His Majesty', would *not* have been on income from government stock, but on dividends from company shares and the like. (He was not in the position of the Duchy of Lancaster, which was, at that time, restricted by statute to invest only in government stock.) Secondly, investment in the private sector would have brought far more likelihood of capital gains, and we know that his father had benefited from advice from banker friends to make such gains. Thirdly, we know he had first-class investment advice which meant that it would not have been wildly dangerous for his investment to be placed in company shares. His relationship with his financial advisers suggests that his capital was not simply placed conservatively in government stock.

Sir Edward Peacock

George V's 'private financial adviser' from 1929 onwards was a Canadian, Edward Peacock, of Baring Brothers merchant bank and director of the Bank of England. John Gore's official biography of George V describes Peacock as a friend of the King who 'did much of the King's private business'.[7] Peacock followed Lord Revelstoke, also of Baring Brothers, in this capacity. Revelstoke had prepared Peacock for the role, holding two dinner parties for men only, sitting Peacock next to the King at the first of these so they could get to know one another.[8]

On Lord Revelstoke's sudden and unexpected death in April 1929, Peacock took over as head of Barings. Revelstoke's brother wrote to the King about the changes, reassuring His Majesty that although Peacock, unlike himself and his late brother, was not a Baring, the bank would remain a 'family affair'. The reply from the King's secretary, welcoming the retention of the family nature of the bank, 'spoke for George V, who had profited so signally from Lord Revelstoke's advice throughout his life'.[9]

Peacock's career is quite remarkable. The son of a poor clergyman, he was a teacher until he was over 30. When he got into banking he rose partly through social connections, but also through being a shrewd negotiator, capable of seeing complex deals through to the end. In Britain he became a favourite of the Governor of the Bank of England, Montagu Norman, and of Revelstoke, who left him a large sum of money in his will. His ascent was on merit, but the route was cleared for him by those born into their positions. He remained grateful to his sponsors and did not initiate a more meritocratic order in the 'blue-blooded' business of merchant banking. Like Revelstoke, his chief sponsor, he was a supporter of the Conservative Party and advised the Conservatives on presentation of policy over unemployment during the 1929 election.[10]

Soon after his promotion, Peacock received a phone-call from Bognor, where George V was recovering from a serious illness, from which he had almost died. Despite his still frail condition (the usually ultra-formal George was in his dressing-gown when he received Peacock), the King wanted to talk to the banker. They spoke for two hours, during which the

King, according to Peacock's later recollections, described Revelstoke as having been his 'best friend' and invited Peacock to continue his work as financial adviser. Thereafter Peacock was called in by the King three or four times a year.[11] In fact, all members of the royal family turned to him for financial advice, and even consulted him on other types of problems. He served four monarchs in all, including the present Queen in the 1950s.[12]

Peacock, in his recollections to Professor Graham of Queen's University, Canada, stressed the distinction between the Civil List and the private investments of the monarch. The Civil List was handled up until 1935 by the formidable Sir Frederick ('Fritz') Ponsonby, who would regularly write in rude and demanding terms to government departments, relaying the latest royal request. To keep him operative in this way, it would not do to have him know the extent of royal wealth, since all the time he had to plead royal poverty to the Treasury or some other government department, as he had done in 1920 with his 'taxi-cab' letter. Thus Peacock recalled how George V would say 'Don't tell Fritz' when the subject of the King's private money came up.[13] Fritz knew there was such, if only from the savings on the Civil List, but he had to be kept in the dark as to the extent of this private capital.

Peacock was 'knighted for his services to the Royal Family', according to John Orbell, the Baring Brothers archivist. George V in 1934 awarded him the GCVO, which carries a knighthood.[14] This was the highest of the honours which, at the time, could be granted purely at the behest of the monarch, not on the 'advice' of the Prime Minister. Peacock's services to the monarch, which earned this honour, should not be interpreted as narrowly concerned with investment. As a leading director of the Bank of England, Peacock was able to perform another service in 1931, at the time of the financial crisis which led to the downfall of the minority Labour government and the formation of the 'National' Government.

The Bank, like the City generally, wanted the minority Labour government to impose significant cuts in unemployment benefit, to help balance the budget and restore 'business confidence'. Ramsay MacDonald's Cabinet was split on this question and lacked any alternative economic perspective to that of the City. The government needed to raise a short-term loan from the American banks to help prop up the pound, with which it hoped to ride out the crisis and not take too many unpleasant decisions. The chances of the government's obtaining the loan would be known on the evening of Sunday 23 August. During the day, the King had seen separately the Prime Minister, MacDonald, Sir Herbert Samuel for the Liberals, and the Conservative leader, Stanley Baldwin. The last two were consulted with MacDonald's permission to see who might form the next government if Labour failed to survive the financial crisis. For the King, who would appoint any new government, it was probably the most crucial day of his reign.

Peacock was in touch with the King throughout the day. This is revealed in an autobiographical essay written by Peacock, not previously used by writers on the 1931 crisis. Peacock describes how George V's private secretary, Wigram, had been instructed by the King to see Peacock to 'find out the true position, and had also said that I was to come to dinner at Buckingham Palace that night to discuss the matter with the King'. To start with, 'I got Wigram to join me at lunch and told him as much as I could.'[15] The two main biographies of George V, by Harold Nicolson and Kenneth Rose, specifically deny that Peacock's dinner with the King had anything to do with the crisis. They seem to have been anxious to protect the King from any accusation, which would have been well-founded, that he was receiving information and probably advice from someone who was not, constitutionally speaking, a 'responsible adviser'. Peacock was not a minister, who, theoretically, would have been responsible to Parliament for any advice given to the King. Moreover, as already noted, Peacock was a Conservative supporter. Wigram during this busy Sunday also consulted Dawson, the editor of *The Times*, twice.[16] This was an adviser that the King shared with Baldwin, the Conservative Party leader, who lunched with Dawson on the same day in order to talk over the political situation.[17]

After his dinner with the King, Peacock phoned from Buckingham Palace to Sir Ernest Harvey, the Deputy-Governor of the Bank of England, at Downing Street, to find out the reaction of the Labour Cabinet to the news from America.[18] The American bankers queried whether the government's programme of spending cuts and extra taxation had the 'sincere approval' of the Bank of England and the City generally. The Cabinet had split on adopting the cuts in unemployment benefit which would have won this approval, and decided to resign. This much Peacock was able hastily to tell the King just before MacDonald arrived to tender his resignation. MacDonald told the King, 'I am afraid, sir, it is all up to you now.' The King replied, 'I can but do my best.'[19] This was to ask MacDonald to split from his Labour colleagues and form a 'National', but in reality primarily Conservative, government to push through the cuts.

The Conservatives and Liberals wanted the cuts in unemployment benefit, but did not want to bear the unpopularity of enforcing a 10 per cent reduction on their own. They would be accused of representing the rich against the poorest section of society. MacDonald, the Chancellor, Philip Snowden, plus Jimmy Thomas, Secretary of State for the Dominions and former leader of the railwaymen's union, were wanted to provide a Labour 'cover' for this policy. The National Government was disastrous for the unemployed and for the Labour Party, who found themselves being denounced by their erstwhile leader plus the handful of other Labour ministers who joined the new caretaker government. In the ensuing election, Labour was reduced to a rump of fifty-two seats in the Commons.

The King's role in the formation of the National Government is still a matter of controversy. However, this author maintains it would not have been formed without the King's having persuaded MacDonald that only he could save the country in the crisis, together with MacDonald's susceptibility to such royal flattery. Peacock, too, did his best to persuade MacDonald to be a 'National' Prime Minister. The King also played a role in persuading Baldwin to serve under MacDonald, which Baldwin saw as threatening his not too strong hold on the Tory leadership, though he might have been persuaded to do this anyway by Chamberlain and the other Tory leaders.

But what is of primary interest here is the way in which the King naturally turned to Peacock, one of the leaders of the City, on this crucial day. For the City was very much present in George V's Court, the King surrounding himself with men who were, or through Court connections became, 'something in the City'. His Lord Chamberlain, Lord Cromer, had briefly been a managing director of Barings and was a director of several companies. He was also a Conservative peer. One of the King's 'Gentlemen-Ushers', Sir Louis Greig, whom *The Times* described as 'a trusted friend' of the King's, was a stockbroker.[20] Wigram, the private secretary, was a director of an insurance company and on his retirement became a director of the Midland Bank and other companies. Sir Frederick Ponsonby, the Keeper of the Privy Purse, was the director of four companies, including two insurance companies. Sir Harry Stonor, another long-time courtier, was the director of a shipping company, and so on. The Court may have had a feudal appearance and was certainly not short of landowners from ancient families, but many of these were also part of the world of finance.

Edward VIII

George V died just before midnight on 20 January 1936. On the evening of the 22nd his will was read by his private solicitor, Sir Bernard Halsey-Bircham. The new King, Edward VIII, was not pleased by its contents.[21] Present at the reading was Wigram, who had been George V's private secretary and who continued in that role for the first six months of the new reign. Wigram recorded that:

> [Edward] was much perturbed that his father had left him no money and kept on saying 'Where do I come in?' We tried to explain that the late King felt that his eldest son, as Prince of Wales for twenty-five years, ought to have built up a nice surplus out of the Duchy of Cornwall and that there was no necessity to provide for him.

Also, he had inherited money from other sources.[22] But Wigram described 'how we failed to comfort the new King. He kept on saying that my brothers and sister have got large sums but I have been left out.'

George V left at least £3 million (at 1991 prices, £100 million) split between his other four surviving children.[23] This figure refers to money and investments, not to the paintings, jewels etc. or to Balmoral and Sandringham. He also left additional money to his wife, Queen Mary,[24] and perhaps his grandchildren, of whom the present Queen is one. It will be remembered from Ponsonby's 'taxi-cab' letter that the grandchildren were the intended beneficiaries of George V's Civil List savings.

Whoever was left money by George V, the new King was not one of them. Wigram continues, 'it was most unfortunate that King Edward VIII was not reasonable' about this fact:

> As a matter of fact it was discovered later that he had tucked away over a million sterling.[25] I tried to assure His Majesty that he would be very well off and there was no reason why he should not save money from

his Civil List and the Privy Purse, as his father had done. His Majesty continued to be obsessed about money.

A new king meant a new Civil List. Wigram, still private secretary in April 1936, received the list of proposals which were soon to be implemented. He expressed his opinion of them to J.D.B. Fergusson of the Treasury: 'From a cursory glance it seems to me that the King has done very well.'[26] Wigram could indeed anticipate savings from the Civil List for Edward.

The 1936 secret report on royal taxation referred to above was drawn up for Neville Chamberlain, because as Chancellor of the Exchequer he had to pilot the Treasury's Civil List proposals through the House of Commons. First, like chancellors before and since, he had to chair the Commons Select Committee of inquiry into the new monarch's Civil List. The committee will generally pass the Treasury measures, which the Chancellor then has to see through the debates in the House as a whole. Generally speaking, there is not too much difficulty, but 1936 was the first time a Civil List was prepared with a considerable number of Labour MPs in the Commons and a number on the Select Committee. So it was as well for Chamberlain to be prepared for any awkward questions he might be asked from the Labour side.

Thus the secret report on taxation matters collected together, for Chamberlain's benefit, 'all that is known publicly on the subject'. This consisted of four parliamentary statements made by ministers on the tax position of royalty from 1842 to 1926. These were included to give Chamberlain an idea of the (very little) information which had entered the public domain regarding matters of royal taxation. In order for the Chancellor to disclose as little as possible to any enquiring Labour MP, he had to be sure how much or how little the questioner might know. If he underestimated the questioner's knowledge, then he laid himself open to being caught out and questioned more effectively than he would wish. If, on the other hand, the Chancellor overestimated what might be publicly known, then he risked giving information away unnecessarily.

A number of Treasury communications at this time show that the top civil servants were hastily preparing some justifications for various royal privileges.[27] They were fearful of Labour uncovering a number of abuses, like the Civil List savings. They need not have worried. Of course, Labour members of a Select Committee can ask questions of the Chancellor. Also, Select Committees on the Civil List have called in relevant Treasury and Inland Revenue officials, as in 1971. But to ask effectively probing questions you need a minimum of knowledge in the first place. The Treasury and its chancellors of the Exchequer have firmly seen their job as to deny that basic minimum, if it touched on sensitive areas. The difference between this 'economy with the truth' and secrecy is therefore often only a difference of degree.

The Treasury has been clearly oriented towards this kind of economy in order to be less than economical with regard to the royal family. This, ironically, from the department whose role was and is to keep public expenditure under control. In this role, the same Treasury mandarins, like J.D.B. Fergusson, had been 'bitter partisans' against those Labour ministers who had held out against cutting unemployment benefit in 1931. Hugh Dalton's diary records how, shortly after the fall of the Labour government and the formation of the National Government in 1931, Fergusson and a colleague, Grigg, were scathing and rude about the ex-Labour ministers Henderson and Graham.[28] For these were the ministers who, though they had accepted other cuts in welfare services, had dug in their heels against the 10 per cent cut in benefit that MacDonald's National Government went on to implement.

Even top civil servants, outside the Treasury, were not to be trusted with admission into the small world of royal finances. A March 1936 memorandum noted with satisfaction that 'the Civil List is of course audited by Sir Warren Fisher' (Civil Service head of the Treasury). The Duchy of Cornwall accounts were also audited by a trusted person: 'What is essential is to keep out audit by the Comptroller and Auditor-General.'[29]

It is unlikely that the latter, a very senior civil servant, was a dangerous republican, but on the other hand he could easily have asked some awkward questions. For instance, why did the Treasury allow surpluses on money apportioned for the various expenses of the Royal Household, by Act of Parliament, to be paid over to the King's Privy Purse? Such enquiries would have disrupted the cosy, but not very accountable, world in which royal finance was organized. It consisted, on the one side, of the royals and a few Palace officials (one of whom was ex-Treasury), plus Peacock, the King's financial adviser, who was on very close terms with leading Treasury officials;[30] and on the other side, of the Civil Service head of the Treasury and one or two others there. The Treasury also closely oversees the Inland Revenue in its dealings with any problems in the tax matters of the royal family as a whole. The Chancellor of the Exchequer, or occasionally the Prime Minister, would every now and then intervene in this little world, their role being to judge whether it was politically expedient to grant the latest royal demand.

There was, however, one other minister whose responsibility included dealing with royal financial demands – the Chancellor of the Duchy of Lancaster. In June 1936 the latter agreed to Edward VIII's transferring to himself almost the entire reserves of the Duchy's No Kin Investment Fund.[31] The fund, amounting to £38,000 (at 1991 prices, £1.23 million), was part of the proceeds from people who died without making a will and with no traceable relatives. Amazingly, their personal and landed property in Lancashire was, and still is, taken by the Duchy, through an ancient right dating back to 1377 (see Chapter 10). The fund, in which the King left just £1,000, had been put aside to pay any relatives not previously traceable who came forward to present their claims at a later date.

The Chancellor of the Duchy, Sir John Davidson, did, however, draw the line against the King's attempt to divert £250,000 (1991: £8.15 million) of the Duchy's capital to his own pocket. Nor would he allow the King to have two years' revenue as an advance on future profits.[32] It may be that Edward VIII was anticipating the possibility that he might abdicate and that he wanted to get as much of the Duchy's money into that personal and private pocket before he gave up the throne. This, of course, he did at the end of the year, when the government would not allow him to marry Mrs Simpson. Or it may be that he felt, even if he remained King, he could make more money with this capital than could the Duchy. For he could play the stockmarket, whereas the Duchy was then legally constrained to invest in British government stock.

The desire to accumulate was combined with a desire to economize – at least on the wages bill and some aspects of the private estates, particularly the great expense of Sandringham. Moreover, Edward already had Fort Belvedere, which he said was his own 'spiritual "Sandringham"'. So he arranged for his brother, the Duke of York, plus Lord Radnor to draw up a plan on how to make economies on the £50,000 running expenses of Sandringham. Part of this cost was the loss that the King's farms at Sandringham incurred, £8,561 in 1935.[33]

Something Must Be Done, and it was. Redundancies in 1936 reduced the total wages bill by £6,150 at Sandringham and by £1,360 at Balmoral, the other private estate of the King. Thus the total wage bill for these estates was reduced to about £42,000 p.a.[34] In retrospect, many royalist books are all too willing to criticize him for such actions. They sound almost republican, contrasting the jewellery and other presents for Mrs Simpson with throwing people out of work in the hungry 1930s. However, this is simply part of the retrospective view that Edward VIII was fatally flawed, which is why he did not do his 'duty' but instead abdicated. At the time, the Treasury saw the redundancies as 'wise estate management'.

When George V came into his inheritance in 1910, he made economies in the wages bill at Buckingham Palace and Windsor, cutting it from £120,418 under Edward VII to £115,643 in his first full year as King. However, after the First World War, because of inflation, it went back up again, though this increase was curbed by the implementation of the 1921 report, described in Chapter 3. Edward VIII made more redundancies at Buckingham Palace[35] and cut all wages and salaries by 10 per cent amongst those who remained.[36] He brought the wages bill down from £148,439 in the last year of his father's reign (1935) so that by 1937 it had fallen over 20 per cent to £117,593.[37] Lady Donaldson, in her biography of Edward VIII, says that 'at the beginning of the reign sanction was obtained, although with difficulty, that no man should be dismissed without alternative employment, but after the formation of the new Household [in the summer of 1936] even this rule was dropped'.[38]

It might be argued that critics cannot have it both ways, by disapproving of monarchs' heavy spending on servants in their various royal abodes and then objecting when they reduce the number of these servants. However, there are four points to make. Firstly, Edward was voted certain sums by Parliament to spend on wages and salaries at Buckingham Palace and Windsor. When savings were made by staff reductions or reducing wages, he pocketed them – no saving was made to the public purse. Secondly, Edward had forged a strong public identity, with the considerable help of the press, as someone who was deeply concerned over the problem of poverty and unemployment, not as someone who added to it. Thirdly, this was the time of the depression, in which finding a job was no easy matter, especially in places like Sandringham in Norfolk and Balmoral in the Highlands. And lastly, many of these jobs were live-in jobs, which would mean losing one's accommodation as well as one's employment.

The Abdication

Edward VIII's abdication in December 1936 and the succession of his brother, the Duke of York, as George VI, posed the problem of how much the former King (now the Duke of Windsor) would be given to maintain him in exile. According to Edward VIII's official biographer, what ensued was a 'long-drawn-out wrangle over money' between the two brothers which 'did more than anything else to poison the atmosphere between the future Duke of Windsor and his family'.[39]

Between Edward's decision to abdicate becoming final, on 7 December, and his ceasing to be King on the 11th, there was much discussion about money. It involved the two brothers and their respective helpers, culminating on the evening of the 10th in a fairly fraught meeting between Edward and the Duke of York. Each brother brought his private solicitor. Also present were Wigram, who was now representing the Duke of York, and Walter Monckton, the Conservative MP and lawyer who was advising Edward. Sir Edward Peacock attended as private financial adviser to the King and Sir Ulick Alexander, successor to the fearsome Ponsonby, as Keeper of the Privy Purse.

Edward, it will be remembered, had been reminded back in January that being left no money by his father was not so bad, as he would save money from the over-generous Civil List, as well as the Privy Purse. In December, it was his turn to recall this argument. He maintained that, now he was abdicating, he could no longer make money from the Civil List. (Though he neglected to mention the £1 million fortune (£33 million at 1991 prices) he had accumulated largely from the Duchy of Cornwall.) He maintained he was 'very badly off'.[40] Therefore, he wanted his father's will changed to give him a share of the money being left to the rest of his family.[41]

He was unsuccessful. Nevertheless, the meeting ended 'quietly and harmoniously', with Peacock's help, according to the Duke of York.[42] Monckton recalled Peacock''s impressive imperturbability throughout the fraught negotiations. A legal agreement was reached, essentially giving Edward £25,000 a year in exchange for surrendering his lifetime tenancy of Balmoral and Sandringham and their contents.[43] Buckingham Palace and Windsor Castle were not part of this deal. They came under the control of the government's Office of Works (now part of the Department of the Environment) and as such were automatically put at the disposal of whoever was King. Edward also handed over the most valuable items of all (especially in present-day terms), the paintings and other works of art which he had inherited as King.

It was sincerely hoped that the government would provide the Duke's £25,000, about £815,000 in current prices, but in case they did not, the Duke of York guaranteed to do so. The royals had indications that the government would provide the £25,000 as part of the new King's Civil List arrangements in 1937, though there are different versions of how strong the indications were. It seems the December agreement was kept secret from the government whilst there was the prospect it would pay,[44] which would be less likely if ministers knew that George VI was prepared to finance his brother.

Yet what became very clear by February 1937 was that both Baldwin as Prime Minister and Neville Chamberlain at the Treasury would block any grant to the ex-King if there was the expectation of Labour opposition and a 'parliamentary wrangle'. Well before the whole matter got to the House of Commons, it was found Labour did object, which effectively put the onus on George VI to pay the Duke's annuity.[45]

What had worried Baldwin, Chamberlain, and also the King[46] was that asking Parliament to provide for the Duke of Windsor could easily lead to queries as to how much he had 'salted away', as Wigram had put it, and as to how he had come by it. Furthermore, if he really needed a grant, could not the King pay for it from his private wealth inherited from George V? How much did George V leave? How had he accumulated this sum? Was not the Civil List too generous if it allowed such accumulation? Winston Churchill, who was a member of the 1937 Select Committee on George VI's Civil List, wrote to Lloyd George about how such perils could present themselves, even without introducing the question of the Duke of Windsor: 'Attlee [the leader of the Labour Party] asked for information about the private fortunes and savings of members of the Royal Family. You will see the drift of this.' Churchill congratulated himself for having managed to sidetrack Attlee away from the danger area.[47]

By February, the new King discovered that he had been misled and that his brother, before his exile, had accumulated what George VI's latest biographer termed a 'huge capital sum'.[48] This made the King distinctly less keen to honour the agreement with the Duke, and at this point he was advised or at least encouraged not to by the Treasury. He wrote saying it was essential that the Duke give him some precise figures. The Duke replied that he would 'prefer not to do so',[49] warning that, if he gave a figure to the King, the King's advisers would be in a position accurately to answer questions about the Duke's wealth, rather than being able to plead ignorance. Edward enunciated a principle which the present Queen followed in relation to the 1971 Select Committee. He said that it 'would be a grave mistake if the private means of any member of the Royal Family were to be disclosed to the Select Committee'. It might mean that such private means could be taken into account in determining the level of state provision for royalty.

Even if he decided to honour the December agreement, the King still had other related worries. One of these was that if the agreement became public, both the press and Parliament might object to the government's planning to fund the Duke's annuity indirectly through an inflated Civil List. This could lead to demands to reduce the Civil List[50] and to leave George VI to pay his brother from his private wealth, the amount of which could become a discussion point.

The King's solution to this was to propose that the Duke should agree to end the December agreement, because he wanted his advisers to be free to tell the Select Committee that he had not agreed to pay the Duke anything. At the same time, the King gave his brother his word that he would in effect honour the terms of the agreement, after the Civil List was passed.[51] Royalist authors concentrate on the Duke's angry reaction, his unwillingness to trust his brother and his stubborn desire to cling to the December agreement. The ex-King told his lawyer that unless he got his annuity, he would assert his right to Balmoral and Sandringham and not simply hand them over to his brother. These authors miss the point that the King was proposing a form of sharp practice in relation to the Select Committee, or that the Duke's objection to this ploy had nothing to do with outrage at the idea of deceiving a Select Committee. It was merely self-interested concern that his brother was reneging on their agreement.

A subsequent stage in the 'endless and acrimonious negotiations'[52] occurred in June 1937, when the government and King attempted to attach to the money the condition that the Windsors should not return to Britain without permission of the King, advised by his ministers. Any unwelcome return to these shores would mean the end of the annuity. Other dilutions of the original agreement were also proposed from the King's side, and further delays caused bitter frustration for the Duke. But some payment had to be made by the King, if only because he had signed an agreement to that effect and because the Duke held the trump card of Balmoral and Sandringham. In July he was threatening, if only in a letter to his lawyer, to prevent the King and the Court from going on their usual seasonal migration to Balmoral in August.[53]

Today, the unedifying row is replayed in the books of royalist biographers. Michael Bloch, very much the Duke of Windsor's champion in his three books on Edward, refers to the 'breach of faith' of the new King in his reluctance to keep to the agreement.[54] Philip Ziegler, on the other hand, Edward's official biographer, refers to the 'lie' that Edward told his brother about being badly off. Because it soured relations between him and his family, Ziegler claims it was 'the worst mistake he made in his life'.[55]

Edward's deception is only partly explained and excused by Ziegler in terms of his being under great pressure at the time of his abdication, plus his abject desire to please Mrs Simpson, who would not be so happy to marry an ex-King without a kingly income: 'Nevertheless, he told a lie for reasons of self-interest, and this cannot be condoned.' However, looked at in the wider context of the history of royal pay demands, Edward was doing little more than conforming to established royal strategy, which has been continued since. This consists of not divulging one's private wealth and pleading poverty.* The only real difference in Edward's case was that the bill for his annuity was not delivered to the Treasury; because of Labour oppositition, it had been diverted to Buckingham Palace.

In the end the settlement, described by Bloch, which took over a year to reach, was that the Duke of Windsor got a lower figure, £21,000 a year. But only half of it was conditional on his only visiting Britain by

---

* Ziegler (p. 326) cites Wigram, who greatly disapproved of Edward, that the latter went beyond concealing the extent of his private wealth by giving an untruthfully low figure at the crucial 10 December meeting. However, Edward felt able to write to his brother a couple of months later, about that meeting, 'naturally *not mentioning* what I have been able to save as Prince of Wales, I did tell you that I was very badly off, which I am considering the position I shall have to maintain and what I have given up . . .' (my emphasis). See Bloch, *Duke of Windsor*, p. 50.

permission of the King, on the advice of his ministers. Part of the agreement by which the sum was paid over was that the new King paid £300,000 for Sandringham and Balmoral (at 1991 prices, about £10 million). This was put in trust and the interest, about £10,000 a year, paid to Edward. The remaining £11,000 or so was to be paid by George VI. This was the part which could be withdrawn if the Windsors returned without permission.

The mother of the royal brothers, Queen Mary, together with George VI's wife (now the Queen Mother) and the senior courtiers were all united in the policy of keeping the Windsors out.[56] They feared that the charisma which had attached to the elder brother for over twenty years might still overshadow the more shy and backward George VI. Thus the family quarrel, after the initial stage when it was entirely about money, became more concerned with keeping out the Windsors. The presence of the ex-King in Britain would interfere with the effort of pumping 'into the once Duke of York what had been pumped of popular affection into the Prince of Wales in the past twenty-five years'.[57]

Taxation on Private Investment Income

George VI inherited about three-quarters of a million pounds from his father, according to Philip Ziegler. Even after buying Sandringham and Balmoral from his older brother, he would be left with £450,000 (at 1991 prices, £14.7 million). Also, he may have saved money from his government annuity when Duke of York.

Whatever George VI was worth in stocks, shares and the like, enquiries were very quickly made on his behalf as to whether now, as King, he could avoid paying tax on the income from his capital. In early January 1937, Sir Edward Peacock was seeking to discover the monarch's tax position as regards private investments. George VI had been King less than a month. Harwood, the ex-Treasury man who became Deputy Treasurer to the King, also took the matter up. It will be remembered that the last time Harwood had busied himself on monarchical taxation matters, he was successful in securing the removal of the tax on the Duchy of Lancaster, in 1933. F.A. Slee of the Inland Revenue replied to Harwood's enquiry, stating the situation as outlined in the 1936 secret report, described at the beginning of this chapter. He reiterated that up to now, where tax had been deducted at source (the rate was then

22.5 per cent), the monarch had not reclaimed the money,* though it was reclaimable.[58]

From here we have to engage in a little informed speculation, together with some elementary deduction. As we have seen, from the preceding account of Victoria and Albert onwards, royals are not afraid to ask for more, and do so regularly. The fact that George VI faced the prospect of paying off his brother would be a good excuse to approach the Treasury for some concession, even though he could well afford the payment. We have also seen that the royals' best prospects for success occur when Parliament does not have to be approached for more money, or at least when MPs are not aware they are being approached. One bounty that the King could extract would be to have any tax deducted at source refunded to him. This we know George V did not generally do. The 1936 secret report stated, 'as regards private and personal estate, income tax deducted at the source *is not reclaimed* by His Majesty . . .' (my emphasis).

In March 1937, in preparation for George VI's Civil List, an updated version of this memo was produced inside the Treasury, for Neville Chamberlain (still Chancellor but soon to be Prime Minister). The wording was practically identical throughout with that of the 1936 document. But the 1937 version, which had been checked with Slee of the Inland Revenue, differs by saying that 'as regards income tax deducted at the source, repayment, though claimable in law, *has not in the past* been claimed' (my emphasis).[59] The latter formulation, compared to the 1936 description ('is not reclaimed'), leaves the future situation open. Thus the significance of the amended wording in 1937 could be that a new practice of reclaiming tax was in the offing. Also, Slee's letter to Harwood had said that the King could reclaim this tax. The Inland Revenue was offering to waive the tax on George VI's investment income. This of course would be too tempting to refuse, but would need ministerial approval, at least from the Chancellor of the Exchequer and maybe also the Prime Minister.

What precisely happened may have been revealed in an intriguingly

---

* The only exception to this was in certain 'special accounts such as the Balmoral and Sandringham Fire Insurance Sinking Fund where, although the investments remained the absolute property of the Sovereign, the income was allocated by Him to certain specific purposes'. (It is interesting that 'Him' is spelt with a capital 'H'. How can you ask someone to pay tax when, like God, he is capitalized?) These 'special accounts', though part of the Sandringham and Balmoral estates, were not considered taxable under the 1862 Crown Private Estates Act.

entitled file listed at the Public Record Office in Kew, amongst the seemingly endless lists of Treasury files. Under the general heading 'Taxation: Income Tax', is the entry for 'Royal Family; Civil List 12 October 1936–23 May 1938'.[60] I applied for this hopefully, as there was no indication in the list that it was closed to public inspection, as many of the files kept at the Public Record Office are. I was told at Kew that the file had been retained by the Treasury, but the latter did not see fit to preserve what might be important evidence in this matter, let alone send it to its proper destination. In June 1991 a parliamentary question from the Scots Labour MP Brian Wilson elicited the response from a Treasury minister that 'this file appears to have been destroyed in 1977. As a result of a clerical error, the Public Record Office was not informed.'[61]

What is known is that in 1952 the Chancellor of the Exchequer, R.A. Butler, publicly stated, in discussing the present monarch's Civil List, that 'the Sovereign naturally, except when her . . . private estates are governed by the [Crown Private Estates] Act of 1862, is free of tax'.[62] If this statement is literally true, then some time between early 1937 and 1952, the monarch started to reclaim taxes which had been deducted at source. The destroyed Treasury file relating to the period 1936–8 may pinpoint the date of this concession, which virtually completed the process, started in 1910, of producing the tax-free monarch.

If income tax on the monarch's private income was removed in 1937 or 1938, this was a stroke of good fortune for George VI. For soon after, income-tax rates rocketed upwards in order to pay for the Second World War. In 1941 the standard rate of income tax, which would have been deducted at source from the King's dividends, was raised to 50 per cent, while the tax thresholds were lowered such that the 1 million manual workers paying tax before the war increased to 7 million in 1943–4. The PAYE (Pay As You Earn) system was introduced to help deal with the associated problems of collecting it all. For these extra 6 million manual workers, paying income tax was a new experience; for George VI it may well have been a past experience. The only tax for which the King was liable was the landlord's Schedule A on rents from Sandringham and Balmoral, but these produced little or no profits.

When Butler said that 'naturally' the Queen pays hardly any tax, it is hard to think of it as natural, but rather the result of a long process of royal pressure and Treasury accommodation to that pressure.

As regards reclaiming tax deducted at source, the pressure may well have been first exerted by Edward VIII. There are three indications that this was so. First, there is the way that Sir Edward Peacock described his relationship with him, which began when he was Prince of Wales. Peacock described how the latter was 'much more interested in and knowledgeable about finance than his father. He liked to talk about investments, markets regardless of his own private intentions; he showed . . . a shrewd understanding of such matters.' Peacock saw much more of Edward VIII on such matters than he did of George V. In fact, Peacock said he became a 'close friend',[63] and the former King refers, in his autobiography, to the merchant banker as 'my old friend'. Peacock recalled how the royal investor on several occasions came to the banker's Connaught Place home at about 7 p.m. to discuss some financial matter on his way to call on the Simpsons. There are similar accounts of how, after the abdication, he is frequently on the phone to his stockbroker in New York or elsewhere.

Thus, apart from telling us something significant about Edward VIII, the keen capitalist, the above suggests that he invested in company shares where tax was definitely deducted at source. He would seem to have been a more adventurous investor than his father. The second piece of evidence is that Edward was, according to Wigram, 'obsessed' about money. He would certainly not have paid any income tax if he could help it. Wigram's account can be suspected of being jaundiced about Edward, but the latter certainly had a capacity to believe himself impoverished when he was not in the least. Thirdly, the destroyed Treasury file which concerns royal income-tax matters was opened in October 1936, whilst Edward was still King, and closed in May 1938, shortly after the conclusion of the financial settlement between the two brothers (though it could be that it deals with other royal taxation matters).

The tax issue did not cease to be important to the Duke of Windsor after his abdication. He wanted his annuity from George VI to be tax-free. Winston Churchill, who had taken the ex-King's side during the abdication crisis and was still upholding his interests, asked for this concession in a letter to the Chancellor, Neville Chamberlain.[64] He seems to have been successful, though the Duke did have to pay surtax on some or all of his investments in Britain when he was living in France after the abdication.[65] However, Walter Monckton managed to secure for the Duke a tax-free status in relation to the French government.[66] This was why they settled on France as their place of exile. In a memorandum the Duke drew up for his wife to help decide where to settle down, he considered having 'untaxed incomes' as most important. Similarly, the Duchess of Windsor, in a letter to her aunt in which she weighs up the same question, lists taxes as the number one factor.[67]

Ideally, they both wished to live in the United States after the Second World War was over. But if they were to live in the style to which they were accustomed (twenty-eight domestic staff and two secretaries), they did not feel able to pay US taxes, especially with servants costing much more there. The American government was extremely unlikely to grant them a tax-free status. One idea of the Duke's was that the British government attach him to the British Embassy in Washington, as a sort of roving ambassador promoting American goodwill to Britain. Of course, he did not want to work too hard, and the job description he drew up for himself emphasized that there should be no specific workload. A nine to five routine was certainly not envisaged. But if he took up this role on an official basis, he could get diplomatic immunity and be free of tax. Certainly, nice work if you can get it, but, as part of the continuing quarrel between the two brothers, the idea was scotched.[68] Perhaps, also, memories of his sympathies towards Nazi Germany may have led the government to believe him unreliable and a risk.

George VI

Those out of work were not to be forgotten at the time of the Coronation of George VI in May 1937. To mark the occasion, the Minister of Labour announced they would receive a special payment of 2s 6d (about £4 in current prices). In the Commons, one Labour MP enquired of the Minister how this mighty sum would be dispensed. 'Will this two shillings and sixpence be paid by instalments or in a lump sum? (laughter).'[69] Cassandra, the *Daily Mirror*'s star columnist, described it as 'the latest insult to the unemployed'. Compared to the grand occasion, the meagre amount was a 'contemptible gesture'.[70]

Different criteria were used to decide George VI's Civil List, which was fixed at about the same amount as his brother's the year before. As with his predecessors, he was able to make transfers to his Privy Purse. These savings, as in 1914–18 and for the same reasons, increased during the Second World War.[71]

Nevertheless, there came a message from F.P. Robinson of the Financial Secretary's Office, Windsor. Robinson had replaced Harwood in this post, and like Harwood was on loan from the Treasury. Robinson stated that the King wanted to be reimbursed for the cost of a special train to visit the Fleet, six weeks after the start of the war, in October 1939. Robinson pleaded poverty, referring to a supposed cut in George VI's Civil List, compared to Edward VIII's. But even the Treasury had to draw the line somewhere. P.L. Smith of the Treasury said that there had not really been a cut in the Civil List at all and that, as visiting the Fleet was a function related to his being King, it could quite easily be paid for out of the Civil List. He noted that during war-time some costs to the King, like that of trains to visit the armed forces, might increase, but there would be a reduction in other expenses (like entertaining). Smith also noted that the King was 'treated very well' by the Treasury over the expenses on his and the Queen's recent visit to Canada.[72]

The same issue of special trains had arisen during the First World War, and the Conservative Chancellor in the Lloyd George coalition, Bonar Law, had recommended that George V foot the bill from his Civil List. The point was that Bonar Law was worried that it might possibly be noticed in the Parliamentary Votes that, whilst the ordinary ranks in the armed forces were being paid very low wages, the King was asking the country to foot substantial bills for luxurious travel. It is recorded that George V did not like having to pay, but 'thought that the avoidance of any parliamentary criticism was of overriding importance'. For the same reasons, in 1939, the Prime Minister's most influential adviser, Sir Horace Wilson, wrote to Robinson at Windsor confirming the First World War precedent. Of course, the Civil List comes from the tax-payer. But the aim was to offload certain expenses on to government departments, so that as much as possible could be saved from the Civil List for the King's private pocket, which was not filling up as quickly as it would have done because of the payments that had to be made to his brother. As we have seen, both here with the two world wars, and earlier with Edward VII's demand during the Boer War to end the tax on his Civil List, war-time is very sensitive for royal finances. The monarchy has to be protected from the adverse publicity which could result from having certain of its demands granted.

A much-quoted anecdote about the King during the war concerns a frugal meal served on gold plate to the American President's wife,

Eleanor Roosevelt, during a visit to Buckingham Palace in 1942. A.J.P. Taylor commented that 'spam on a gold plate' would be a good motto for the whole reign. The royals and their staff were, of course, subject to rationing during the war, though when the King and Queen had important guests they could obtain extra rations.

The official in the Royal Household, Frederick Corbitt, who had been responsible for procuring its food, published his recollections in 1956. These covered the war years, and he recalls keeping the ration books of the King and Queen and staff members in a safe in his office. However, food from one's own farms and estates was not subject to rationing. Corbitt recalls that 'food from Sandringham, Windsor and Balmoral was used extensively throughout the war to supplement the ordinary rations. Salmon from the Dee [on the Balmoral estate, which also supplied grouse] was an especially useful item.'[73] Unfortunately for George VI, he was not that fond of salmon. The dairies at Windsor supplied butter, which was used moderately at the royal table.

There is no mention of 'spam on gold plate menus' in Corbitt's book. Moreover, for the King's weekly lunches with the Prime Minister, small decanters of whisky and brandy were provided, plus cigars for Churchill. One of Churchill's ministers, Lord Reith, dined at the Palace in July 1941, after the imposition of rationing, without too much hardship. He records his dinner at the Palace as cold jelly soup, ham mousse and cold chicken, strawberry ice and strawberries and cream.[74]

Perhaps the war led the King to be more frugal in other respects, though judging from his purchases of jewellery he was not entirely so. Leslie Field describes how he 'loved sapphires and had a connoisseur's appreciation of the stones'. He 'purchased many pieces of sapphire jewellery from Cartier as gifts for Queen Elizabeth and for his daughter, Princess Elizabeth'. In 1942 he bought the Queen a brooch consisting of gold flower chips, with clusters of cushion-shaped sapphires and brilliant cut diamonds in its centre.[75] This she could add to her enormous jewel collection. And in April 1944, for Princess Elizabeth's 18th birthday, he gave her a Cartier bracelet of square-cut sapphires and diamonds.[76]

In war-time, Civil List expenditure on entertaining and wages drops, allowing savings. As his father had done in the First World War, George VI made a donation of £100,000 to the Treasury from these savings. But he waited until 1948 to do so, at a time when he was forced to make some concession because he was asking for more money for Princess Elizabeth (now the Queen) following her wedding to the Duke of Edinburgh. The Princess had just had a rather sharp increase, on reaching her 21st birthday in April 1947, taking her from £6,000 to £15,000 a year (at 1991 prices, from £105,000 to £260,000). However, after her marriage she would apparently need a great deal more money. The Keeper of the Privy Purse, still Sir Ulick Alexander, was dealing with the Treasury and putting forward figures for the increased annuity, which were eventually whittled down to a proposal for £50,000.[77]

Alexander did not deal with the King's private finances; Peacock still did that, though as a director of several companies including a large insurance company and a South African gold-mining company, Alexander could have assisted with the King's investments. In the same way that Peacock recalled how George V had told him, 'Don't tell Fritz [Ponsonby]', the previous Keeper of the Privy Purse, about his private investments, so George VI gave the same instruction. 'Don't tell Ulick,' he would say, and Queen Elizabeth (now the Queen Mother) would say the same.[78] But the King did not entrust Peacock with all his investments. William Hill-Wood, of another merchant bank, Morgan Grenfell, was a friend of the King's, and his nephew recalled how his Uncle Willy was asked by the King to look after some of his personal investments on the same discreet basis as Peacock: 'Hill-Wood reported regularly to the King on his finances, keeping details of the account to himself.'[79] Sir Ulick had to push the Treasury hard, declaring the royal coffers empty. It would not do to remind him that there were other, private, coffers. The fewer people who knew the details of such matters the better.

The 22-year-old Princess Elizabeth, as she then was, received an increase from £15,000 to £40,000 a year in recognition of her now being married, the Commons Select Committee having trimmed £10,000 off the original figure put to them. (The Duke of Edinburgh was to receive £10,000 a year.) Nevertheless, this increase represented some difficulty, in what was supposed to be a period of austerity. This was why the Labour Chancellor of the Exchequer, Hugh Dalton, referred to Princess Elizabeth's need for a large rise, at this time, as 'so delicate'.[80] The Labour government in these years never tired of emphasizing the task of reconstruction after the war, such that many ordinary items of consumption were rationed. In fact, because of the general period the government felt it inappropriate for there to be a general public holiday for the wedding of the heir to the throne.

Dalton showed that Labour could respond to royal requirements. But in this case the increase had to be passed by Parliament. This was why he had to reject the first proposals that came from the Palace. Like Dalton, the King was worried about 'any acrimonious debate on the financial affairs of the Royal Family, or from the putting of detailed questions on this subject to Alexander [Keeper of the Privy Purse], who would appear as a witness before the Select Committee'. Yet the King was torn because 'he said he could not go on indefinitely making the additional provision [for the Princess] from his own resources'.[81] So a compromise, relatively favourable to the royals, was arranged. The King made his contribution of £100,000, from his war-time Civil List savings, towards the increased cost of the annuity to his elder daughter and the £10,000 for her new husband. Ninety per cent of the Princess's annuity was made tax-free by the Treasury.[82]

A few years later, there was another Labour Chancellor of the Exchequer for George VI to deal with. On matters of welfare, the post-war Labour government had introduced a whole range of free items through the health service. Aneurin Bevan, the founder of the NHS, had resigned in 1951 when charges were introduced to help pay for British participation in the Korean War. Gaitskell went to Buckingham Palace to tell the King about the budget and the dispute in the Party over the imposition of charges on, amongst other things, false teeth. Gaitskell reported in his diary that the King said, ' "he [Bevan] must be mad to resign over a thing like that. I really don't see why people should have false teeth free any more than they should have shoes free," waving his foot at me as he said it. He is of course a fairly reactionary person,' Gaitskell concluded,[83] despite the fact that he himself was in favour of charges for false teeth. When it came to money from the state for the royals, somehow a different standard entered royal thinking. The state paid £77,000 (at 1991 prices, £1.1 million) to the King's Privy Purse for personal expenditure, like the upkeep of Balmoral and Sandringham. Also, all his clothes were paid for from the Privy Purse,[84] and probably his shoes too.

As with the situation after the First World War, the 'nest egg' (as Alexander described it)[85] of savings on the Civil List from before and during the war faced the prospect of being slowly eroded by inflation. But after the First World War, boom and inflation soon gave way to slump and deflation, when the King's representatives implemented a policy of wage cuts. After the Second World War, there was no slump, and wage cuts would have seen empty servants' quarters at Buckingham Palace. In fact, the royals had great difficulty as it was in recruiting suitable servants. In 1947, the 'normal' situation of savings going to the Privy Purse started to go into reverse.

Inflation, and the difficulty of getting servants in conditions of full employment,[86] caused wages and salaries to increase, but only to slightly over the amount that was allocated by Parliament for them. The most the allocation of £134,000 for wages and salaries was exceeded by, in any one year, was £4,726 in 1949.[87] There was not much of a 'wages explosion' at the Palace and it paid notoriously badly. The Civil Service Union (now part of the National Union of Civil and Public Servants), which recruited amongst the 'below stairs' staff, had yet to make much of an impact on wages. It had received recognition from the King in 1946, but this was a limited recognition, as Palace officials would not deal with the union directly, no doubt thinking it beneath them. All negotiations had to go through the Ministry of Labour.[88] And it was not until well into the 1950s that the union had much of an effect, the older servants having been against it.[89] Only in the 1970s did Palace officials agree to negotiate directly with CSU officials.

It was on Household Expenses (Class III of the Civil List) that the increase was concentrated. Between 1947 and 1951 the government accordingly relieved the Civil List of some of these expenses, the largest being for fuel, lighting, and the upkeep of Buckingham Palace Gardens. Also, the earlier form of VAT, Purchase Tax, was refunded on items bought for state and ceremonial purposes. One can't help speculating about whether there were pleas for help from the King which led to this government munificence, even in the days of 'austerity' under Attlee's Labour government. The Civil List was thus saved £50,000 a year, diminishing the drain on the Privy Purse 'nest egg', but not preventing it entirely.

Despite subsidizing Class III of the Civil List from his Privy Purse after the War, there was enough accumulated from 1937 to 1945 to mean that, over the whole of George VI's reign, a net profit was made. This amounted to £101,000, even after the repayment of the £100,000 in 1948.[90] Also, George VI and Queen Elizabeth still received, in the post-war years, their combined annual Privy Purse income from the Civil List of £110,000, plus payments of between £90,000 and £100,000 a year from the Duchy of Lancaster (in all, about £3 million in current prices). The Office of Crown Lands (now the Crown Estate) also contrived to pay him over £30,000 during his reign.[91] One would imagine that such sums still allowed a good deal of accumulation. However, George VI, who died when he was only 56 years old, would have found inflation eating into this accumulation more and more had he lived much longer. Then he would no doubt have applied to Parliament for more money. This would have led to questions about his private fortune, and whether a King who benefited from tax concessions and other favours really needed the extra money. It is precisely this scenario which occurred in the present reign in the early 1970s.

II

Elizabeth II

6

The Queen's Civil List, 1952–71

At the outset, it is important to deal with a very long-serving argument on behalf of the monarchy. For over a century, queries over the cost of the monarchy have been met with the claim that really the monarchy costs the country nothing, even that the tax-payer makes a profit out of the institution. And most recently it has been deployed by the Palace, the *Daily Telegraph*[1] and Woodrow Wyatt in *The Times*[2] in defence against calls for the Queen to be taxed on her private fortune.

The argument in question states that in 1760 the King surrendered the Crown Lands (now called the Crown Estate) to Parliament in exchange for a Civil List,* for the duration of the reign. Ever since, British monarchs at the beginning of their reigns have agreed to renew this 'bargain' or exchange. It is maintained that because the net rents from these lands, which go to the government, have increased so much, the monarch would be much better off if he or she were to reclaim the lands.

The real point of the argument is that we should not carp and criticize at the costs of the monarchy, given the profit to the public purse. This was the view forwarded by the Queen's representative when she applied to Parliament for an increased Civil List in 1971. In one form or another, this argument is raised every time there is a full-scale debate on the Civil List in the House of Commons and on countless occasions in certain newspapers, magazines and books.[3] Replying to claims that the Queen should pay tax, Charles Moore in the *Daily Telegraph* in July 1991 maintained that the

---

* To be precise, though, the Civil List dates from 1698, but was paid to earlier monarchs on a different basis. See Chapter 1.

Queen 'does badly' out of the Crown Estate arrangement. The estates 'produce about £60 million a year for the public purse; the Civil List amounts to a mere £7.9 million'. Woodrow Wyatt in *The Times* made the same point. The latter publications seemingly put no reliance on the case for the Queen's Crown immunity from tax, for they did not even mention it.

Mr Moore also did not mention the items which are funded by government departments and which together cost many times more than the Civil List – the Royal Yacht, Royal Train, Royal Flight, upkeep of Palaces, telephone bills, annuities for other royals, staff pensions, salaries of press officers etc.

A somewhat more realistic version of the argument would, however, include the latter costs, and calculate that the annual expenditure on the monarchy at £53.5 million* and the amount paid over from the Crown Estate (£57 million in 1989–90) are comparable.[4] For a complete figure for the cost of the monarchy to the state, however, one would have to include what *The Economist* once called the Queen's 'indirect earnings' from her tax exemption,[5] together with the cost of royal protection, for which no official figures are given and which will add some more millions, if not the £100 million a year suggested in one recent newspaper article.[6] Also, the cost of the British monarchy is many times greater than that of a non-executive presidency, even that of a richer country. The German presidency, because it does not have to support relatives of the President, provide a presidential yacht etc., costs only about £10 million a year (see Introduction).

Leaving aside which is greater, the Crown Estate's revenue or the cost of the monarchy, would a new monarch have the right to say, 'Unlike my predecessors, I shall forgo a Civil List, but I want the Crown Estate back, because its lands are mine by hereditary right'? In 1885 Queen Victoria was 'very willing that the "bargain" should be reopened, so as to give to the Crown its property instead of the Civil List'.[7] Prince Charles has apparently suggested it would be good for the monarchy to reclaim the Crown Estate profits.[8] Its right to do so has been acknowledged in the Civil List Acts passed at the beginning of each reign – but is this right operative? A *Daily Telegraph* editorial in 1991 centred on the idea that it was.[9]

* See Chapter 8 for details of how this figure is arrived at.

We shall answer this question within the established legal and constitutional framework. This means forgetting that the origins of the hereditary right to the Crown Estate lie in the not so legal, but highly effective, seizure of the Norman Conquest and subsequently in all manner of other seizures – including those of monastery lands under Henry VIII.

The answer, or 'advice', that any government would give a monarch who demanded back 'his' or 'her' Crown Estates would simply be that, regrettably, it was not possible in the modern era. And that would in itself settle matters. It may be true that government ministers and civil servants have usually been careful to maintain the formality that a new monarch can reverse the so-called bargain of 1760. But it is no more than a formality. For the monarchy's own sake, the government of the day (of whichever party) would seek to protect the monarch from the consequent embarrassment of such a step back into the eighteenth century.

Moreover, within the royal camp, Sir Frederick Ponsonby, despite employing his usual vigour on behalf of George V's finances in 1920, was careful to deny that the King or his successors had any right to the Crown Lands. He stated correctly that 'it is an essential part of the Constitution that the Sovereign should be dependent on Parliament for the Civil List and should not receive money direct from Crown Lands'.[10] In other words, the outcome of the struggles of the seventeenth and the late eighteenth centuries was to subordinate the monarchy to Parliament, financial dependence being an essential feature of that development. Thus, the representative of the King relinquished any practical, or even theoretical, right to the return of the Crown Lands.

However, this does not mean Ponsonby (or other monarchists) would let go of this particular bone. In spite of there being no royal right to these lands, Ponsonby argued that the Civil List was really paid out of the net profits from them. As these had, in the years before 1920, clearly overtaken the Civil List, then 'there is no reason why Parliament should not behave generously and allow the Sovereign to profit by the increased value of the Crown Lands'. Also figuring in the calculations of the Keeper of the Privy Purse were something called the 'Small Branches of the Hereditary Revenue'. These are an assortment of revenues which were worth about £50,000 in 1920.[11] (They had been surrendered to Parliament in 1830.)

Despite the fact that, even formally speaking, by 1920 the Civil List had long since ceased to be paid from any special fund supplied by the

Crown Lands, or the Small Branches of the Hereditary Revenue, the figures for the proceeds of the Crown Lands and the Small Branches are reproduced faithfully in each of the six main Select Committee Reports on the Civil List this century. They always exceed the Civil List, and thus seem to confirm the calculation that the nation has profited from the monarchy.

Ponsonby was not the last courtier to use the rising Crown Lands/ Estate revenue to justify a royal claim for more government money. During the last Select Committee on the Civil List, in 1971, the late Lord Cobbold, the Queen's Lord Chamberlain, argued 'that the public purse has had an extremely good bargain' from the rising Crown Estate revenue, which 'seems to be a strong justification for the claim now being put in for the Civil List'.[12]

Even as a negotiating point on behalf of the monarch, it has long been recognized *privately* within the Treasury that references to the pre-1760 situation are irrelevant. In a memorandum on Ponsonby's request for more money in 1920, Sir Warren Fisher, Civil Service head of the Treasury and Auditor of the Civil List, respectfully dismissed Ponsonby's reference to the appreciation of Crown Lands revenue:

> The fact is that in the days when the Sovereign drew these Revenues he was liable for a great many items of ordinary civil expenditure now borne on Votes or on the Consolidated Fund, including the salaries of the Diplomatic Service, of the Judges and of the First Lord of the Treasury and Chancellor of the Exchequer. *That these Revenues have increased greatly in value is therefore to my mind not altogether relevant* . . .[13] (my emphasis)

Indeed, the expenses of civil government have increased at a far greater rate.

As with the King's tax exemption in former times, the Crown Lands and other assorted revenues did not belong to the monarch as a private person. This was reflected in the law. In 1760, when George III surrendered the Crown Lands revenue to Parliament, he could not have owned them privately, for as King he was prevented from owning any land in a private capacity. It will be remembered that it took the 1800 Crown Private Estate Act to enable him to own land privately. The public status of the Crown Lands was well understood in the early eighteenth century before their surrender. Thus in 1702 Parliament prohibited their sale, partly because of the fear that future monarchs might sell them off to assist their becoming financially independent of Parliament. Yet these properties were still used for political purposes. The valuable properties in central London were frequently let out, at far below their market rent, to MPs and peers in return for giving parliamentary support to the ministers chosen by the King. Walpole, as 'Prime Minister' from 1721 to 1742, deployed the Crown Lands in this way to maximum effect in exerting the 'influence' of the Crown.[14]

Therefore, the Crown Lands contributed in two ways to the running of the government. Firstly, by providing some minor cash revenue to the King, and secondly, as a means of political bribery. This was really as good as cash from the point of view of the King and his ministers, because much of the Civil List cash was also used for the same purpose of patronage – in the form of sinecures and pensions. The historical expert on the Civil List of the eighteenth century refers to it as being 'uniquely the private pasture of the political class'.[15] It was not until well into the nineteenth century, when the rich ceased to graze off the Crown Lands, that these properties started to realize their potential as a money earner. In the eighteenth century they had brought in something like £6,000 a year, very little even in those times.*

In the 1952 debates on the Civil List, three Conservative backbenchers regurgitated the notion 'that the Crown, in fact, hands over to the state more money every year than is voted on the Civil List, so that it does not cost the tax-payer one penny'.[16] As in Civil List debates this century, Labour speakers denied this, following the earlier tradition set by Radical Liberals. After Hugh Gaitskell had spoken in this vein from the Labour front bench, the Conservative Chancellor of the Exchequer, R.A. Butler, went out of his way to agree with Gaitskell, 'from the historical angle'. Butler thus clearly disowned the arguments of his own backbenchers. 'It should be clear', he said, that the Crown Lands and other hereditary revenues 'were originally the moneys that ran the country', and not the private property of the Sovereign.[17] (Here, in action, was a literal

---

* It was this state of affairs that caused Adam Smith in his *Wealth of Nations* to argue in 1776 that the public revenue would benefit more if they were sold off at market value to relieve the National Debt. It remains to be seen whether a present-day Conservative government would risk offending royal sensibilities by privatizing the Crown Estate, given its link, albeit tenuous, with the Queen.

example of 'Butskellism', the term used to describe the 'consensus' between Conservative and Labour front benches in the 1950s and 1960s.)

'No more than a useless legal fiction', was how, in 1968, the Tory Bow Group dismissed the old Crown Lands argument.[18] But this did not prevent a great number of others in their party reverting back to the myth of the Crown Lands in later debates. Even a Labour Prime Minister, Harold Wilson, did so in 1969.[19] The *Daily Telegraph, Daily Express* and Conservative MPs have in the 1980s employed the Crown Lands/Estate argument to emphasize what a good deal the public purse gains from the monarchy.[20]

An Embarrassment of Riches

Generally speaking, the idea that the state does well out of the monarch's surrender of the Hereditary Revenue refuses to die, because it serves the purpose of excusing the expense of the monarchy and, most recently, the Queen's tax exemption. However, paradoxically, the monarchists understate their case.

It is not just the land under the management of the Crown Estate that the state benefits from. There is also the 120,000 acres of forests that were transferred from the Crown Lands to the Forestry Commission under a 1923 Act. Mention of this land is only ever considered in dusty old official reports. If the next monarch were really able to take back the Crown Lands/Estate, he would under that Act be entitled to considerable compensation for this woodland from the government.[21]

Monarchists have also tended to forget the other hereditary revenues of the Crown, which were also part of the 'bargain' of 1760. If one accepts the Crown Lands/Estate argument, one could go on to show how the state has profited from all the other Hereditary Revenues of the Crown it acquired in 1760 and subsequently. For instance, royalists hardly ever mention one of the items of the Small Branches of the Hereditary Revenue, *Bona Vacantia*, surrendered in 1830. This mainly derives from the belongings of those who die intestate (without leaving a will) and without traceable relatives. *Bona Vacantia* (literally ownerless or 'vacant' goods) is administered by the Treasury Solicitor. The government derived an income from this source of £5.1 million in 1989–90,[22] about the same as the cost of the

Civil List.* Mention of this form of revenue is passed over, probably because royalists do not wish the monarchy to be associated with this sort of income.

There have been other, much more considerable omissions, such as the Hereditary Post Office revenue (hence the 'Royal' Mail) and the Hereditary Excise duties, which had been largely levied on beer, cider and spirits. These, like the Crown Lands, were surrendered in 1760.

One of the several Treasury confidential memoranda drawn up in 1936 refers to these revenues. The Treasury official pointed to the rents of the Crown Lands and the Small Branches and stated how much they brought in to the government. But then, his report noted, there were also further Hereditary Revenues. A monarch's entitlement to these is as strong, or as weak, as his claim to the Crown Lands. As regards the Hereditary Excise, 'there is no doubt that some proportion of the duties at present collected may be regarded as still part of the Hereditary Excise revenue of the Crown', though 'what that proportion is it would be difficult to say'. Nevertheless, the official took the view that it was 'clearly impracticable' for the Hereditary Revenues, including the Crown Lands, to be restored to the monarchy.[23]

Still, for *public* consumption the Treasury has implied, though not actually stated, that the monarchy provides revenue rather than just consuming it. This has been done, during this century, by providing tables of figures for Select Committee reports on the Civil List, giving the revenues of the Crown Lands and the Small Branches of the Hereditary Revenues. So why, alongside these figures, have we not had tables for the other and more considerable Hereditary Revenues?

For one thing, it would have led to an embarrassment of riches. It was a patent absurdity to say that the profits, or some portion of the profits, of the Post Office were really owned by the monarch and that his successor could reclaim them. In order to keep afloat the argument that these hereditary revenues do belong to the monarch, and are merely surrendered for the duration of one reign, millions of hypothetical pounds in revenue from excise on alcohol and from the Post Office had to be jettisoned. It was not until 1969 that an Act formally repealed any right of the monarch

* However, income arising from *Bona Vacantia* in both Cornwall and Lancashire is still under royal control, as we have seen in the latter case with Edward VIII and the Duchy of Lancaster's No Kin Investment Fund. See also Chapter 10.

to the Post Office revenues.[24] As for the Hereditary Excise, the 1702 Crown Lands Act still remains on the statute book (1 Anne c.7, s vii), which theoretically entitles the revival of a special tax on alcohol for the royal coffers.

Further, it is repeatedly neglected that George III's hereditary revenues were not the only income he surrendered to Parliament in 1760. In fact, he had earlier been voted by Parliament what were known as Temporary Revenues, which he also gave up. These were revenues which had been traditionally voted to the King only for his reign, and were not considered his by hereditary right; hence the term Temporary Revenues. They consisted of customs duties (tonnage and poundage) and various other excise duties. They were not voted to George III's successors, but clearly, if there were to be a return to the pre-1760 situation, these too would have to be restored.[25]

The Temporary Revenues were, in fact, included in the 1837 Select Committee Report as part of what the monarch could reclaim. But in the twentieth century these revenues, together with the Post Office and the Hereditary Excise considered above, have never been included in any public statement of what the monarch might theoretically claim back. If they had been, it would imply that the monarch could demand billions of pounds, or that the nation is gaining billions of pounds through the post-1760 Civil List arrangements.

Moreover, apart from the gigantic amounts, a constitutional monarch could not 'own' the right to collect taxes like customs and excise. The receipt of such revenue implies a monarch with real power, whereas income from landed property does not necessarily have the same constitutional overtones. Thus it is the Crown Estate revenues which are selected for the specious argument that the tax-payer gets the monarchy for nothing, and so forth. It is long since time to put this argument to rest. As we have seen, the Civil Service Head of the Treasury, Warren Fisher, did so in 1920, when it had been necessary to put in some perspective, at least within government, George V's claim for a bigger Civil List. Treasury files in subsequent years indicate that Fisher's view had become the established one on this subject. Also, for the 1952 Civil List debates, it appears that the Chancellor, R.A. Butler, was briefed accordingly.

Yet in 1991 the Treasury were highly enthusiastic in recommending and providing Woodrow Wyatt's article from *The Times*, in which the

Crown Estate argument featured prominently. Perhaps what earlier officials recognized has been forgotten, or the pressure of work makes it easier to refer to a published article. What is clear is that the Treasury should know better about the status of the Crown Estate.

The Civil Lists of 1952 and 1971–2

When the present Queen succeeded in 1952, she was dealt with generously, just as other monarchs had been. That year, the Civil List was relieved of the wages bill for industrial staff engaged on the maintenance of the Royal Palaces.[26] This transfer of liability for certain costs from the Civil List to government departments was a continuation of the process that had been going on for a number of reigns.

Annuities for other royals had always been separate from the Civil List, though also settled at the beginning of a reign. In 1952 these totalled £160,000, with extra provisions for when the 2-year-old Princess Anne came of age, and extra still when she married. Royal annuities have generally given more to princes than princesses, but both have always received an increase on marriage.

Traditionally, Civil Lists had been set for the duration of the reign, which had caused no real problems before the war when inflation was low and when for periods there was deflation. In 1952 Labour suggested ten-yearly reviews of the Civil List to deal with inflation. This was rejected as involving too much parliamentary scrutiny into the 'delicate' matter of royal finances. The government solution was to include in the Civil List of £475,000 a minimum allowance for inflation of £70,000. From this annual sum, a fund would be built up in the earlier years of the reign to cope with inflation in the later years. Butler and the Treasury intended that the Queen would not have to come back to Parliament for more money. They expected that this arrangement would give the Civil List the necessary elasticity to cope with the anticipated decline in the real value of money, even over a long reign. Using surpluses in this way also meant that they could no longer be diverted to build up the monarch's private fortune. Stopping this abuse of the Civil List, practised from 1830 onwards, was the end of an era. The need to cope with post-war inflation, rather than Treasury zeal to stamp out the misuse of public funds, had wrought the change.

Yet from the royal point of view things did not go smoothly. In 1959,

Lord Tryon, the Queen's Keeper of the Privy Purse, expressed royal concern over the rising expenditure of the Civil List: 'I feel the time has come to ask for certain items to be put on the Vote of various Government Departments, in order to save the Civil List.'[27] Action duly followed, and the Civil List was relieved of the costs of the Royal Train in 1960 and of royal visits abroad in 1961. Also around this time, much, though not all, of the costs of entertainment incurred when foreign heads of state visit the Queen in Britain plus the salary of the Marshal of the Diplomatic Corps were transferred.[28]

But these transfers served only to delay the Queen's coming back to Parliament to ask for more money. This occurred, in 1971, after the Civil List fund to meet inflation ran out. As was traditional, an all-party House of Commons Select Committee was set up to consider the Queen's request for more money. But for the first time the evidence given to the Select Committee, together with various memoranda, was to be published. Used carefully, along with other sources, the Select Committee has a good deal to teach one about royal finances.

As the various costs of monarchy were more and more met by government departments, Civil List expenditure was increasingly devoted to paying those who worked for the monarch. The problem of inflation for the Queen came to be mostly the rising wages and salaries bill. Average rates of pay for full-time employees rose by 174 per cent from 1953 to 1970, according to the Keeper of the Privy Purse.[29] This was a figure for all full-time employees, covering the upper-class 'Members of the Household'; the white-collar employees, known as 'Officials' and 'Clerks'; and the housemaids, footmen, chefs, chauffeurs etc., who are referred to as 'Staff'. 'Staff', according to Douglas Keay's book, published in 1983, must address the higher grades as 'Sir' or 'Madam'.[30] Each group has its own separate place to take meals.*

The Civil Service Union which represented the staff grade in the Royal Household put the increase enjoyed by their members at a somewhat higher rate, of about 200 per cent for the same period.[31] If indeed the higher rate is applicable to the staff, then this would have kept them well above inflation, which was about 80 per cent from 1953 to 1970. But

---

* The Duke of Edinburgh attended in March 1981 a conference organized by the Industrial Society, of which he is patron. The purpose of the conference was to seek ways to break down the barriers between 'Them' and 'Us' in the world of work.

200 per cent was only the same increase in earnings generally in force over this period. Moreover, it was a 200 per cent increase on what was a very low level in the first place. It had been kept low before the present reign in order to allow maximum savings from the Civil List for the monarch's private fortune, and the low wages persisted. John Dean, who was Prince Philip's valet, describes how charwomen in the early 1950s were paid less than two shillings an hour (£1.30 in 1991 prices). He, at the top of his scale, earned £250 a year (£3,200 in 1991 prices), and maids only about half as much.[32]

By 1971, about 75 per cent of the staff were in the Civil Service Union (now part of the National Union of Civil and Public Servants). The Palace officials still refused to deal directly with the union, negotiating only through the Department of Employment, a situation which the union had been consistently trying to change since 1963.[33] The union evidence to the Commons Select Committee on the Civil List in 1971 refers to the still relatively low wages creating difficulties for the Royal Household in finding and keeping staff, despite the 'glamour' of royal employment. To help ease the labour shortage, a certain number of foreign staff had been recruited. In the kitchens the foreign employees were mostly Spanish.[34]

The memorandum to the Select Committee from the Keeper of the Privy Purse straightforwardly referred to market constraints, to explain why the Queen had increased staff pay: 'Particularly in recent years, in order to recruit and retain good quality staff, individual rates of pay have been raised so that they *now* bear comparison with those paid in employment outside the Royal Household'[35] (my emphasis). This is equally straightforwardly an admission that previously Palace pay could not bear this comparison. The union took some of the credit for the 'particularly sharp increase in pay . . . during the last four or five years'. The increases often came in the form of the Queen's representatives accepting the principle of Civil Service comparability. But even after the increases in the period 1966–71, the comparability principle for the large bulk of the staff brought their pay up only as far as low-paid Civil Service grades, like messengers.

Nevertheless, the Civil List arrangements of 1952 could not cope with these increases. This was true despite a cut in full-time employees, paid from the Civil List, from 421 in 1953 to 375 in 1970. It might be suggested that an increase in the Civil List was necessary, not for the benefit of an extremely wealthy monarch, but primarily to assist an unfortunate, low-paid group of workers. This indeed was the line taken by Labour's Denis Healey, when Chancellor of the Exchequer in 1975, to try to overcome the objections of his backbenchers to further increases in the Civil List.[36] Those representing the Queen at the Select Committee preferred to avoid mention of low pay and to refer to the problem as inflation in general terms. Had they spoken out forcefully for the staff, whose union they still refused to negotiate with directly, they could have increased any sense of grievance entertained by the footmen, housemaids, pages, chefs, kitchen staff, coachmen and chauffeurs.

In fact, the union in its initial written evidence referred to 'a good deal of dissatisfaction on pay and overtime arrangements' amongst Royal Mews staff (coachmen and chauffeurs). The latter's claim was settled before the union representatives appeared before the Select Committee. The CSU stance was that, whilst working for the Queen was a privilege, their members should have rates of pay in keeping with earnings obtainable outside the Royal Household.

There is another reason why it is not surprising that the Queen's representatives did not couch their request for an increased Civil List in the language of trade-union protest against low pay. This is their upbringing and background. The late Lord Cobbold, who assumed the role of the Queen's chief representative before the Select Committee, was from an old banking and brewery family. Before becoming the Queen's Lord Chamberlain, he had been Governor of the Bank of England (1949–61), having been first introduced into the Bank by Sir Edward Peacock, George V's private financial adviser, and Charles Hambro. The Keeper of the Privy Purse, Lord Tryon (two years below Cobbold at Eton), was the son of a former Conservative Cabinet minister.

The monarchy exists in a lavish form. As long as this is the case, then there will be numerous servants needing pay increases to keep them at least abreast of inflation and the standards of the wider society. Yet this did not mean that the tax-payer had to provide. The Queen had other sources of revenue. Roy Jenkins, then Labour's deputy leader (subsequently leader of the SDP, now Lord Jenkins of the Liberal Democrats), pointed out that, even employing a very conservative estimate of the Queen's private fortune, 'it would still produce a tax-free income which would perhaps more than double the size of the Civil List'.[37] In fact the Select Committee were told that some of the Queen's private money had been used to assist some of her relatives in dealing with inflation.

The revenues of the Duchy of Lancaster, which the Queen received, could also have been tapped. Duchy money was in fact employed to meet her own Civil List deficits in 1970 and 1971, just as it had been used in 1921 when George V suffered a temporary deficit on his Civil List. In the 1980s, when there were a number of minor shortfalls, another source of revenue was discovered – profits from admissions to the Queen's Gallery and Buckingham Palace, Windsor Castle and Holyroodhouse in Edinburgh, and profits from the souvenir shops.[38] One wonders what other funds like this might exist, which could be put towards the Civil List.

It should also be borne in mind that the Queen's difficulties were only with the Civil List. There were no problems with the much larger source of government funding to the monarchy, via government departments. Even after the increases in the new Civil List in 1972 for the Queen and corresponding increases for other members of her family, these constituted at that time only about 30 per cent of government spending on the monarchy, the other 70 per cent or so coming from the Ministry of Defence for the Royal Yacht and for the Royal Flight and from the Department of the Environment for the upkeep of the Palaces and so on.[39]

The public were first alerted to the 'crisis' in the Civil List in 1969, by Prince Philip, and there was no doubting whom he expected to foot the bill. On American TV, Prince Philip voiced publicly what he had been saying privately for over a year (according to Andrew Duncan's *The Reality of Monarchy*). 'We go into the red next year', he told his interviewers on NBC's *Meet the Press*. He continued, flippantly, 'now inevitably if nothing happens we shall either have to – I don't know, we may have to move into smaller premises, who knows? We've closed down – well, for instance, we had a small yacht which we've had to sell, and I shall probably have to give up polo fairly soon, things like that.'

Another Prince Consort, it will be recalled, in 1850 listed the types of thing he felt were expected of an English gentleman. Before polo became popular in this country Prince Albert mentioned things like 'a Moor or a Forest in the Highlands of Scotland', which, like Prince Philip, he feared he could not afford. In the twentieth century, these requests were left to royal representatives like Sir Frederick Ponsonby, who, like Philip's moving to 'smaller premises', made mock-threats of appalling prospects

– George V going to open Parliament in a taxi-cab. But Albert's and George V's royal claims were, wisely, voiced privately, kept within the small world of royal finances. Now the Queen's husband, probably without premeditation, brought the whole matter crashing out into the open. And royalty asking for more money is not a pretty sight. Andrew Duncan says that efforts to secure cuts in the tapes of the programme were given up when it was realized that British journalists were present as observers.[40] The embarrassing pleas of poverty were shown a few days later on British TV.

Philip's mock-threat of impending cutbacks brought forth one mock-solution. A group of London dockers, drinking in their local pub in Bermondsey, professed themselves much moved by the Prince's request on behalf of the royal family. On hearing that the Duke might have to give up polo, they wrote off to him informing him of their intention to start a collection to buy him a polo pony.[41] (The offer was graciously declined.) But not all responses to the Duke's broadcast were as generous. The Labour government's meeting of the Inner Cabinet of 11 November was largely devoted to what response to make to the controversy stirred up by Philip. Barbara Castle, then Secretary of Employment, in her diaries records a general lack of sympathy at the meeting for Philip, whose 'wife was one of the richest women in the world'.[42] Even Harold Wilson, perhaps thinking of the royal standpoint in the ongoing negotiations between the Queen's advisers and the Treasury, departed from his usual devoted royalism. He pointed out that most rich people felt they should spend a good part of their wealth on 'charitable and public purposes. It takes royalty to assume that all their private income is to be kept to themselves and accumulated and that they are not obliged to spend any of it on seeing them through their public life.'[43]

Prince Philip's remarks may have been stated jocularly, as his defenders stress, but they were not simply a joke. The Queen's husband was referring to grievances which were being pressed by the royal family in the negotiations with the Treasury. He created a unique situation for the monarchy, by going public. Earlier monarchs' attempts in 1904, 1905 and 1920 to increase the Civil List in mid-reign had remained secret, nipped in the bud by ministers who pointed out the consequences of the parliamentary debate which would be required.

It was also unique in that, since the introduction of the new form of the Civil List in 1830, so that it no longer paid for any aspect of civil government, monarchs had made a profit on the Civil List, right up until the end of the last reign. They had been able to save money from the sum allotted for wages and salaries and other expenses, which the Treasury allowed them to transfer to their 'Privy Purse' (see Table 6:1). The idea of making a loss would have been experienced as a great and unwelcome change.

TABLE 6:1

Savings on Civil List[44]

		£	approx. value at 1991 prices £
Victoria	(1838–99)	653,768	34.4 million
Edward VII	(1902–9)	261,592	13.8 million
George V	(1910–35)	487,000	16.1 million
Edward VIII	(1936)	31,156	1.0 million
George VI	(1937–51)	101,158	2.0 million

(The figures have been reduced to take account of George V's and George VI's repayments to the government of £100,000, in 1916 and 1948 respectively; and of George V's donations to war-time charities.)

Harold Wilson sought to quiet the storm of publicity over Philip and the Civil List by making a statement to the Commons. He mentioned the detailed discussions which had taken place between Treasury officials and the Queen's advisers during 1968–9 on this 'delicate' matter. Wilson said the government had decided a Select Committee should be set up to look into the Civil List, but, probably for electoral reasons, he wanted to postpone the issue until after the next election. He may also have sought delay because Barbara Castle and others, though not republicans, wanted a Select Committee to investigate the private fortune of the Queen. Edward Heath, as leader of the Conservatives, agreed that this whole question of money was 'delicate' but wanted a Select Committee now. That Wilson could brook delay, in such an 'urgent' matter, was too much for Sir Arthur Vere Harvey (Conservative). Emotionally, he demanded to know, 'Has the Prime Minister a soul?'[45]

The Select Committee was instituted after the 1970 election, which the Conservatives won. The Queen conveyed to Parliament a 'Gracious Message' – this being the title of royal requests for Civil List money.

The only alternative to raising the Civil List, so far as the Queen and the government were concerned, was for the government to step in and meet still more expenditure previously borne by the Civil List. However, this expedient was now virtually exhausted. As Anthony Barber explained, the large majority 'of the total cost of services connected with the Monarchy is already borne by the Votes and the number of possibilities remaining for further transfers is therefore limited'.[46] However, the Chancellor was able to find two such costs. One of these concerned 'responsibility for the whole cost of State Visits to this country, which are at present financed in part from the Civil List'.

The matter of who paid the extra costs during state visits, it will be recalled, had a wider significance. The monarch in 1910 had agreed to pay this charge from his Civil List, and in exchange the Civil List was relieved of income tax. This presumably explains why handing over the remaining part of this charge to the government was left to the last. No public mention was made of the historical connection with the tax issue.

The other transfer from the Civil List to the Votes was 'the costs connected with the Royal Victorian Order'. The latter refers to a group of honours, including knighthoods, which are handed out by the Queen for services to the royal family and which are purely in her gift. It was one of these, for instance, which was given to Edward Peacock, the King's private financial adviser, by George V. The private nature of these honours would, one might have thought, have prevented their being met from the public purse.

Houghton's Plan

Why not complete the historical trend from the mid-eighteenth century, whereby the Civil List paid for less and less? Why not let the government take over directly the whole financing of the monarchy, lock, stock and barrel, instead of funding part of it indirectly through the Queen's Civil List? This was the solution forwarded by Douglas Houghton (now Lord Houghton), the Labour frontbencher,[47] who was no radical when it came to the royal family. Houghton's plan took at face value the Palace's definition of the financial problem. From that starting-point he devised a scheme to deal with the difficulties caused by inflation.

Houghton also rather too readily agreed with the Queen's Lord Chamberlain, Lord Cobbold – and with the Chancellor of the Exchequer – that, apart from the Privy Purse, 'the Civil List includes no element of "pay to the Queen" '. It was simply, as Cobbold had said, money provided for 'what we have termed "Head of State Expenditure" '.[48]

Houghton contended that the frequent 'misunderstandings' of a 'pay rise for the Queen' would be removed if the minority of the funding of the monarchy, still dealt with through the Civil List, was taken over by the state. The state would directly pay all the managerial, white-collar and manual staff (many of the latter were already paid Civil Service rates). The wine and food bill, upkeep of the royal carriages, royal garden parties and all other expenses would be similarly handled. As inflation meant these bills would increase, the state would again pay, just as it did with all government expenditure. No one could say the Queen was getting large pay increases as the funds would not be routed through her hands. The Queen would still be given a generous allowance, for her own use, to be kept quite separate.

Houghton argued forcefully that a new body be created, the Commissioners of the Crown, which would take over and be responsible to Parliament for all the expenditure relating to the royal family. As he was at pains to stress, this would not involve that much extra parliamentary scrutiny, for already the great majority of expenditure was borne by government, and theoretically could be debated in the House of Commons. Houghton's scheme became the policy of the Labour Opposition. Beyond Labour's ranks, it was supported by at least one Tory newspaper, the *Daily Express*, as well as by the *Observer*. The *Daily Telegraph* noted there was a feeling amongst Conservative MPs at one point that 'the opportunity might have been taken to introduce rather more radical reforms of the time-honoured system of financing the Royal Household than the [Select Committee] report proposes'.[49]

Why did the Queen, through her advisers, object to this proposal? Firstly, take the question of visibility. This cut both ways. Houghton's plan would have prevented the Civil List being misunderstood as all going into the Queen's pocket, but as Houghton himself pointed out, various costs of the monarchy were strewn around various departments – the Royal Yacht was paid for by the Department of Defence, the upkeep of the Palaces by the Department of the Environment and so on. By grouping together all these charges under the one heading of the Commissioners of the Crown, the real cost of the monarchy would become much more visible.

Secondly, the work of the Queen's 375 full-time employees was not simply concerned with the public functions of a head of state. Many of the servants exist also very much for the Queen and her family's private benefit. For Labour, Joel Barnett (subsequently Chief Secretary to the Treasury, 1974–9, now Lord Barnett) suggested that 'almost certainly' the staff carried out 'personal duties' for the Queen.[50] One does not want to get drawn into the minutiae of whether, if one of the Queen's footmen walks one of the Queen's corgis, this is done privately for Her Majesty or on behalf of the head of state. But a great deal of the work of the Royal Household has little or nothing to do with the tasks of the head of state. For instance, when the Queen is at Balmoral from August to October, she is essentially off-duty and on holiday. Nevertheless, during her Highland stay there are about 120 servants, mostly brought up from Buckingham Palace or Windsor, who are paid from the Civil List. Similarly with her stays at Sandringham. (See Chapter 11 on the Queen's private country homes.)

The late Stephen Barry was for eleven years one of Prince Charles's two valets. Before that he was for four years a footman in the Queen's service, including being a 'nursery footman', helping out young Andrew and Edward's nanny, who also had a nurserymaid for assistance. Barry's was one of the jobs that had escaped the several efficiency surveys to which the Palace administration has apparently, from time to time, been mercilessly subjected. He was able, in one of his books (written with the journalist Unity Hall), to give the servants' perspective – 'the Royals do absolutely nothing. Everyone who works in the Palace has a function and the end result is cosseting the Royals.'[51] By paying them from her Civil List, the Queen makes sure this process continues. She is able to keep the reins of patronage within the Household in her own hands. Of course, if they are paid for out of the Civil List it is still the tax-payer who pays, but via the Queen. This gives her much more power than if the whole staff perceived themselves as pretty much like civil servants working for the state.

As Lord Cobbold put it in rejecting Houghton's proposal:

although the [Royal] Household is in one sense a Department of State, it is also a family administration and the two things are slightly intermingled and it is not a straightforward department . . . It is almost an item of principle that the Queen regards these people as her own servants and they regard themselves as her servants. I think they have the idea of the dignity of the Monarchy, which is supported by the idea that the Queen is controlling her own Household.[52]

In his earlier written evidence to the Committee, when it came to justifying the cost of the wages and salaries of these employees, he had not noticed this intermingling and lack of straightforwardness. Then, wages and salaries were emphatically said to comprise 'head of state expenditure' pure and simple.[53]

Cobbold, as a former Governor of the Bank of England, was presumably felt to be much more authoritative in putting forward the Queen's case, contradictions and all, than the Queen's Keeper of the Privy Purse. Though Cobbold as Lord Chamberlain was Head of the Queen's Household, when it came to presenting evidence to Select Committees on the Civil List, this had always been the task of the Keeper of the Privy Purse. In 1971 the occupant of the latter post at least had the name to fit the task – Lord Tryon.* He appeared with Cobbold before the Select Committee, but left the burden of presenting the Queen's case and answering the trickier questions to Cobbold. The latter had also been able to lend his weight to negotiations with the Treasury, where he would have been very well known to those who mattered. (He was also the last Lord Chamberlain to censor the London theatre until this power was removed in 1968.)

Houghton tried in certain ways to reassure Her Majesty about his proposal. He stated that hiring procedures could be carried on as informally as before for the Queen's more personal staff.[54] Yet, on the other hand, Civil Service procedure for 'hiring and firing and pensions and conditions of service and transfers, hierarchy, promotion' etc. would be applicable for the bulk of employees. Houghton's reply to Cobbold shows that his reform could lead to further changes than the ones he wanted or anticipated:

> The central issue appears to be one of control. Who is to be in ultimate control of the Royal Household? Is it to be the Queen or Parliament? Here again, I speak with great respect. If the Monarch could manage without coming to Parliament, there could be only one answer. In

---

* Some innocent pleasure was had on a *That's Life* programme a few years ago about the surname of the present custodian of the Privy Purse, Sir Shane Blewitt.

other words, she would run her own Household and pay for it . . . [but] the expenses of a constitutional monarchy are the responsibility of the state.[55]

All this could be the thin end of a long wedge. At some time in the future, the Commissioners of the Crown may not be so sympathetic to the monarchy. As much as Douglas Houghton and Labour protested that the Queen would really find the reform quite acceptable, this could not be true. Perhaps it might even affect recruitment to the Members of the Household level. (The latter was, and still is, almost totally upper crust and remains totally white; see Appendix B.) The monarchy is not so easily recast in a mould of Labour's making.

Moreover, the state's further intervention into the finances of the monarchy, handled previously with such delicacy by the Treasury, might lead to the Queen's tax exemption coming into question. The Conservative majority stood firmly in the way of Houghton, and all that his changes might bring.

7

Hidden Subsidy:

The Queen's Tax Exemption on Her Personal Fortune

In Chapter 5, we took the history of royal tax-paying and non-tax-paying up to the year 1937. We speculated that at about this time George VI stopped paying income tax on his private investment income – up until then, the most significant tax still paid by the monarch. By July 1952, R.A. Butler could tell the Commons that 'the Sovereign naturally, except when her or his private landed estates are governed by the [Crown Private Estates] Act of 1862, is free from tax'.[1] Assuming this bare statement to be true, then at some time between 1937 and 1952 the monarch had dropped the previous practice of not reclaiming tax normally deducted at source from investment income.

Butler's remark was an oblique reference to the Crown immunity argument – that the Queen is not liable to any tax unless specifically made so in a piece of legislation, and that otherwise she enjoys the same immunities from taxation that 'the Crown' does. In Chapter 1, it was contended that this argument is outdated and therefore should not apply to the Queen's private fortune. When there had been monarchical government, the monarch's tax exemption did have a logical basis. The King or Queen imposed taxes and spent the bulk of them on the business of government. For a monarch to tax himself or herself would have been pointless. No extra revenue would be raised. By 1830 all vestiges of royal control over government finance had disappeared, and with it the rationale of the monarch's tax immunity.

Butler's statement was not widely reported, if at all, and in fact those who wrote about the monarchy, from different perspectives, did not know about the Queen's freedom from taxation or that it was justified by Crown immunity. In the following years they stated that she did pay income tax. Some of these writers had turned for information to a government booklet, *The Monarchy in Britain*, put out by the Central Office of Information; others had also consulted the Queen's courtiers.

The booklet, which is updated every two or three years, is still being produced by the COI as a guide, 'to be used for reference purposes in preparing articles, speeches, broadcasts'. It stated: 'The Queen does not pay income tax on the Civil List, but does on income arising from her private estates.'[2] Butler, when it came to paying tax, had correctly limited his statement to 'private *landed* estates' (my emphasis), which is all that the 1862 Act covers.* What the booklet did was to note that the Civil List escaped income tax, but as regards the Queen's private income to refer only to what in practice was the very minor exception to that immunity – the private estates. Thus the formula devised for the COI guide was extremely economical with the truth.

The wording in the booklet was reasonably interpreted, by those who felt that the Queen's tax position must be a reasonable one, to mean that she paid tax on all incomes arising from her private fortune. Thus monarchist authors absorbed and compounded the misleading impression contained in the COI booklet. Dorothy Laird wrote a very detailed book, *How the Queen Reigns*, in 1959, for which she received considerable help from courtiers. She wrote: 'income from the Queen's private estates *and so on* is liable for tax' (my emphasis).[3] Subsequent writers were less tentative.[4] By 1969, the Conservative MP Norman St John Stevas (Leader of the House of Commons, 1979–81, now Lord St John) was quite emphatic: 'It is sometimes thought that the Queen is not liable to pay income tax but this is not the case. She pays tax on her private income.'[5]

The COI booklet came to be misleading even as regards the Queen's private landed estates, Sandringham and Balmoral. As we shall see later in the chapter, from 1963 the only tax the Queen paid on her estates were local authority rates. 1965 saw the introduction by the government of a new tax, capital gains tax, but the Queen does not pay this either.[6] (The Labour government a year later did specify in the relevant Act

---

* The 1862 Act repeated the provision in the original 1800 Act, described in Chapter 1, that the private estates of the monarch should be taxable. From now on we shall refer to the 1862 Act because it is the more recent one.

that the Queen should pay Selective Employment Tax on the staff she employed, but the tax was abolished by the next Conservative government in 1971.)

The June 1971 edition of the COI guide had carried the usual evasive formula. The necessary corrections were not made until the December 1973 edition, *after* the Select Committee Report of December 1971 officially stated that the Queen paid no tax, and after considerable publicity in 1971–2 about her tax situation. The COI booklet had also, up until 1971, managed to omit any mention of the Prince of Wales's tax privileges.

If, for some reason, the situation had been reversed, and the Queen and the Duchy had paid tax, but the booklet had stated they did not, then one could be sure that a correction would have taken place very quickly. The relevant Palace official, with whom the booklet would have been cleared before publication, would have demanded a full revision of the offending passage. We may recall in this connection how Queen Victoria demanded from Gladstone that his government rebuff Dilke's accusation that she avoided paying tax.

In 1971, with the Queen's 'pay claim', as the press generally referred to it, in the pipeline, media interest in the Queen's tax situation grew. We see the use of the 'private estates' formula as a smokescreen at last being penetrated and *some* of the truth of the Queen's total tax exemption being uncovered. On 18 April 1971, John Whale writing in the *Sunday Times* described how courtiers 'point to a [tax] liability under the Crown Private Estates Act 1862; they forbear to say that both forms of tax specified in that act are obsolete'. However, he refrained from coming out and saying that the Queen enjoyed a general tax exemption on her private income, for this was not known before December, when it was officially established for the first time.

The first parliamentary debate to touch on the tax exemption took place in May 1971, when the Commons agreed to the composition of the Select Committee to look into the Civil List. It was agreed that the republican MP for West Fife, Willie Hamilton, be a member of the Select Committee. Hamilton did not mince his words when it came to talking about royalty, and his membership undoubtedly enlivened the proceedings of the Committee. Hamilton, who left the Commons in 1987, has often been portrayed as an isolated joker in the 'sensible' Labour pack, because of his republicanism. It is true that most Labour

MPs did not share his republicanism, or if they did, they did not attach the same importance to it as he did. But, as *The Economist* pointed out, it was not just the left in the Labour Party in 1971 who shared Hamilton's objections to an increase in the Civil List.[7]

On 20 May, in reply to a Labour MP, the Chancellor, Anthony Barber, argued that 'the Queen's resources in her private capacity' should not be investigated. Her investment income was not to be tapped to meet the expenses of the monarchy; it was up to the state to provide the Queen with an adequate Civil List. However, the right-wing and monarchist Labour MP Reginald Paget (later Lord Paget) maintained that the tax privileges of the Queen would have boosted her private fortune, and that the Select Committee should consider this hidden public subsidy when deciding what amount the Civil List should be.

Nor was this simply a Labour point of view. The *Sunday Telegraph* earlier in May had argued that the private fortune could not 'be left out of the reckoning altogether, even under the "rate for the job" concept, for in a sense the fortune is itself part of the rate. It has grown as a result of a unique royal privilege: no death duties are paid on the Sovereign's estate' (this fact was revealed even in the earlier uncorrected editions of the COI booklet). If the writer had been aware of the income-tax exemption, he would surely have pressed his point more forcefully.

Not lacking in forcefulness was the *New Statesman* on 28 May 1971, a week after the appointment of the Civil List Select Committee and the exchange in the Commons between Barber and Paget. 'THE ROYAL TAX AVOIDERS', in large bold letters, appeared on its front page, above an article written by the paper's editor, Richard Crossman. This article made a great impact, notwithstanding the journal's small circulation, because up until the previous year Crossman had been a senior Labour Cabinet minister. Also, despite one or two imprecise comments in the press and Parliament about secret tax privileges, it simply had not registered with the public that the Queen might not pay taxes like everyone else. Crossman later recalled that about two-thirds of the hundreds of letters he received said 'how terrible it was [of him] to suggest . . . that they did not pay their taxes'.[8]

Crossman, like Whale and the other commentators, did not know the exact tax position of the monarch – that she paid no income tax at all. The style of Crossman's article was trenchant, but for lack of hard information, he made only the vague assertion that 'on much of her income she pays no income tax'. When the truth was revealed in December, even he described himself as surprised at the complete exemption enjoyed by the Queen.[9]

In the meantime, the Queen and her officials were not revealing what the monarch's real tax situation was, not even to those in the media who could usually be counted upon to defend the monarchy to the hilt. At times of trouble for the monarchy, traditionally, the monarch's private secretary would have a word with the editor of *The Times*, who would pass his inside information to the readers in a suitably discreet and authoritative sounding editorial. *Times* readers would be reassured that any carping voices raised against the throne carried only badly informed and unsound arguments.

However, *The Times* could not have been receiving the raw material from the Palace with which to render its usual service. On 29 May its leader writer professed not to know the Queen's tax situation. Apart from calling Crossman 'gratuitously offensive', *The Times* largely agreed with him and politely dismissed Barber as wrong for trying to exclude any consideration of the Queen's private resources:

> In so far as the Queen's income and estate has certain tax exemptions not available to her subjects, they may be said to be possessed 'in right of the Crown', and it has for long been established that revenues enjoyed 'in right of the Crown' are taken into account when consideration is given to the Civil List.

The *Financial Times* also chose the words 'gratuitously offensive' to describe Crossman. Yet its article of 3 June 1971 was more radical than Crossman's, by making explicit what had been implicit in other comment, that the relevance of any tax exemption meant it should be disclosed how much it was worth to the Queen. The Select Committee should:

> ascertain from the Inland Revenue . . . whether the Queen actually pays income and surtax on her private income, at the full rate. If so, it should in all reason be left private. If not, details of the private holdings, and the tax reliefs thereon, should be ascertained and published.

The aim, the article concluded, was to discover the 'total resources available to the monarchy' in order to gauge what increase, if any, the

Civil List needed. Also, the Select Committee 'should recommend that estate duty [now called Inheritance Tax] be paid on private possessions of the Queen's'. If not, the Queen should retain the use of Sandringham and Balmoral only if she relinquished ownership to a public body, like the National Trust.

It was left to Robert Blake (made Lord Blake in the same year), the Conservative Oxford don and constitutional expert, to gallantly and, it seems, single-handedly mount a defence of the tax exemption, in the *Spectator* of 12 June. Unfortunately, he did not appear to know exactly what he was supposed to be defending. The best he could do was to ask, rather lamely, 'is there not at least a case for the view that the Queen is not like anyone else, and that the traditional exemptions, *whatever they may be*, should continue?' (my emphasis). Did we really want the Queen to have to use 'tax accountants and the other experts who advise the very rich' on how to minimize their tax bill? 'Why should there not be this single exception to the ordinary rules? There is only one Queen of England.'

Though there were Palace-inspired articles in the press about how the Queen's wealth was being greatly exaggerated,[10] the tax issue was assiduously avoided. In June, the Treasury did submit a short memorandum to the Select Committee on the Queen's tax position,[11] followed by Treasury and Inland Revenue witnesses appearing before it. However, Committee members, including Hamilton, were sworn to secrecy until the Select Committee reported.

Publicly, in May and June, monarch and government decided to tough it out in silence. They intended to wait and see what happened when the Civil List was debated in Parliament at the end of the year, in a situation more under government control. One tactic the government used, according to *The Times*, was to time the debate on the large, but overdue, increases in MPs' salaries to fall on the same day as the main debate on the Civil List.[12] This allowed Conservative ministers, MPs and some newspapers to argue that the general Labour approval of their own pay increases contrasted unfavourably with their objections to a supposedly similar rise for the Queen. The timing of the two main debates on the Civil List, which contained much Labour querying of the tax exemption, just before Christmas (14 and 21 December), could have had a similar inspiration.

The Select Committee Report was published on 2 December. In response to the considerable public pressure, the government agreed for the first time to publish considerably more accompanying data than was usual. At last the public was told of the Queen's tax exemption. The government's proposals contained in the report, of course, said nothing about curtailing this dispensation. But the proposals had to be debated in the Commons, something which monarchs have always dreaded.

The Commons Debates on the Tax Exemption, 1971–2

The December 1971 debates on the Civil List took place almost exactly 100 years since Dilke's speeches, the last time that the monarch's tax status had been much of a public issue. Though of course in the meantime it had often been a secret issue between monarch and government.

Conservative newspapers like *The Times* and the *Sunday Telegraph* had in May detached themselves from the cause of monarchical enrichment. Now, drawn back into line with the publication of the Select Committee Report, they welcomed the report's acceptance of the government's proposals to considerably increase the Civil List, and forgot all about the bearing that the tax exemption had on the matter. However, the business press was more independent. *The Economist* argued that, without knowing the 'Queen's indirect earnings' from her special exemption, all discussion about what amount the Civil List should be was mere 'arguing in the air'. Similarly, the leader in the *Financial Times* on 3 December reiterated the significance the paper had attached to the tax exemption six months earlier. More predictably, perhaps, the *Guardian* (political columnist Peter Jenkins) and the *Daily Mirror* took much the same view.[13]

As with Houghton's plan for a separate government department to finance the monarchy, which the Conservative majority on the Select Committee had rejected, the whole tax/private wealth question concerned the private and public faces of the Queen. After twenty Select Committee meetings and a lengthy parliamentary debate the week before, Roy Jenkins, then the Deputy Leader of the Labour Party, finally realized this, reaching the same conclusion that the *Financial Times* had expressed back in June. Jenkins would also have been able to draw on his experience as a former Chancellor of the Exchequer, which included the negotiations with the Palace during 1968–9. He told the Commons on 21 December, as the veil lifted from his eyes, 'I think it may be that one did not see the issue with total clarity previously – that the vital point is disclosure.' In order to see if we should continue tax exemption, he said, we should need to look at how much the Queen had benefited from it since 1952: 'But if that is objected to' – as an invasion of privacy – 'then the logical corollary, with the adequate state provision [via the Civil List] which is now being made, would be to move to a normal tax position.'[14] This statement of official Labour policy was greeted by 'loud Labour cheers'.[15]

Jenkins's colleague, Richard Crossman, claimed that the monarchy had shown 'almost indecent arrogance' by refusing information to the Select Committee on the Queen's private fortune. While that fortune 'retains the privilege and the monopoly of being tax-free it is not private income in the sense that any other citizen's income is private. Therefore it is a matter of public concern.'[16]

In the late nineteenth and early twentieth centuries, government ministers stated that, in judging how much the Civil List should be, the private resources of the monarch could indeed be of legitimate public concern. Moreover, this principle was conceded even though Queen Victoria and Edward VII *did* pay income tax. In 1873, the question of disclosure arose during the debate on the Crown Private Estates Bill, which had been devised to remove a remaining legal obstacle to Victoria's bequeathing her private estates to her successor. The Solicitor-General was quite emphatic that when the next Civil List came to be discussed, 'the House could call for a return even of personalty [personal wealth] before granting the sum which they thought necessary to support the dignity and power of the Crown'. The Prime Minister at the time, Gladstone, also stated that a very high private income could in principle lead the government to reduce the Civil List.[17]

In 1901, when it came to passing a Civil List for Edward VII, the Solicitor-General's promise of 1873 was, in a sense, put into effect. The extent of the new King's private fortune was indeed revealed by the Chancellor of the Exchequer, Sir Michael Hicks-Beach. He told the Commons that 'it is a fact which cannot, I think, be too widely known that the present King has no personal fortune'.[18] The Chancellor justified the proposed level of the Civil List on the grounds that Edward VII did not have any money of his own to subsidize his regal lifestyle. The implication of this argument was clear, whether Hicks-Beach would have welcomed it or not. It meant that if a monarch did possess sizeable private funds, she or he should receive a correspondingly reduced Civil List. Subsequent chancellors and their Treasury officials have not, however, embraced this implication.

In the 1971–2 debates, Barber, Whitelaw, Stevas and the other Tories stayed off the whole issue of the Queen's tax exemption and personal fortune, finding it altogether too delicate. They either airily dismissed the matter as irrelevant[19] or, better still, did not mention it at all. Most Labour MPs were baffled at the origins of this tax exemption, as well as having no idea how much it was worth to the Queen. One Labour MP, John Grant (Islington, East), asked three times what was the basis for this exemption. Here is Anthony Barber's reply, as Chancellor of the Exchequer, in the third of these debates, where it was the central issue and he could hardly avoid some sort of response: 'There is also room for argument about certain factors – such as . . . the private resources of the Queen – and about the extent to which, if at all, these factors are relevant.' Barber went on to say 'I have made my views clear on this subject', that he respected the views of the Opposition, but 'we must beg to differ'.[20] Making his views on the exemption clear, or known in any form, is exactly what he had not done. Stevas, who contributed very fully to the debates, came up with no argument for it, even when pressed. This is not surprising, as two years earlier, in the article quoted above, he had gone out of his way to deny its existence. Whitelaw, as Leader of the House, was also at a loss on the matter, in the first debate. The best he could do was to say that the whole matter of tax exemption had been covered by a previous Conservative speaker, 'and I do not think there is any need for me to say anything further'.[21]

The speaker whom Whitelaw considered to have covered the subject was a former Tory minister, John Boyd-Carpenter. Having been a junior minister at the Treasury at the time of the 1952 Civil List, he was able briefly to divulge the Crown immunity argument that held sway within the Treasury: 'As taxes are raised in the name of the Crown and indeed the express recommendation of the Crown', it was improper, even 'ludicrous', to tax the wearer of the Crown.[22] However, Barber must have had little faith in this line of argument, for he did not employ it, even when being hard pressed for an answer by the Opposition.

However, the monarchy nowadays does use this defence. The Queen's press secretary, Charles Anson, told me in 1990, without great conviction, that 'taxes are raised in the name of the Sovereign and therefore she's not taxed'.

It was logical for monarchs in bygone days to be exempt from taxes because they really did raise taxes and govern the country; taxing themselves would have been pointless. Now only the name remains, and the exemption is claimed on a purely private fortune. And even regarding the hardly vital contribution of supplying the name, matters are not clear-cut. On the one hand, we still have *Her Majesty*'s Commissioners of Inland Revenue, while near the beginning of every annual Finance Act, on whose authority tax revenue is raised each year, the archaic formulation about imposing taxes 'to defray Your Majesty's public expenses' remains intact. Similarly, each Finance Act contains much 'humbly beseeching' of 'Your Majesty' to accept the proposals. Yet on the other hand, reality very often intrudes into the make-believe. Each of these Finance Acts starts off matter-of-factly, saying that tax revenue is needed for 'the National Debt and the Public Revenue'.

The Treasury mandarins, by way of explanation, had provided a brief memorandum for the Select Committee. This was a good deal less informative, one imagines, than those drawn up privately within the Treasury, like those of 1936 and 1937 discussed earlier, which summarized the whole history of royal tax-paying. The memorandum for the Select Committee stated baldly that 'as part of the Royal Prerogative, the Queen is not liable to pay tax unless Parliament says so either explicitly or by inevitable inference. There is no distinction for this purpose between the private and public aspects of the Sovereign.'[23] But as we noted in Chapter 2, this mystical Royal Prerogative is far from absolute on royal tax matters. It was recognized, even by Edward VII and as long ago as 1901, as susceptible to government 'advice'. Therefore, it does not even require legislation in Parliament to have the Queen pay taxes (though that would be quite straightforward to arrange – a clause in the annual Finance Act would suffice).

Ministers and expert witnesses from the Treasury and the Inland Revenue, who appeared before the Select Committee, were at pains to hide such episodes as Edward VII's having being forced to pay income tax. Defending the anachronistic Royal Prerogative argument was difficult enough anyway. If it had been known that the escape from income tax had been of relatively recent vintage, then the appeal to the ancient rights of the monarch would be shown to lack even the required antiquity.

Legal Precedents and the Queen's Tax Exemption

When John Strudwick of the Inland Revenue had appeared before the Select Committee, he was obliged to elaborate on the Treasury statement about the Royal Prerogative and monarchical tax. He said he took the wording of the general principle of the Queen's tax exemption from Lord Watson's judgment in the case of Coomber *v.* Justices of Berkshire 1883, which went all the way to the House of Lords.

This case concerned whether a Berkshire police station should be subject to Schedule A income tax, which was then levied on landed property. The Lords' verdict declared that Crown immunity, which covered departments of central government, should be extended to the police station, which thus did not have to pay.[24] Can the fate of a humble Berkshire police station in the late nineteenth century hold the key to the tax exemption of Her Majesty's personal fortune, then or now? Not surprisingly, at no point in this legal contest is anything mentioned of Queen Victoria's personal fortune. Throughout the legal judgments of Lord Watson and Lord Blackburn in 1883, there is constant reference to the 'public purposes' served by the building in question. In all such cases this has been the guiding principle as to whether a person or organization is entitled to Crown immunity from taxation. By the Crown, Lords Watson and Blackburn meant central government, whose 'law and order' function was being discharged by a Berkshire police station.

Lord Blackburn, the senior judge, in reaching the same decision about the police station, did mention the monarch's tax exemption, but from an earlier era. In a 1790 case the King was said to be exempted from the duty normally paid on post-horses, which were carrying an express letter from the Governor of Portsmouth to one of His Majesty's Principal Secretaries of State. What was relevant was that those horses were used 'not on any private business whatever, but wholly related to the public concerns of this kingdom'.[25]

In the 1790 case the term 'the King' was used because at that time George III functioned as head of government, even though his own head did not always function so well. By the nineteenth century, when monarchical power declined, judges started to use the more impersonal term, 'the Crown', to refer to government (and indeed would often refer to 'the government' and 'the public' without any form of royal reference).[26] So, whether it is 'the King' in the eighteenth century who is exempted, or 'the Crown' subsequently, it was really the government which was so exempted. Because the 1883 judgment, cited hopefully by Strudwick, constantly refers to public purposes, it serves only to highlight that the monarch's private fortune fulfils no such public function in the modern era and should be taxed.

As John Griffith, Emeritus Professor of Public Law, London University, has put it:

> the principle that emerged from the many legal cases in the nineteenth and twentieth centuries was that for a body to be recognized as part of the Crown, its purposes had to be both public and part of central government. Therefore it seems to me that the income the Queen receives on her private investments is not money she receives on behalf of the Crown, but on her own behalf, and as such should be taxable.[27]

Strudwick cited another case, dating from 1954 (the Legal Department of the Inland Revenue have assured me that, to the best of their knowledge, there is no more recent case that might bear on the Queen's tax exemption). This case, similarly, had nothing whatever to do with the Queen's personal fortune – the question before the House of Lords being the tax status of the custodian of Enemy Property seized during the Second World War. Lord Asquith, one of the Law Lords hearing the case, stated purely in passing that 'the Sovereign is personally immune not only from rates and Schedule A but from all direct taxation. This is clear but irrelevant to this case.'[28] Strudwick claimed that this was the most recent case in which there were 'authoritative pronouncements'.

However, far from being 'clear' or 'authoritative', this was simply a comment made in passing, with no examination of the monarch's tax situation. Nor, of course, was the judge obliged to explore that avenue, for as he himself commented it was not relevant to the case he was then considering. In fact, he was quite wrong to say that 'the Sovereign is personally immune . . . from rates and Schedule A'. At that time, the Crown Private Estates Acts did bind the Queen to pay these taxes.* Nor is there any understanding of the tax-paying past of the monarch. This would have shed a very different light on matters, especially the 1901 episode when the government totally ignored the question of Crown immunity and simply told Edward VII to continue paying income tax.

Then there is the question of inconsistency, or having your cake and eating it. The Queen's Crown immunity from tax assumes that the Queen can be referred to as the Crown, which is equatable with the whole vast machinery of government. Yet this immunity is claimed for the Queen's private income. On a legally questionable and certainly anomalous basis, the monarch has latched on to a privilege which is more appropriately enjoyed by the Crown, in the sense of its being the government. However, the Queen rejects the liability of disclosure and accountability, considered essential in the finances of Ministries and Departments of the Crown, by pleading that, as regards her private fortune, she is a purely private person. This right was invoked during the Select Committee, when Roy Jenkins requested, as a member of the Committee and a former Chancellor of the Exchequer, to be told the extent of the Queen's personal wealth and was refused by the Queen. All that Lord Cobbold could do was to quote the Queen, who dismissed certain estimates of £50 or £100 million as 'wildly exaggerated'. Barber denied that Her Majesty's refusal to provide any unexaggerated figures was on government 'advice'.[29] Furthermore, when Strudwick was asked by Douglas Houghton how much the Queen received in repayment of any income tax deducted at source, he replied 'that is a question I think we must refuse to answer as being detailed information about tax of an individual'.[30]

This deft switch from public to private, from the Prerogative of the Crown to claiming the rights of the ordinary citizen, and back again, is characteristically employed as regards the financial affairs of the monarch. Faced with taxation, she is the Crown. Faced with disclosure, she is a private citizen.

---

* One possible explanation for this glaring error is that Lord Asquith was not thinking of the Queen's private income at all. He referred, it is true, to 'the Sovereign' being 'personally immune' – but as the Crown is considered a person in law and sometimes the term Crown and Sovereign are used interchangeably, then he may have simply meant the government. Similarly with the other Law Lords, Morton and Tucker, who also referred to their immunity of the 'personal revenue of the Sovereign' and 'the Sovereign personally'. When it comes to the legal concept of the Crown, confusion abounds.

The above examination of the Queen's tax status has looked at the legal and constitutional arguments that have been put forward to justify the Queen's tax exemption. It helps us understand why Conservative ministers in 1971 were unenthusiastic about propounding any version of the Crown immunity case, even in the absence of other arguments. Rather than being purely a technical discussion of the law, it is also a way of demonstrating that the legal claims for exemption do not correspond to the role of a modern constitutional monarch, who no longer rules and who is no longer at the centre of government finance. Nowadays, the question of the Queen's tax immunity reduces itself to the argument for and against naked privilege.

If the tax exemption was so clearly justifiable, why then did the Queen's advisers allow and encourage misconceptions to be spread, by authors and politicians, suggesting she did pay tax? Why was the removal of the tax on the Duchies and the private investments kept secret? For the simple reason that, were any of this known, there would have been an outcry about the country's richest person not paying tax, whilst more and more wage-earners were being sucked into the income-tax system.

Labour in 1971 had stated in the House of Commons, albeit with due deference, that the Queen should either disclose the extent of her personal fortune so that the value of the tax exemption could be seen, or pay her taxes. Though when in office and the Civil List had to be dealt with once more in 1975, Labour forgot its adherence to the pay or disclose policy, though many Labour backbenchers, like Michael Stewart, a former Foreign Secretary, urged that the Queen should pay tax.[31] Some have argued that Labour capitulated on the Queen's finances because the position of respect enjoyed by the monarchy would have made ending the exemption an unpopular move. But in fact an opinion poll taken a few years later, in 1978, was to show that 66 per cent thought that the Queen should pay income tax.[32] More would surely have agreed had it been specified that she should pay on her private fortune alone.

Many, including Crossman, though a fierce opponent of royal financial privilege, have argued that it is generally only the intelligentsia who would wish to deny the royals their financial privileges, whereas it is the much more numerous 'working-class socialists who are by and large staunchly monarchist'. However, in the 1978 poll less than a third of the professional and managerial group thought the Queen was too rich. This rose as one went 'down' the social scale to just under half of unskilled workers who thought the Queen too rich. Similarly, in a December 1971 poll concerning the Queen's Civil List increase (from £475,000 to £980,000, or £6.1 million in 1991 prices), 31 per cent of Conservative supporters thought the increase too high, whereas 74 per cent of mainly working-class Labour thought it too high.

Whether people supported the monarchy a lot, a little or not at all, just over half (according to the December 1971 opinion poll) thought the Civil List increases too high. The large majority of letters to the *Daily Mirror* voiced this view. They represented a gut feeling that with low old-age pensions, the unemployed and other people suffering genuine hardship, there were better ways of spending the money. They may not have understood the finer points of royal finance, but who would say that they were wrong? Two Welsh widows wrote that they were 'in no way opposed to the Royal Family', but were 'very embittered about the increase in their money'. Prevented by illness from working, they could 'hardly afford food or proper heating'.[33] It was also the double standard which hurt. Two pensioners were 'hopping mad at the cash award to the Royal Family. Coming on top of the Minister of Social Security's statement that pensioners could buy more this Christmas, it was the last straw.'

Labour's inability to diminish royal privilege can be attributed not so much to 'public opinion' as to the general conservatism that traditionally grips Labour once it gains office. (Though, most recently, with Neil Kinnock's warm agreement to the Conservatives' new system of paying for the Civil List in July 1990, this process has occurred before office has been won.)

If Labour forms the next government and attempts to introduce the 'fairer society' Neil Kinnock wants, then at the least it should ask that the richest person in the land makes her contribution to that end. It would hardly be impossible to bring about. The case presented in this chapter attempts to show how little likelihood there would be of an effective argument against a government which sought to end the tax exemption. The twentieth-century history of the monarchy's tax situation demonstrates the acute vulnerability, experienced in royal and government circles, about special tax privileges for the monarch.

Mr Kinnock need not have been so defensive when the subject was broached in an interview in the *Independent on Sunday* in March 1991. The Labour leader argued that he was more worried about the £5 billion a year that was lost through off-shore tax arrangements than the Queen's tax exemption. Yet one concern does not preclude the other. There is no reason why he should not seek to end both anomalies. And if he is not offended by the most prominent and dramatic case of tax avoidance, it suggests he would be less than zealous in closing the generally available loopholes.

The Poll Tax, the Council Tax and Business Rate

The last remaining taxes paid by the Queen, mostly on her private estates, have not been very burdensome for someone of her income. Some of these have now been removed. Though there may have been some royal prompting, their removal occurred mainly because of changes in the taxation system, and the way the Treasury has interpreted the effect of these changes on the Queen whereas earlier royal successes in repelling the Inland Revenue, which involved very large sums of money, were a product of regal pressure.

The principle of Crown immunity does not apply if an Act mentions the Crown, and the 1862 Crown Private Estates Act specifically mentions the monarch, stating that the monarch should be taxed 'in the same manner and form in all respects as if the same estates . . . [belonged to] any of Her Majesty's subjects'. However, as stated at the beginning of this chapter, the egalitarian phrasing is less forceful, in practice, than it sounds. Up until 1971, it was even used to imply that the Queen paid income tax on all her private income. It served as a useful hook on which to hang a deceit.

Yet even as regards her private landed estates, Sandringham and Balmoral, the 1862 clause had a very limited application. The Act was held to apply only to taxes on the private landed *property* of the monarch, and not on the *person* of the monarch.[34] Tax on rental income from land (Schedule A income tax) was judged to be applicable, because it was effectively applied as a tax on property. However, in 1963 there was a convenient change in the method of collecting tax on this form of income. It switched to being more clearly a tax on the person of the landlord and it gave Her Majesty a loophole, through which she duly escaped. Also, the Inland Revenue representative told the Select Committee in 1971 that the Queen was not liable to tax on any farming profits made from the land she farmed herself. This too is a tax on the person and therefore said not to be applicable.* The Sandringham Estate Office's pamphlet, describing the royal estate, claims that the Queen's farming operation has become, in recent years, highly efficient and profitable. Therefore, the Inland Revenue's view is no longer of purely academic importance.

Insisting on the distinction between property and person should have meant that the estates were liable to death duties, but the Treasury has decided otherwise (though, very significantly, earlier in the century the Solicitor-General of the day advised the Prime Minister that death duties were chargeable – see Chapter 11).

What all this means is that after 1963 it was held that the only form of tax for which the Queen could be liable was the local rates at Sandringham, Balmoral and other private properties. Only the rates were held to be a tax on her private landed estates (until they were scrapped in favour of the Poll Tax in 1989 in Scotland and 1990 in England and Wales). The new Council Tax is planned to come into effect in 1993. Half of this tax is a tax on the person, like the Poll Tax, but the other half is a property tax, and the Queen will presumably have to pay at least that for Balmoral and Sandringham, though the legislation has yet to be drafted at the time of writing. If she pays the property element, this would amount to about £400 a year on each property. Even if she paid the tax in full, it would leave the Queen much better off than when the old domestic rating system applied. Those in the highest band (Band H), no matter how valuable the property, will only have to pay three times the amount that those in the very cheapest ones pay.

When the much-hated Poll Tax was introduced, the Queen came in for a certain amount of adverse publicity. Unlike the domestic rates which it replaced, it is a tax on the person. Since she would hardly miss the sorts of sums involved, she might have volunteered to pay the tax as an 'act of grace'. But this would lead to suggestions that such graciousness be extended to cover income tax, where millions of pounds are involved. What she has done is to follow the example of some other wealthy landowners and pay the Poll Tax of her staff at Balmoral and Sandringham (in many cases previously she may well have been paying their rates).[35]

* However, Roy Bartlett, an expert in tax law, has argued that farming profits are made taxable by the 1862 Act and that rental income is still taxable, notwithstanding the tax changes in 1963. See his article, 'Taxation and the Royal Family – I', *British Tax Review*, 1983, pp. 99–112.

In the wave of publicity surrounding her escape from the old domestic rates, together with that surrounding its successor, the Poll Tax, it was completely forgotten that the Queen has to pay the new Uniform Business Rate, which was introduced at the same time as the Poll Tax and will survive alongside the new Council Tax. As the name suggests, it is levied on businesses. Unlike the Poll Tax, it is a tax on property, and parts of Balmoral and Sandringham contain business property, particularly Sandringham (estate offices, workshops, souvenir shops etc.). Therefore, for 1990–91 the Queen was liable for £38,283 for Sandringham and £1,184 at Balmoral,[36] though she may well be eligible for transitional benefit at Sandringham. Interestingly, as yet, there seems to have been no mention of the Queen's paying the Business Rate. When there was hostile comment in the press about her not paying the Poll Tax, one might have thought that the Palace Press Office would have used this as a counter and pointed out that, contrary to what many newspapers have said, it is not true that the Queen now pays no form of tax at all. However, such a defence would invite the question that, leaving legal technicalities aside, since she pays one particular tax without any special privileges, why does she not then pay other taxes in like fashion?

The Queen is also liable to Stamp Duty under the 1891 Stamp Act. But in his 1990 budget, John Major removed this duty on the purchase of stocks and shares. This will be useful for her share-dealings. Besides the Uniform Business Rate, the only taxes left are therefore Stamp Duty when buying property and indirect taxes like Customs and Excise and VAT (which in some cases is reclaimed).

Prince Charles

The Prince of Wales is not covered by the Civil List and gets no annuity from the government. He does, however, live at Kensington Palace, which is maintained by the Department of the Environment, from the over £20 million a year it pays out on the upkeep of the various Palaces in royal occupation.[37] His income comes from the Duchy of Cornwall, the tax-paying history of which was explored in Chapter 4. It is now held that the Duchy is not liable to tax, on the basis of the 1913 Law Officers' Opinion. Their Opinion was reaffirmed in 1921 when the Prince of Wales secretly escaped income tax on his Duchy of Cornwall rents.

Mr Strudwick, referring to the legal opinion of the Attorney-General and Solicitor-General in 1913, was suitably apologetic to the Select Committee, as well might have been:

> Their answer, I am afraid, which is all I have, does not really take us much further, because they simply said [that Crown immunity applies] . . . also to the Prince of Wales in his capacity as Duke of Cornwall. This result arises from the peculiar title of the Prince of Wales to the Duchy of Cornwall. That is all they said.

It was on this occasion that Strudwick added, without irony I assume, 'what the peculiar title is, I am afraid I cannot say'. Even Harold Wilson was highly sceptical about the legal opinion.[38]

We also noted that it was indeed peculiar that the Prince of Wales could benefit from Crown immunity, as he is not yet the holder of the Crown. This point is very thoroughly expounded in an article in the *British Tax Review* of 1983, by R.T. Bartlett, Honorary Research Fellow in Law at the University of Exeter.[39]

So for tax purposes the Duchy of Cornwall is part of the Crown. Yet when asked by Willie Hamilton whether the Duchy was 'the private property of the Duke', Sir Patrick Kingsley, Secretary of the Duchy, answered 'yes'.[40] For other purposes he did not want to stress too much the business about the Duchy's being part of the Crown. This is because there is a controversy, of over 150 years' duration, which argues that the Duchy should really have been surrendered to the state, like the other Crown Lands. As with the Queen's private fortune, there is an opportunistic use of the confusions surrounding the whole question of what the Crown is and what it is not. Legally, the concept of the Crown is not so much a grey area as a 'mess', to use the description used 100 years ago by a notable Cambridge historian of law, Professor F.W. Maitland.[41]

Prince Charles does not pay death duties, capital gains tax or income tax on his Duchy revenue, but he does make a 'voluntary contribution', as did his great-uncle the Duke of Windsor, in lieu of income tax. This is in fact not so voluntary, because it is the product of negotiation between the Treasury and the Keeper of the Privy Purse, on behalf of the Prince, and ultimately depends on government 'advice'. In 1969 the outcome was that when Prince Charles reached the age of 21 later that year the Treasury would be paid 50 per cent of the profits of the Duchy (before then they had taken considerably more).[42] At this time, when rates of tax were far higher than now on incomes of this scale, this constituted a considerable saving. On his marriage in 1981, Charles's payment was lowered to 25 per cent, with Treasury approval;[43] thus he received the largest married man's allowance in the country. At the time of writing, the top rate of income tax is 15 per cent higher at 40 per cent. As the net revenues of the Duchy now run at over £2.5 million a year, this saving is worth £465,000 annually.[44]

What income the Prince receives outside of the Duchy, in his own name, is liable to tax in the normal fashion.[45] This is also the case with the other royals, who cannot shelter behind Crown immunity. This is not to say that they do not use the methods available to ordinary wealthy individuals and families for reducing their tax bill, which their accountants can advise them on. Nor are they totally left without state help in tax matters.

Other Royals

With the royal annuities, we leave the murky area of the Crown and things become a little clearer, though not always more defensible. Under income-tax law, other royals can claim tax relief for expenses which are 'wholly, exclusively and necessarily incurred in the performance of the duties in respect of which the annuities are payable'. As noted in Chapter 4, since 1922 such royals enjoy the special privilege of an automatic minimum of 80 per cent tax relief on their annuities. They are also free to make out a case to the Treasury that their expenses are greater than 80 per cent. If convinced, the Treasury can allow them up to 100 per cent.

With rising inflation between 1952 and 1971, and fixed annuities, the royal annuitants found the Treasury sympathetic in the assessment of the expenses they submitted. Only the Duke of Edinburgh was held to 80 per cent. Of the other annuitants in 1971, three – Princess Margaret, the Queen Mother and the Duke of Gloucester – received 100 per cent tax relief and Princess Anne received almost 95 per cent exemption.[46]

In the Select Committee, Jeremy Thorpe, the then Liberal leader, asked what procedure was followed in determining these percentages. The answer from the Civil Service witness is not reproduced; the line of asterisks shows there was an answer, but that they subsequently objected to its being published. Nor were any figures presented to the Select Committee about the relevant expenses. Instead, strenuous assurances were given by Sir Douglas Allen, Permanent Secretary to the Treasury, that there was a very thorough review of expenditure to make sure no element of private expenditure was included in the total claimed as allowable expenses. The main area which had to be watched, said Sir Douglas Allen, was servants' wages. Another problem area was said to be expenditure on clothes by royal ladies. Evidently, it was difficult to draw the line sometimes, 'but we have built up a fair degree of experience over the years of the kind of expenditure the [royal] households require, and the knowledge of what is going on, what standards are justified'.[47]

One wonders, in the case of the late Duke of Gloucester (father of the present Duke), who was allowed the full 100 per cent exemption, if the vigilance of the Treasury on this matter might have been insufficient. The wages of Peter Russell, the Duke's butler in the early 1960s, would have been considered one of the relevant expenses. Russell gives the servant's perspective, in his 'serve and tell' book *Butler Royal*, the best of this genre. Running the Duke's bath was an important duty. The bathwater for his evening bath had to be several degrees hotter than the one for the morning and a thermometer was provided for the sake of exactitude. The valet had to lay out the shaving equipment, unscrewing the tops of the bottles and his toothpaste. There had to be a cigarette next to every ashtray, and a matchbox in a solid silver cover with a match jutting out so that he didn't have to open it. Other essential work of the staff, which was necessary for the performance of his public duties, included the cook's cutting the bread, which went with the Duke's fried egg, to the same circular shape. The potatoes he ate had to be of the same size 'and the kitchen maid spent many hours cutting them into shape'.[48] No doubt the wages of the two chauffeurs were considered an allowable expense only for the proportion of their time that they drove the Gloucesters to their public engagements. It is a shame that the servants' view of things was not presented to the Select Committee.

The royal annuitants, it was frequently stressed, 'are taxable like any other subject on their income and property'.[49] And so they are in theory. It's just that in practice, when it comes to the tax relief it grants against their annuities, the Treasury treats them very differently from any other subject. Lord Cobbold admitted as much with regard to the Queen Mother. Here we note a distinct straying from the original view that her annuity was totally devoted to her expenses, incurred in the course of carrying out her royal duties. He suggests that there are other considerations:

> It has always seemed right and proper to me – this is my personal view – if I may so put it, to think in the Queen Mother's case more in terms of services rendered over the years of peace and war than to try to relate expenditure to the actual official duties of later years.

Moreover, Cobbold felt that a sizeable portion of her expenditure was devoted not to carrying out royal duties, but to maintaining a more 'elaborate Household' than other royals. This Cobbold deemed to be necessary because she was a former Queen Consort.[50]

The 80 per cent tax relief is a minimum figure and the Treasury does not investigate whether the expenses incurred (however one may define them) ever fall below 80 per cent. This would seem to have occurred in the case of the Duke of Edinburgh, who in 1971 was still of working age. The Chancellor, Anthony Barber, had stated about the annuities that, 'to some extent they also represent . . . compensation for the fact that the Queen's closest relatives are precluded from earning a living in the ways open to the rest of us'. When Lord Cobbold was asked what consideration there was in the Duke of Edinburgh's annuity for such compensation, he said between £15,000 and £20,000 (at 1991 prices, £100,000–£134,000). Lord Cobbold referred to 'the high salary which he would undoubtedly command in the outside world'.[51] This sum should, of course, be taxable, because it is stated to be a form of income, not representing the expenses of his office. Moreover, Cobbold noted that, apart from the need to pay him this 'salary', there was another need for him to 'build up savings for the future', which was also being catered for in the new sum for his annuity. On the latter point, Richard Crossman commented in the *New Statesman* that for someone married to the 'richest woman in the country, this seems an unnecessary refinement of royal social security'.[52] It is ironic that Cobbold, when he was Governor of the Bank of England, regularly urged government to rein in on public expenditure.

The Duke's earning potential may well not have been assessed at so high a figure if he had not married the Queen, but if we take Lord Cobbold to be correct, then this figure of £15,000–£20,000 comprises 23–30 per cent of the Duke's increased annuity for 1972. This is without the portion he was given to build up his savings. Therefore it is not possible from Cobbold's figures to say that as much as 80 per cent of his annuity was going on expenses.

Perhaps if Lord Cobbold had cared to elaborate further, we might have also learnt that there were still other considerations, concerning Princess Margaret, who has regularly fulfilled the least number of engagements, and so on. Clearly the annuitants will have claimed for more than 80 per cent tax relief, as they had asked for higher annuities than Barber and the Treasury eventually gave them. This meant that even the usually obliging Treasury had not accepted the figures for expenses that they had submitted. Barber admitted that the figures that he proposed and were later passed constituted a compromise between Treasury and royals.[53]

Today, the Palace takes the view that all the annuities are fully used for official expenses. This is apparently accepted by the Treasury and, one learns, none of the annuities is any longer taxed, even in part.

It should be remembered that all the annuitants have private means. For instance, Princess Anne 'is able to draw funds from the trust fund set up for her by the Queen'.[54] Similarly, Princess Margaret will have inherited money from her father, George VI, and when she was only 12 years old she was left £20,000 by the Society hostess Mrs Ronnie Greville (£470,000 in 1991 prices).[55]

In the summer of 1990, at the end of the Parliamentary Session, it was announced that all the payments to the royals would increase sharply, but be fixed for ten years to avoid the unseemly comment about 'royal pay rises' that accompanied the annual increases. The new allowances are supposed to provide more than they need in the earlier years of the nineties, to provide a surplus from which to cope with inflation in the closing years of the decade. The new figures, together with the previous amounts, are shown in Table 7:1.

The second group of royals considered in this section are less closely related to the Queen. Before 1976 the Queen was allocated a lump sum as part of the Civil List and distributed it at her discretion to mostly her first cousins. This lump sum was increased along with the rest of the Civil List in 1971, causing the *Sunday Telegraph* to comment that 'some of the extra payments to minor members of the royal family are, to say the least, debatable'.[56] Because they received the money at the Queen's discretion and not as part of a legal and binding contract, Princess Alexandra, the Duke of Gloucester and the Duke of Kent did not pay any tax at all on these sums.[57] Since 1976, they have received their money from the Queen. (To be precise, it is paid by the government, which is refunded by the Queen from her Duchy of Lancaster revenues.) This new arrangement has not altered the way in which these three receive their payments, totalling £630,000, free of income tax.

TABLE 7:1

	£ 1991–2000	£ 1990
Queen Mother	640,000	439,500
Prince Phillip	360,000	245,000
Duke of York	250,000	169,000
Princess Anne	230,000	154,500
Princess Margaret	220,000	148,500
Dowager Duchess of Gloucester	90,000	60,500
Prince Edward	100,000	20,000
	1,890,000	1,237,000

The third group consists of Prince Michael of Kent and, previously, of Prince Richard of Gloucester, who as 'younger sons' were to receive nothing at all, either from the Queen or the government. But neither were they expected to carry out any public engagements, as are the other royals. Because of his brother's early death in 1972, Prince Richard came to inherit the title of Duke of Gloucester, carrying with it promotion to the second group and leaving Prince Michael alone in this unfortunate category. Here, the government and the Queen have drawn the line; nor does he receive any special tax privileges, though Princess Michael did say, during a radio interview on *Woman's Hour* in 1983, that her husband had inherited money from his mother, father and his grandmother (Queen Mary), which gave him a private income.[58] This money in turn will have derived from George V's savings from the Duchy of Cornwall and subsequently the Civil List and the Duchy of Lancaster. (We may recall George V's worries in 1920 for anticipated grandchildren, like Prince Michael.) As with all the above royals, a (palace) roof over one's head is provided for Prince Michael, free of charge.

8

Government Expenditure on the Monarchy, 1975 to the Present Day

In 1974 the Queen planned to embark upon the modernization of her 365-room mansion, Sandringham House, using her own funds. But on 6 February 1975 the Queen's Press Secretary announced that 'the Queen felt that although the improvement work could be carried out, it would be insensitive and inappropriate at a time when so many people were facing economic difficulties'.[1] There was, however, a more compelling reason for delaying this expensive project. For in only six days time, the Prime Minister, Harold Wilson, was due to tell the Commons that the Queen needed a further cash injection to keep up with inflation, though the matter had not been discussed in Cabinet. The evening before Wilson's announcement, Barbara Castle, then Secretary of State for Social Services, went to Buckingham Palace for a reception. She detected what she thought might well be:

> a bit of royal softening up – particularly as the refreshments were modest in the extreme, demonstrating that the royal economy drive is really on: nothing but whisky and some almost undrinkable white wine. Not even a canapé in sight. The Royal Family were waiting in line in force . . . Altogether a great night of royal salesmanship.[2]

The 1971–2 Civil List arrangements had failed to anticipate the increase in the level of inflation, up from 8 per cent in 1971 to over 20 per cent in 1974. In 1971, the method eventually decided upon had been to settle the sum of the Civil List above what was thought to be immediately necessary, paying the surpluses into a fund which would

137

be drawn upon to meet the demands of inflation over the next five years or so. Only when this fund had been exhausted would it be necessary for Parliament to be approached for a further increase. Moreover, this would be effected by a Treasury Order, which could only be debated in the Commons in a very restricted way. And there would be published on such an occasion, or at least every ten years, a very brief report from the three Royal Trustees. They are, on the government side, the Prime Minister and Chancellor of the Exchequer (greatly influenced by the Treasury mandarins), together with the Keeper of the Privy Purse who represents the Queen.

However, inflation overtook this plan as it had overtaken, though more gradually, the 1952 Civil List. In 1974, the Civil List was relieved of one further cost, when the upkeep of the Buckingham Palace Press Office was transferred to the government's Central Office of Information.[3] But this was not enough, and in 1975 it was arranged for yearly upratings to maintain the value of the Civil List. It was now a Labour government, under Harold Wilson, which was in the position of catering to the royals. Roy Jenkins had said in 1971, about Houghton's plan to set up a Department of the Crown to finance the monarchy, 'I strongly suspect that we shall do something very near to this when we [Labour] next have to make arrangements in this area.'[4] But Labour in office, prompted by Treasury officials, proved to be as loyal to the throne as the Conservatives. Houghton's scheme to abolish the Civil List was forgotten by both the Prime Minister and his Chancellor, Denis Healey. Houghton himself had gone to the Lords, and Willie Hamilton was ignored when he reminded Wilson and Healey that, only a few years earlier, Houghton's scheme had been Labour policy.

Neil Kinnock, eight years away from the Labour leadership and still a left-wing backbencher, also spoke enthusiastically in favour of a Crown Department to 'clear away the many mists that surround the whole question of the Queen's personal and private wealth and the tax-payer's contribution to the Queen and the remainder of the Royal Household'.[5] But it was not just the Labour Left and the maverick republican Willie Hamilton who objected to their government's timidity in the face of the monarchy. Barbara Castle's diaries note that 'the most serious threat of backbench revolt [against the new Civil List increases] came not from the left-wing Tribune group but the centre-right Manifesto group'. The latter put down an Early Day Motion in the Commons demanding 'full information concerning the effects of the Sovereign's immunity from taxation . . . on her private wealth'.[6] Similarly, Robert Kilroy-Silk, now a TV presenter but in 1975 a new Labour MP, urged the Prime Minister to consider appointing 'a Royal Commission to examine the financial position of the monarchy'.[7]

What Labour did with the Civil List in 1975 was to implement the approach that Barber had first advocated back in May 1971, just before the Select Committee had been set up.[8] This was to have the Civil List increases voted through Parliament annually, like any other piece of government expenditure. Barber and the Treasury had later discarded this method as involving too much parliamentary scrutiny, but in reality there is very little scope for parliamentary enquiry into the sums that government spends each year. So Labour obligingly returned to Barber's original plan, which would provide the desired annual increases, and Harold Wilson announced the Queen's agreement with this change.

To make this alteration, fresh legislation was needed, and this led to more parliamentary debate, echoed in the press, covering much of the same ground as in 1971–2. The Queen felt compelled to make two voluntary financial contributions, described below, in addition to the gesture of deferring the building work at Sandringham. No doubt there was a certain amount of annoyance at the Palace with the politicians in general for not getting their act together, to obviate the need for further embarrassing debate on the monarchy. Cobbold had told the Select Committee in 1971 that at the Palace they were 'very much hoping' that some method could be found which would 'automatically, or semi-automatically' make the Civil List inflation-proof.[9] This was not achieved, and even though the annual increases passed through the Commons smoothly, in later years they attracted a certain amount of unwelcome media attention.

What Cobbold had wanted was to agree with government an index and link it to the Civil List, so as to give automatic annual rises without any fuss. However, this would create an awkward precedent. Government ministers of whichever party was in power would appreciate that trade unions could argue for increased wages, saying that if the Queen should be insulated from inflation, so should their members. Facilitating such comparisons is not what the monarchy is there for.[10]

Once the Civil List was out of the way, the renovation of Sandringham, described in February 1975 as 'insensitive and inappropriate', with 'so many people . . . facing economic difficulties', went ahead. Yet the numbers facing economic difficulties mounted through 1975, as unemployment increased from 791,800 in February to 1,200,800 by December. The modernization was completed by November 1976.[11] Whilst waiting for the alterations to be completed, the royals had to make do with the eight-bedroomed Wood Farm, also on the 20,000-acre Sandringham estate. The *Daily Telegraph* gave an unofficial estimate that the renovation had cost £400,000 (at 1991 prices, £1.4 million).[12]

In May 1979 Mrs Thatcher's Conservative government was elected and soon set about cutting public expenditure. It seemed the royals were not to be spared this painful process. Accordingly, in January 1980, the Chief Secretary to the Treasury, John Biffen, stated in answer to a parliamentary question that 'the government's search for economies in public spending applies to expenditure on the Civil List'.[13] The Palace Press Office response to Biffen's statement was that 'like everyone else these days, the Queen has to be economy-minded'.[14] Yet in March, the government found it necessary to give Princess Anne an extra £23,000 a year (at 1991 prices, £46,600), an increase of almost twice the rate of inflation. This was said, by a Palace spokesman, to be necessary to fix the roof and guttering at her Gatcombe Park home.[15] The one-off cost of fixing the roof of the Phillips's house hardly seems to justify a permanent increase in the Princess's annuity.

Governments, of course, accept the lavish level of funding provided by the Queen's Civil List. Nevertheless, if one looks at the period from 1975 to 1990 as a whole, *increases* in the Queen's Civil List have been fairly tightly controlled by government. The Civil List has increased over this period by 3.6 times, the same rate as prices have risen. At the same time, it has had to meet some extra costs. When HMSO (Her Majesty's Stationery Office) changed its legal status in 1980, it ceased to supply stationery and office supplies free to the Palace. This was very much against the historical trend, which has been for the Civil List to pay for less and less. Further costs were incurred from 1982, when the Civil List invested in data-processing equipment. This would reduce costs in the long run but in the meantime had to be financed.

Thus in the early 1980s a number of press accounts, inspired no doubt by the Palace Press Office, now funded by government, told of the pressure on the Civil List, which required economies if the Queen was to make ends meet. The headlines pronounced 'QUEEN'S CASH HIT',

'THE PALACE IS FEELING INFLATION PINCH', 'THE ECONOMICAL QUEEN CUTS HER COSTS' and so on.[16] In 1980, the Civil List grant of £2.9 million was insufficient to meet expenditure by £108,710. The shortfall was reduced in 1981 and all but eliminated in 1982.[17]

The journalists who wrote the stories described the deficits (totalling just under £200,000) as being met from the Queen's 'private fortune'.[18] However, whatever they were told, the official report from the Royal Trustees which came out in January 1984 stated that because of the 'exceptional circumstances the deficit on the Civil List for 1980, 1981 and 1982 was met from the [Royal Palace] Presentation Fund'. This is the fund formed from the profits on admission charges and souvenir sales to members of the public who visit the Queen's Gallery next door to Buckingham Palace, Holyroodhouse and Windsor Castle. Usually the surplus, after meeting staff expenses of 130 employees and costs of preserving the works of art, is invested. Further Civil List deficits, totalling £319,254, were also met from this source in the 1980s.

It will be recalled that in the past the Queen had been happy to transfer the bulk of the costs of the monarchy to government departments. By 1990, 90 per cent of government expenditure on the monarchy was met by various departments,[19] leaving the Civil List to be used mainly to pay her staff, an arrangement which gives her control of the Royal Household. (She does not, however, pay for the occupational pensions to retired employees. This has been left to the government since 1936. The bill for 1989–90 was £1.04 million.[20]) Any significant economies in the Civil List would always be likely to involve the Household payroll.

In 1982 the full-time employees were cut by twenty to 346 (though this was still more than the 337 employed full-time in 1975).[21] The *Sunday Telegraph* noted in March 1982 that 'instead of employing an army of cleaners at Buckingham Palace, the Queen has contracted out cleaning in all but the most sensitive areas of the Palace'. Also at about the same time some clerical work and catering services were contracted out. In the following year, the *Sunday Telegraph* noted that Palace officials were 'reticent' as to whether there had been any redundancies or not.[22] In 1987, after a management review, the salary bill was reduced by 12 per cent in real terms, and in 1991 full-time employees paid from the Civil List were down to 265.

The Royal Trustees Report of 1990 states that 'wages and salaries are comparable to those in the Civil Service'. The 1984 report stated that 'since 1972 they have received increases similar to those awarded to members of the Civil Service'. (Conditions of service are, however, not linked to those of the Civil Service.) Receiving the level of increase which applies in the Civil Service is not an advantage, however, since in the 1980s the government has kept Civil Service pay increases below the level of increases in the private sector. And generally, whatever progress has been made in pay and however the alignment with Civil Service pay has been worked out in practice, the pay for the bulk of the staff has to be described as low.

For instance, in July 1987, Buckingham Palace advertised for a footman, at the Truro Job Centre in Cornwall, to be aged 19–26, 'of excellent appearance, manner and family background, and easily checked'. The pay was a mere £4,700, rising to £5,400 over five years. It did include living-in, but live-in servants do not get London allowance. A similar advertisement, displayed in a Norfolk Job Centre, in 1988 offered £5,000–£5,700.[23] In November 1989, the *Daily Mirror* described footmen as getting a rise bringing their wages up to £6,121.[24] There is no reason to believe that the staff who work for the Queen are anything but loyal, but loyalty to the monarchy does not provide hard cash. Many staff 'moonlight' and do outside catering jobs at weddings, receptions etc. The royals know about this; when they attend a reception, they may be waited on by one of their own footmen.

Once having left royal service, some former staff have committed the ultimate disloyalty, by going into print. When Prince Charles's valet, after sixteen years of royal service, produced a book on his former royal master in 1983, he was following in the footsteps of the valet to Charles's father, whose book on Prince Philip came out in the mid-1950s. The motive may be pure gain, the desire for recognitioin or a desire to give their account of life at the Palace. Like other 'serve and tell' books by ex-royal servants, both referred pointedly to low pay, though protesting loyalty to the royal family,[25] and one can't help feeling that the contrast between that low pay and the wealth of the royals played a part in encouraging the former servant to cash in on his inside knowledge.*

When I asked the Queen's Press Secretary, in July 1990, for some

---

* For a long time now, the Palace have had employees sign a document committing them to lifelong confidentiality, which the Queen's solicitors have enforced by taking several ex-servants to court. Charles's valet got round this by publishing in the United States, where it would have been more difficult for his former employer to pursue the matter through the courts.

up-to-date figures on wages and salaries paid to those employed by the Queen, I was met with a polite but firm refusal. He would refer, in a purely general way, only to the link with Civil Service pay levels. This is the Royal Household reacting as a private household, which need not be publicly accountable. Yet it is not so private that the Queen offers to improve the lot of her lower-paid workers from her private, tax-free investment income. Also, when asked to justify the use of public money, one learns it is to finance the *public* duties of the royals.

As regards the white-collar staff, one job was placed in the classified ads of *The Times* in May 1987. A report elsewhere in the paper commented that the Palace 'is, it seems, far from generous in the salary stakes. While rank-and-file secretaries all over London can easily command between £10,000 and £15,000 a year, Her Majesty's Privy Purse Office is . . . offering just £7,987 for a confidential personal secretary, rising to £9,780' (plus free lunches and a parking space).[26] Neither are contractors, who since the early 1980s have provided cleaning and catering services, known for their high rates of pay or generous holiday arrangements, let alone union protection for their employees.

Significant financial discipline has been exercised to keep the Civil List from increasing too fast. But in reality this is largely a charade, because what really counts is the much larger expenditure on the monarchy, borne on the cost of the Departmental Votes. This much less visible sum has risen well ahead of inflation and the official estimate for 1990–91 is £46.2 million. This is ten times greater than the amount allocated in the comparable year of 1974–5, £4.64 million,[27] though prices increased only 4.6 times over the same period.

The £46.2 million is a higher figure than it would otherwise be because of 'exceptional' renovations at Windsor Castle. But it is in fact a representative figure when one also assigns to 1990–91 a portion of other recent exceptional expenditure, not included in the above figure, such as the three new jets for the Queen's Flight. Similarly, one should spread the cost of the major refit of *Britannia* in 1987 over a number of years, including 1990.

With the Civil List, the royal annuities and Royal Household pensions coming to a further £7.3 million, this makes £53.5 million. However, this is not the total figure because it includes nothing for royal protection, which must be some millions more. (Neither Buckingham Palace nor Scotland Yard will discuss anything to do with security, including its cost.) Nor does this figure include the cost of the Queen's tax exemption.

If we look at the picture over the whole reign, we see the same parity as there was in the period 1975–90 between the increase in Civil List spending and the rise in prices. Both increase during 1952–90 by about twelve times. Keeping the Civil List down was, of course, in large measure achieved by shedding various charges to government departments. Known expenditure by government departments increased from £343,000 in 1952–3, the first year of the Queen's reign,[28] by 135 times to £46.2 million in 1990–91. This increase is eleven times greater than the rate of inflation.

Yachting with *Britannia*

One factor in this considerable jump in expenditure was that in 1952 there was no Royal Yacht. *Britannia*, which came into service in 1954, is a considerable item to maintain. The Royal Yacht is in fact an ocean-going liner, 125 metres long with a gross tonnage of 5,862 tonnes. A review in the *Observer* of the various luxury yachts used by the world's super-rich put *Britannia* as only second in size to the Saudi King Fahd's yacht, and larger even than the yacht belonging to the world's richest person, the Sultan of Brunei. *Britannia* has a full crew of twenty-two officers and 254 men. When in harbour, the number is only one third less.[29] The wages bill for this contingent, in the latest figures available, those for 1970, exceeded that for the Royal Household. The yacht is used for state visits abroad, but also for personal pleasure. For instance, it has often been taken to Cowes, where Prince Philip goes for the yachting at the end of July or for special royal birthday celebrations. It is also used in August to transport the royals at a leisurely pace to Balmoral, with the Queen and Prince Philip stopping off for the odd official engagement. And, of course, it is for royal honeymoons.

The running costs of *Britannia*, met by the Ministry of Defence, of £9.3 million in 1990–91,[30] exceeds the Civil List, which was £5.06 million for the calendar year 1990. The cost of *Britannia* has not just drawn criticism from predictable quarters. Conservative newspapers have often queried the sums spent on it, particularly on its many costly refits, which are additional to its normal running costs. In 1980, just after Mr Biffen's announcement that the Civil List would have to make some economies, it was announced that *Britannia* was having another refit, costing £5 million. Charles Irving, Conservative MP for Cheltenham, thought 'the Ministry of Defence must have gone totally barmy. This yacht was re-equipped only about five years ago.'[31] (Actually it was four.)

In 1987 there was a very major refit, which came to £19 million on top of the normal annual operating cost.[32] To put this in perspective, it is about the same price ($29 million) that the Manhattan property tycoon Donald Trump paid the Saudi Arabian arms-dealer Adnan Khashoggi for his yacht.[33] This was also in 1987, when Trump was at his financial peak. As a more modern ship, it might not have been a bad buy for the Ministry of Defence, as a replacement for the ancient *Britannia*, which has needed more and more money to keep it seaworthy to royal standards. But even if Her Majesty could have made do with a ship 40 metres shorter than *Britannia*, it would not fit the royal image to have a ship previously owned by someone else, let alone an arms-dealer. Nor would it be politic for the Ministry of Defence to commission a new yacht, as this would more obviously raise the issue of royal extravagance. Making do with one's old yacht does not seem quite so extravagant as ordering a new one, even if the eventual cost is much greater. No doubt the tradition attached to *Britannia* is another factor.

After the 1987 refit, proud dockyard workers who had worked round the clock to complete the job on time were not at first allowed to bring their families aboard to show them the results of their labour. 'We are being treated like serfs,' the union representative, Neil Skinner, was quoted as saying. Buckingham Palace said, 'we can't keep the ship in pristine condition if we have hundreds of workers walking around her'.[34] In the end, though, the workers were allotted a time to show their families around the ship.

In 1938, when the old Royal Yacht *Victoria and Albert* was scrapped, the Navy minister, Duff Cooper, put forward a proposal for a replacement. He told his Cabinet colleagues that a useful way to justify building a new Royal Yacht would be to argue that it could double as a hospital ship in time of war.[35] This was only a rationalization, for in the event of the Second World War the plans for this 'hospital ship', were shelved. After the war, the Labour government felt that building a Royal Yacht hardly squared with its austerity programme, which included the rationing of many basic foodstuffs. But just before leaving office in October 1951, it gave way and ordered the yacht to be built. *The Times* greeted the news with great satisfaction in its leader. It had not been 'seemly' for George VI to have to charter a liner when he had 'occasion to go afloat in state'.[36]

For many years, the hospital ship idea was wheeled out as an answer to critics of the expense of *Britannia*. Yet during the Falklands War in 1982, another ship, the holiday liner *Uganda*, had to be requisitioned as a hospital ship when it turned out that *Britannia* used the wrong type of fuel and would therefore have required its own refuelling tanker in the South Atlantic.[37] It is ironic that such an oversight should have occurred when the Duke of Edinburgh was a frequent user of the ship and had spent twelve years in the Navy. And he remembered that when *Britannia* had been built, he had been 'very interested in every detail of her design'.[38] Moreover, Prince Charles, in the 1970s, had also been a naval officer who had commanded a ship for a year. That the fuel problem was overlooked suggests that during *Britannia*'s many refits, its use as a hospital ship was not taken seriously, and that its participation in naval exercises was not particularly useful. After the Falklands War, in 1984, at the cost of £6 million, *Britannia* was converted to the more economical diesel, enabling it to use the same fuel as the rest of the fleet.[39] *Britannia* cost £2 million to build in 1954 (£25 million in 1991 prices), but the total cost of refits since then, in current prices, has been £92 million.[40]

In 1986, *Britannia* was fortuitously in the right place to rescue Britons trapped in the Yemen. But while the notion of its use as a hospital ship has been none too convincing, a new justification for the cost of *Britannia* has surfaced. About once a year, it is made available for business seminars whilst it is docked in foreign ports or in the Port of London. The idea is to sell British goods and services abroad. For instance, in March 1989, the Governor of the Bank of England and the chairmen of the Stock Exchange and Lloyd's held a seminar for foreign diplomats, promoting the businesses of the City of London.[41] A Ministry of Defence spokesman listed a further five such business seminars aboard *Britannia* in foreign parts in the 1980s. This hardly constitutes an intensive use of *Britannia* for this purpose. These public-relations days may well help raise a little business for British firms, but it is hard to see how such a minor operation could add up to the estimate of the Defence spokesman, that they had brought Britain 'several hundreds of millions of pounds' of business. Rather than enthusing over *Britannia*'s record of attracting business in a commercially competitive world, it seems as if he was trying to justify the existing way the yacht is used.[42]

The Ministry of Defence also provides the Queen's Flight. In 1981, when the Conservative government's policy of cutting expenditure had a high profile, it seems to have been sensitive about visible extravagance and delayed replacing the 1960s Andover turbo-props. It finally did so in 1986, acquiring two British Aerospace 146 jets plus a third in 1990, at a total cost of £40 million.[43] In addition there are two Westland helicopters. The Central Office of Information pamphlet on the monarchy describes the arrangements for using the Queen's Flight:

> The Queen, the Queen Mother, the Duke of Edinburgh and the Prince of Wales are entitled to use it on all occasions. At the Queen's discretion it is also made available to other members of the Royal Family, but only on official duties.

This means that the senior royals can use the Queen's Flight for *personal* as well as official journeys, even if the lesser royals cannot. In 1971 the Queen's Flight employed the services of about 180 officers and men. For 1990–91, the running costs were £6.7 million. A minority of this cost is attributable to Defence ministers and military brass, who are entitled to use the aircraft free of charge, 'with Her Majesty's approval and subject to availability'. Other ministers who are entitled to use it have their departments billed for the cost. In 1979, the Royal Family's flying time was 433 hours compared with 115 hours for ministers and other VIPs.[44]

Another item of royal transport is the Royal Train. In 1990–91, £1.4 million was provided for its day-to-day running costs.[45] Like the yacht and aircraft, the new Royal Train is built and equipped with security as well as luxury in mind. A portion of the £7.5 million cost of the new Royal Train, announced in 1985, was to make it withstand 'rockets, bombs and machine-guns'. When Scotland Yard advised that there were still security loopholes, an extra £2.5 million was spent.[46] When Queen Victoria travelled by train, the entire length of the line was patrolled before the Royal Train passed. Then as now the main threat to royal safety was perceived to come from Ireland, and after a Fenian bombing and other actions in England in the late 1860s, extra precautions were taken.[47]

The upkeep of the Queen's Palaces – Buckingham Palace and Windsor Castle – is taken care of by the Department of the Environment

(Holyroodhouse is paid for by the Scottish Office). Kensington Palace and St James's Palace, where other royals live, are also maintained by the DoE. Unless there are the kind of recent large outlays on boat, train and planes already mentioned, the maintenance of the buildings is the largest single item, for 1990–91 running at £25.6 million (which includes sums being spent on 'exceptional work' at Windsor Castle). That Prince Philip in his 1969 NBC interview suggested, even if in jest, that he and the Queen 'may have to move to smaller premises' particularly annoyed one member of the Labour Cabinet at that time, Richard Crossman. He pointed out subsequently how Buckingham Palace was maintained by the government and not out of the Civil List.[48]

There is also the cost of police time – to protect the royals from the IRA, international terrorists and random persons of unsound mind. When the royals travel, local police are also involved in providing security, but the core of this work is carried out by the Royalty and Diplomatic Protection Squad of the Metropolitan Police. No separate figures for the cost are available, but it means that, in addition to the 265 full-time and seventy-seven part-time employees paid from the Civil List, eighty or so industrial staff who maintain the buildings, paid by the Department of the Environment, and a dozen Press Office staff paid by the Central Office of Information,[49] there are yet more personnel involved in the maintenance of the monarchy. A further 180 keep the Queen's Flight airborne, 276 keep *Britannia* afloat, and more keep the Royal Train on the rails. For two months in the year the army provides 120 Scottish soldiers who guard the Queen at Balmoral. There are more at Sandringham and Balmoral. More than a thousand in all.

It is evident that the money spent on the monarchy through government departments is not under the same fairly tight control as is the much more visible Civil List. We can see the difference between the two different forms of financial discipline in the case of one particular item, the transferring of costs in 1981 for stationery and office supplies from HMSO to the Civil List when the government made HMSO a semi-autonomous Trading Fund.* As the Royal Trustees Report put it, 'significant economies' were made in spending in this area. In fact,

---

* Such a transfer was not repeated when British Telecom was privatized. The latter no longer provided telephone calls free, but the Department of the Environment stepped in to pay the bills. The Post Office still provides free postal services. See the COI booklet *The Monarchy in Britain* (1988), p. 15.

after the changeover expenditure was reduced by about half in real terms (compared to 1979–80, just before the changeover).

The Queen's Voluntary Contributions

In recommending increases to the Civil List, both Conservative ministers in 1971 and Labour ministers in 1975 were relieved to be able to emphasize certain financial contributions the Queen seemed to be making. There were three ways in which the Queen helped out with Civil List expenditure. In 1971 she offered to forgo the £60,000 p.a. the government had paid to her Privy Purse, together with another item amounting to £3,000. In early 1975 she offered to contribute £150,000, for that year only, towards the £420,000 increase in the Civil List. And at the end of 1975 came the biggest of all, the previously mentioned contribution of relieving the government 'for the time being' of the necessity of paying out to her three cousins,[50] who in 1991 received collectively £630,000. All these contributions were recommended as being most generous by government ministers. However, in Chapters 3 and 4, we have seen that, whilst royals have made 'voluntary contributions' before, there has always been a hidden snag as regards any benefit to the Exchequer.* This was true as regards both George V's and George VI's contributions from war-time Civil List savings, and George V's donation in the cause of National Economy in 1931.

As regards the Queen, we know that she has made no savings from the Civil List, as had the previous five monarchs. This was ruled out by the form of the Civil List settlement in 1952, as described in Chapter 6. All the contributions discussed above were funded from the Duchy of Lancaster revenues, but they still left plenty of money for the Queen's personal use. In 1976, the first year the Queen footed the bill for her cousins, it totalled £118,000, leaving a surplus of £267,000 from the £385,000 she took from the Duchy revenues. By 1989 this surplus had grown tenfold, far ahead of inflation, to £2.79 million

---

* In fact, it was in 1974, the year before the Queen's offer to pay her cousins, that the bulk of the costs of the Buckingham Palace Press Office, £48,000 in 1975–6, were transferred from the Civil List to the Votes. This transfer was not disclosed until the mid-1980s. If it had been announced at the time, the Queen's offer would have appeared less generous. Since then, to cater to increased media interest in the royals, this cost has increased at twice the rate of inflation.

(£3.19 million drawn out from the Duchy less £400,000 to the cousins).

But over and above that, at the time of the three contributions, was the mounting sum which the Queen kept by not paying tax. They gave ministers, and monarchists generally, something to point to at a time when critics were complaining of the cost of the monarchy, and seem to have been an attempt to buy off criticism cheaply, and distract attention from the tax exemption. The amounts that the Queen gives with one hand are public and praised. What she takes with the other hand in terms of freedom of taxation is secret.

If it is secret, how then can we know that the value of the tax exemption was actually increasing through the 1970s? Firstly, there is the point that the Civil List and Duchy of Lancaster revenues (used in the first half of the reign largely for upkeep of Sandringham and Balmoral) should have taken care of practically all personal expenditure.* And of course expenditure by government departments takes care of the large items like the upkeep of palaces, the Royal Yacht etc. What requirements remain are often met from the assorted and often valuable gifts that the Queen has received and continues to receive from foreign heads of state and business organizations. Therefore there is nothing much else to do with the income on her private investments except plough it back into further investments. The purchases of land for the years 1971–87 also count as investments and suggest no shortage of money.

In 1971, the very year of Her Majesty's Gracious Message to the House of Commons asking for more money, lest they 'go into the red', the Queen bought the Polhampton stud in Hampshire, which she had hitherto only rented.[51] There she kept her thoroughbred yearlings, before they were sent into training for the racecourse.

In 1976 the Queen bought from R.A. Butler his home, Gatcombe Park in Gloucestershire, to give to Princess Anne. Butler was the Chancellor who had guided her 1952 Civil List through Parliament. He received the purchase price of about £750,000 from the money that he and other politicians had felt the Queen should acquire. Or perhaps Her Majesty paid rather less: as Butler's biographer, Anthony Howard, has noted,

---

* An exception would be the money probably needed to subsidize the Queen's horseracing enterprise. See Chapter 11.

'the transaction . . . did not provide Rab with complete satisfaction'. Butler told his biographer 'more than once' and with some feeling that 'the Royal Family, you know, drive a very hard bargain'.[52] Perhaps Prince Albert's hard-headed approach to buying property cheaply, noted in Chapter 1, had been revived in some way, more than a hundred years after his purchases of Osborne and Balmoral.

As described earlier, by November 1976 Sandringham House had been renovated at a cost of something like £400,000.

The following year, the Queen bought for her daughter the 600-acre Aston Farm, Cherington, next door to the 730 acres of Gatcombe Park.[53] The Queen retained the ownership and since the couple's separation has rented it to Mark Phillips.

In 1978, the Queen acquired 6,700 acres close to Balmoral. The Delnadamph estate had what Balmoral had lacked, a good grouse moor, and had recently come on the market at £750,000. The Palace spokesperson said the Queen had bought it to avoid 'the ever increasing cost of renting grouse-moors'.[54] Also on the estate was a twelve-bedroom house, Delnadamph Lodge, and several cottages. The main house, according to the *Daily Telegraph*, was once considered as a wedding present to the Prince and Princess of Wales. However, it was not so used and by 1987 had clearly fallen into disrepair, the property being offered to the army for demolition practice.[55] The army said the demolition would be carried out free of charge. Though in a remote position, it is a shame to think that it could not have served some better purpose – perhaps for those who could otherwise not afford a holiday in the picturesque Highlands. At least it might have been made available for such use outside the two months or so the royals use Balmoral.

Since 1979, the value of the tax exemption will have declined. Other things being equal, the Thatcher government's reduction of income tax, particularly in the higher tax brackets, means that the Queen now benefits less from not paying tax. However, this does not involve any reduction in Her Majesty's actual income. Also, assuming the Queen's income is still rising, we can expect the value of the tax exemption to be growing again.

In 1982, another estimated £750,000 bought the West Ilsley stables in Berkshire, where Major Dick Hern was already training some of the Queen's racehorses.[56] According to the Queen's stud manager, the purchase price came from selling her top-class filly, Height of Fashion, so although it is yet another acquisition, in this instance it was not paid for from the Queen's investment income. One could say that it was made possible by previous royal investment in the racehorses from which Height of Fashion was bred. Bought from the Sobell family, the stables at West Ilsley contain more than a hundred horse-boxes and stand in more than a hundred acres. Also included were thirty houses and a lads' hostel.

Lastly, there is the sum, estimated in the press to be £5 million, paid by the Queen for the new home built for the Duke and Duchess of York. The five-acre site in Sunninghill Park, near Windsor, was acquired from the Crown Estate, and the planning prohibitions against building on 'green belt' land were overcome. Originally, the Tory Berkshire county council had rejected the application, made in the name of Flitcham Nominees Ltd, by refusing to consider it except on 'straightforward planning' grounds. But the final decision lay with the local Bracknell council. The latter accepted the view that the royal couple's need for seclusion and security – the nearest neighbours are 200 yards away – overrode the normal planning situation.[57] The design of the new house, according to the tabloid press, who watched it gradually taking shape, does not seem to have left anything out. It has a helipad, swimming pool, tennis court, cinema, billiards room, stables and garaging for six cars, with separate staff quarters for six people. The Yorks have thus been able to leave their former home, Castlewood House, also near Windsor, where they lived rent-free in one of King Hussein of Jordan's spare country houses.

Another Increase and More 'Economizing': the Civil List for the 1990s

In July 1990, the Prime Minister, Mrs Thatcher, announced to the Commons that the government was planning to increase the Civil List sharply from £5.09 million to about £7.9 million a year. The new figure is intended to stay the same from 1991 to 2000, and thus end the system of annual increases. The £7.9 million sum is planned to produce surpluses in the early years which will be employed to mop up the deficits that inflation, anticipated to average 7.5 per cent, will cause in the later years (7.5 per cent was the average rate of inflation during the 1980s). The other royals are also being paid on the same basis. It is in fact a return to the arrangement that had briefly been in place from 1972 to 1975. Mrs Thatcher referred to the new set-up as having been approved by the Queen, but why was the 1975 system of yearly upratings ended?

Mrs Thatcher, under questioning in the Commons, recommended the new system as giving 'much more dignity' to the monarchy. In other words, there will be no more annual announcements of increases in the Civil List, which triggered embarrassing articles about 'pay rises' for the royals. Mrs Thatcher also claimed the new arrangement would assist in long-term planning, because the Royal Household would know its income for the next ten years.[58] This latter argument can be discounted, because government spending in general manages to exist on a basis of annual financing, which does not preclude an element of longer-term planning.

Mrs Thatcher reintroduced the old story of 'royal economizing'. She described how the £7.9 million figure was based on rather less than a 7.5 per cent inflation rate, because the Queen would make a contribution in terms of 'efficiency savings', which would reduce spending by a total of £5 million during 1991–2000. She said these savings would result 'from continuing improvements in management, in line with the best financial practice'. And indeed an accountant, old Etonian Michael Peat from the royal auditors Peat, Marwick, McLintock, has been drafted in for two years to tighten things up financially. He is a latter-day equivalent of Ralph Harwood, whom the Treasury supplied to the Royal Household in 1921 to fulfil a similar function.

Because 70 per cent of the Civil List goes on wages and salaries, this would appear to be the area where the bulk of the savings would come from; and Mr Peat's firm had already sent in work-study experts in 1989 to run the rule over staff at Windsor. The savings could also come from another source which was not mentioned anywhere. The anticipated surpluses, which will accumulate in the early 1990s, will earn interest before being used up by 2000. At a rate of 10 per cent they will provide the £5 million by themselves. Also, before the new set-up is introduced there will be an increase of 16 per cent, nearly twice the rate of inflation, on the Civil List.

Should the rate of inflation exceed 7.5 per cent, there is a safety net. The government has powers under the last Civil List Act to make extra payments to the Queen and other royals. So the press comment about the royals entering an era of tough budgetary constraint is rather silly. Also, as argued above, the attention to keeping down the costs of the

Civil List has not been matched by the effort to keep down the spending of government departments, which involves far greater sums.

It could be said that this was only a different method of paying the royals, and as such was unlikely to create any fuss. However, changing the Civil List arrangements, essentially to protect the royals from annual publicity about their finances, could be expected to raise all the same issues as had been debated in the Commons in the 1970s. That the government wished to head off any such debate is apparent from the manner in which the new measures were made public.

Robert Harris of the *Sunday Times* described how, 'as a piece of news management, this was a classic'. It was announced 'at the fag-end of the [Parliamentary] session', when MPs were thinking of their summer holidays. 'MPs learned of it only two hours in advance. They were allowed twenty minutes to ask questions.' The increased awards to the other royals – including Prince Edward's increase from £20,000 to £100,000 – 'were not even read out but buried in a table in *Hansard*'.[59] Before announcing the increases, Mrs Thatcher had consulted the Labour Party leader, Neil Kinnock, who gave his warm approval. This made it possible for the government to get away with breaking the news in the way it did. He may even have made the new measure itself possible. For if Labour had opposed it, saying that there waas no reason for the Queen to avoid public scrutiny, then the government might have dropped the whole idea of the ten-year Civil List. Labour opposition would have stirred up controversy and thus partly defeated the object of the new measure.

It was all a strange contrast to Neil Kinnock's statements of the 1970s about the monarchy. He was then, by all appearances, a republican. In 1975 he had found the royals 'outrageously overpaid'. He wanted 'a job inspection of Her Majesty as an employer', given the 'widespread rumours that much of her staff is seriously underpaid'. He drew attention to the 'immense riches' of the monarchy, compared to the 'immense strain' suffered by those in poverty and near poverty.[60] He voted against the Labour government's Civil List Bill and resigned his job as Michael Foot's parliamentary private secretary.

Robert Harris, who has written a biography of Kinnock[61], fears that the Labour leader has now succumbed to the royal embrace. Looking at matters from the so-called 'middle ground' of British politics, he credits Kinnock with having abandoned old-fashioned left-wing ideas and brought the Labour Party up-to-date. But, Harris says, there is no corresponding need to adapt one's views on the royal family. For 'nothing has changed there in the past fifteen years, except that it has grown even bigger and richer'. Harris feels that Kinnock has not simply adopted a more 'sensible' approach to the royal family for a party leader wishing to avoid controversy. With the new Civil List and his tribute to the Queen Mother for her 90th birthday, what he has done is 'to roll over on his back and wave his arms and legs in the air'. Labour leaders have always made suitably respectful comments on similar occasions. Yet Kinnock telling the Commons that the Queen Mother had 'genius' and 'greatness', and much more besides,[62] is the kind of flannel usually associated with the more reactionary Tory backbencher.

On the Civil List, it was left to the firmly royalist Tory backbencher, Anthony Beaumont-Dark, to suggest that the Queen should pay tax on her private income and also her private wealth, like everyone else.* As Harris concludes, having a Tory MP taking a stance well to the left of the Labour front bench means that 'revisionism has gone far enough'.

---

* Mrs Thatcher responded by saying that 'the Queen has not been subject to tax for a long time' and rejecting the idea she be taxed now. Was Mrs Thatcher suggesting that, earlier in her reign, the Queen had paid tax on her private income?

III

The Royal Fortune

9

The Queen's Wealth and Its Uses

In their survey of Britain's richest 200, *Money* magazine in March 1988 placed the Queen as far and away the richest person in the country, as have other such surveys. *Money* calculated her total worth at £3,340 million. In the same year, *Fortune*, the American business magazine, thought it was a hefty £1,800 million or so more (at $8,700 million), making her the fourth richest person in the world.[1] The Queen is without doubt the wealthiest person in Britain. No one has had the monarchy's total freedom from the attentions of the Inland Revenue. No one has so many personal expenses paid for by the state. No one in Britain has a jewellery collection to compare with the Queen's, comprising mostly presents to her and her predecessors. These are the three motors of royal accumulation, which are unique privileges of the monarch – tax exemption, state subsidy and presents given to her in her capacity as head of state.

There are many other valuable possessions, notably the royal art collection. Precision over figures for the Queen's wealth is not really possible. Even though she may employ the computers at Buckingham Palace to calculate, probably not even the Queen herself can know the value of her multitudinous assets. As the Texan one-time billionaire Bunker Hunt once said, someone who knows how much money they are worth is not worth much.

What would certainly have baffled the Texan approach to money matters is that the Queen has, it seems, at least *eight* different legal statuses of ownership. Nor is it just Texans who get perplexed, because these categories are not always clearly defined and nowhere is an overall view of royal wealth presented. This chapter attempts to remedy that situation by exploring the many highways and byways of the Queen's fortune, but it has to be said that once you get to a certain level of wealth, it becomes extremely difficult to put a precise figure on assets. Her Majesty is way beyond that level.

For instance, both the leading writers on the royal jewels in the Queen's personal possession describe them as being of 'incalculable value'.[2] Andrew Morton took an interesting stab at valuing them by consulting a top valuer, Laurence Krashes of Harry Winston in New York. However, he did not have access to the jewels themselves, but had to rely on photographs and what information is publicly known. He described his task as 'like landing a plane in fog without radar'. The figure he came up with was £35.6 million. Morton also says, with reason, that the jewels would probably bring ten times Krashes's valuation because of their royal ownership – i.e. £356 million. Morton acknowledges that there are undoubtedly other royal jewels which are not known and have not been photographed, and their value could not therefore be included.[3]

Then there is the Queen's extremely valuable and extensive postage stamp collection, assembled by her father and grandfather. As with the jewellery and the other valuables, the price the stamps would fetch would depend on the exact circumstances in which they were put on the market. Also, the prices that extremely rare items would fetch (whether stamps, paintings, jewels or whatever) are hard to predict because they are not constantly on the market, and do not therefore acquire a known price.

Where items are insured, this would give us some figures to work on, but such figures are secret.* All in all, it seems best to eschew the various 'guesstimates' that are made every so often. We can nevertheless obtain a very real idea of the vast wealth of the monarchy, in its various forms, which are:

1 Government Property
We start, firstly, with the most public of the eight types of ownership. It is purely nominal. The Queen can no longer really be said to own the Navy or the law courts or any part of government machinery, even if it is said to belong to that very ambiguous entity, the Crown. The same is true when on much rarer occasions part of the state, like a naval

---

* The Royal Collection is insured just for damage, other than by fire, theft or total loss. The costs are met out of the Royal Palace Presentation Fund (described in previous chapter).

ship, is said to belong to 'Her Majesty in right of the Government of the United Kingdom'. Also in reality just as nominal is her title to the Crown Estate, discussed in Chapter 6.

2 *Legally Inalienable Property*

This refers to the actual, not purely theoretical, ownership of assets – which are said to be 'inalienable'. This covers the three palaces used by the Queen – Buckingham Palace, Windsor Castle and Holyroodhouse in Edinburgh – plus Kensington Palace and St James's Palace, occupied by the other royals. For the government, the Treasury Solicitor has defined the palaces legally as 'non-surrendered Crown Property', which 'are vested in the Sovereign and cannot be alienated'.[4] They have to be passed on to the next monarch. Lord Cobbold in his submission to the Select Committee in 1971 placed the Crown Jewels, kept at the Tower of London, in this category. However, unlike the Palaces, they are hardly ever used by the royals. There are, though, other jewels in the Queen's possession (a minority of such) which are most probably owned in the same way.

3 *Inalienable by Custom*

Cobbold stated that:

> [he] would not presume to deal with the legal technicalities. But for practical purposes, there is a clear understanding, accepted by Her Majesty and operated by the Officers of my Department. It is as follows: The Royal Collection is regarded as covering all pictures and works of art purchased or acquired by all Sovereigns up to the death of Queen Victoria, and also certain property acquired [since then, at the discretion of subsequent monarchs].

This seems rather like the second category, only it seems to work on the basis of understandings within the Royal Household, as opposed to being fixed from outside by the government. These collections include a wide variety of artefacts, not just paintings, sculptures and drawings. There is the greatest collection of Sèvres porcelain in the world, plus elaborate and finely worked furniture, jewel cabinets, tapestries, carpets, chandeliers, candelabra, clocks, ancient armour, guns, swords, daggers, bronzes, plate, glass, coins etc. The Royal Library at Windsor houses the collection of fine prints, rare books and original music manuscripts by Mozart, Mendelssohn etc. There are also the extensive historical documents of the Royal Archives, which were not mentioned by Cobbold. These most likely come under this heading. All these varied possessions, too, are of incalculable value.

4 Lesser Properties

These are properties which the Queen has at her disposal for her servants, courtiers and family. They are referred to as 'grace and favour' or 'official residences'. There are hundreds of them – 310 were listed in 1947.[5] Most of these are fairly ordinary, but some are very fine indeed. Not all are covered by the same legislation and the matter is legally very complicated (most are maintained by the Department of the Environment, and others by the Crown Estate and are thus covered by the Crown Estate Act 1961, s. 5, s.s. 5). Some or all of these properties can be sold.

5 The Duchy of Lancaster

The monarch automatically inherits the Duchy's properties and investments. The Duchy's status, as we have noted, conveniently oscillates between being purely private and being part of 'the Crown'. Moreover, there is a controversy over whether the monarch owns the Duchy at all, which is examined in the next chapter. But officially, at any rate, it is held to be a distinct and separate type of ownership.

6 The Duchy of Cornwall

If there is no Prince of Wales, the monarch has to shoulder another Duchy, that of Cornwall, and hold that estate also. This does not apply to the present Queen, nor would it apply to Charles when he becomes King, because he has sons. But it did apply to Edward VIII and George VI (though they gave the Duchy's profits to the government).

7 The Queen's Private Estates

These are Sandringham and Balmoral, with the recent additions of the grouse moor, the racing stables and the stud, together with any other landed property the Queen owns. *Fortune* magazine in 1987 alluded to much larger landholdings, saying that she is 'reputedly one of the largest landowners in Manhattan' and 'also has large holdings in France and West Germany'. But the article provides no evidence at all.* What makes the landed property a separate category is that

---

* I drew a blank at *Fortune* in trying to follow this up further. I was told that the London and New York freelancers who provided the information for the article no longer work for the magazine. Their source seems to have been a *News of the World* article. The Queen's Deputy Private Secretary has stated, 'Her Majesty neither owns nor part owns' such property (*Daily Express*, 1 March 1991).

it is covered under the legislation of the 1800, 1862 and 1873 Crown Private Estates Acts, discussed in Chapters 1 and 7.

8 *Private and Personal Wealth*

This comprises non-landed assets, which, with the exception of willing such property, are not covered by the Crown Private Estates Acts or any other such legislation. This obviously includes the Queen's investments in stocks and shares, bonds and bank deposits; and also her racehorses. But it also includes a great deal of the paintings, furniture, etc. which are not deemed part of the Royal Collections. The great majority of the Queen's jewellery, even though she feels that many items are 'heirlooms',[6] must also rank as private. Similarly the stamp collection.*

None of these categories is watertight in practice, because of the archaic and also newly manufactured complexities of royal ownership. There is a significant amount of royal opportunism, sanctioned by the Treasury, about allocating a form of wealth to the most advantageous class or indeed to more than one class simultaneously. We have noted in Chapter 7 how, in order to gain tax exemption, private investments are described as belonging to the Crown, with all the connotations of Government Property (category 1). But when it came to the matter of disclosure, the Queen's investments were purely Private and Personal Wealth, like those of any other individual (category 8).

When it comes to enumerating those private assets, Cobbold shows a great desire to minimize them and to suggest that, for instance, the bulk of the privately owned jewels were really heirlooms and thus in effect part of the Royal Collections (category 3). Similarly, 'the Stamp Collections made by George V and VI, though they are private collections, are, for practical purposes, regarded and operated in a similar way to the Royal Collection of Pictures and Works of Art'.[7] In this way, Cobbold was trying to make more credible the idea that estimates of the Queen's private wealth as being £50 million (£335 million at 1991 prices) were 'wildly exaggerated'.

Understandably, the royals themselves sometimes get confused. Lord

---

* George VI's collection of decorations in the form of medals and ribbons was said by his official biographer to be 'among the most complete in the world'. These, though, were not mentioned in the evidence to the 1971 Select Committee.

Mountbatten described the royal Palaces in 1971 as 'state-owned'.[8] However, as described above, they fall within the second category of Legally Inalienable Property. Thus the mildly amusing scenario, occasionally proposed, of 'privatizing' the Palaces in royal occupation, first requires them to be nationalized. The Queen cannot sell the Palaces, but it is inconceivable she would want to. Apart from the force of tradition requiring monarchs to live in existing palaces, selling them commercially would mean that any subsequent owner could exploit the former royal connection in an embarrassing fashion. Buckingham Palace as an hotel would hardly be in keeping with the 'dignity of the monarchy'. The Legally Inalienable classification also carries with it the great advantage that the government picks up the bill for the maintenance of the Palaces (over £20 million a year).

During the 1971 controversy over the Queen's wealth, Lord Mountbatten, described by his official biographer as the 'shop steward of royalty', gave advice to one of his trade-union members. This was his nephew, Prince Philip, whose wife was applying to Parliament for more money from the government. The problem was that the Queen faced the accusation of being sufficiently wealthy already and not needing an increased Civil List. Mountbatten wrote, 'it is true that there is a fortune, which is very big, but the overwhelming proportion (85%?) is in pictures, objets d'art, furniture, etc. . . . The Queen can't sell any of them, they bring no income.'[9]

Mountbatten's advice to Prince Philip was to take the type of union action that the members of other unions would find difficult – make sure there was a sympathetic piece in *The Times*. The article should make just this one point about the art treasures. 'So will you please believe a loving old uncle and NOT your constitutional advisers.' Doubtlessly the latter, in the form of the Chancellor of the Exchequer and perhaps the Prime Minister, were telling the Queen to make no intervention, lest they further fuel the public debate on the matter. Moreover, their advice is supposed to be followed by the monarch.

Five days after Mountbatten's letter to Prince Philip, it was the *Daily Telegraph*, not *The Times*, which was selected for the sympathetic piece (though the day after that, *The Times* did carry on its front page an article making the point about the works of art and other royal collections). The *Telegraph* piece was essentially a statement by John Colville, who had been private secretary to the Queen when she had been Princess Elizabeth. He had married a lady-in-waiting to the Princess and his mother was a long-serving lady-in-waiting to Queen Mary. Colville told the newspaper that if the Queen 'has got more than two million today I'll eat my hat' (£2 million was the same figure he said Edward VII had left in 1910, when prices were eight times lower than in 1971). He claimed his informant on these matters had been a member of the royal family.[10] But when questioned by another newspaper, it seems his royal informant had not told him about the Queen's present wealth. His £2 million figure, he said, was based on 'commonsense and historical knowledge – I certainly had no inside information into the Queen's wealth'.[11] He did not even make clear whether the £2 million consisted only of investments like stocks and shares or whether it included land, jewels and other possessions. The privately owned jewels by themselves would then have been worth more than £2 million.

The Palace Press Office duly said that £2 million was 'a considerably more realistic guess than some of the absurd figures of between £50–£100 million that have been bandied about recently'. It was a royally inspired attempt to get the media to think more in terms of £2 million, but the press generally did not grant Colville's estimate much credence, and no more was heard about it. Ten days later, Lord Cobbold, Lord Chamberlain to the Queen, read from a prepared statement to the Select Committee, in which there was no mention of £2 million or any specific figure at all. Cobbold said the Queen felt that ideas that her private wealth amounted to between £50 and £100 million 'can only arise from confusion about the status of the Royal Collections, which are in no sense at her private disposal'. Such figures were 'wildly exaggerated'.[12]

The Art Treasures

In the above *Times* article, a Palace official was quoted as asserting that various assets like the works of art 'belong to Britain'. But when it comes to defining ownership more precisely, these treasures seem to belong very much to the Queen. Lord Cobbold said they were one category of 'the Queen's possessions, public and private' (Inalienable by Custom in our classification). So even if the understanding is that she must pass them on to her successor, they are nevertheless hers as Queen. And she hardly needs to sell them to make ends meet.

In fact, some of the works of art are not inalienable. Lord Cobbold more precisely defined the Royal Collection as 'all pictures and works of art purchased or acquired by all Sovereigns up to the death of Queen Victoria'. Other later items, unspecified, have been added to the collection. This delimitation leaves a good deal of the art treasures outside of the Royal Collection, and therefore part of the Queen's Private and Personal Wealth, pure and simple. Some of these may eventually be added to the Royal Collection, but this will be purely at the discretion of the monarch. The Queen and Prince Philip have built up a collection of modern artists, and at one time a committee of experts advised on such acquisitions. These include an outstanding Lowry ('The Carriage'), as well as paintings by Graham Sutherland, Paul Nash, Edward Seago, Sidney Nolan, de Grey and many more. Also, the Queen Mother owns a number of valuable paintings, including some by Impressionists like Monet and Sisley.

As regards the Royal Collection proper, during the present reign great improvements have been made in public access. Mostly lesser paintings are on display at the State Apartments of Kensington Palace. Some of the masterpieces are on display at Windsor and Hampton Court. A number of items from the collection are loaned to galleries and museums in Britain and abroad. The greatest progress was made with the opening, in the early 1960s, of the Queen's Gallery, adjacent to Buckingham Palace. In 1958, the Duke of Edinburgh had sent for the Minister of Works (who nowadays would be a junior Environment minister) and suggested that the ruined private chapel, hit by a bomb during the war, be rebuilt as an art gallery open to the public. There were already two other private chapels at the disposal of the royal family, so they could spare it. The minister thought the Duke's suggestion 'a most excellent idea and a splendid piece of public relations by the Monarchy'.[13] There was also a financial motive behind this change. Though the cost of reconstruction would be paid for by the government, the gallery was to charge admission and make a surplus. This money would be used to maintain the royal works of art, relieving the Civil List of the charge.

Thus it would be wrong to see the Royal Collections as totally locked away in the Palaces as they were in Victoria's day. Her successors, Edward VII and George V, cared little for paintings. Sir Oliver Millar, a former Surveyor of the Queen's Pictures, states that one has only to look at their homes (Sandringham, Marlborough House, York Cottage), which 'reveal the inborn philistinism so prevalent in the ruling classes in that confident age',[14] in order to see this. Yet as regards the paintings, George V 'had his father's intensely proprietary attitude towards his possessions', and though he lent pictures to exhibitions, he did not like art historians writing about them.[15] Most of the greater accessibility occurred whilst Sir Anthony Blunt (the Soviet agent) was Surveyor. Had he helped subvert former royal restrictions on public display?

Treasures there are in abundance. They are priceless. The historian J. H. Plumb had access to them and was dazzled:

The royal treasures of the British monarchy are of an unparalleled magnificence and variety. Works by almost every great master of painting are to be found in the royal collection – one of the finest of all Vermeers, magnificent Rembrandts, Rubens of spectacular quality. Portraits from Holbein to Winterhalter . . . Hundreds of drawings by Leonardo da Vinci, exquisite examples of Michelangelo and Raphael; in paint or in pencil there is masterpiece after masterpiece.

The decorative arts are represented in furniture, bronzes, china, plate and glass and jewels. The collection of armour 'would equip a regiment of princes'.[16] By the time of his second book on Britain's 'Royal Heritage', Plumb put it into perspective. He asserts that only the Louvre, the Metropolitan Museum in New York, the National Gallery and the Victoria and Albert Museum in London can better the Queen's collections 'in quality and range. If the Queen's collections were placed in one building, it would take its place immediately as one of the most outstanding museums in the world.'[17]

This is not exactly what has happened. In 1962, the Queen's Gallery was opened, which added greatly to public accessibility. But in describing this gallery Plumb has to move down several gears. He ceases to celebrate the vastness of the Royal Collection. Instead he becomes suddenly concerned that London had previously lacked 'small and intimate galleries', and thus the new gallery filled an important gap.[18] This is a polite way of saying that much of the collection, not on display elsewhere, would remain unshown for long periods of time. Sir Oliver Millar, in charge of the Queen's pictures until 1988, was also defensive about the size of the Queen's Gallery in his book.[19] If the art treasures were publicly owned, then more would be on display than actually is the case. The Tory Bow Group's pamphlet on the monarchy in 1968, six years after the opening of the Queen's Gallery, observed that 'so much' of the Art Collection 'is rarely seen in public'. The *Daily Telegraph* in 1987 felt that 'the rather conservative exhibitions which have already taken place' at the gallery 'show us only the tip of the iceberg . . . of so vast a collection'.[20]

Harold Jackson in the *Guardian* was disappointed in 1985 with 'the tiny and pretty tedious display of the royal Fabergé collection . . . [in] the poorly arranged Queen's Gallery'.[21] When I went in 1988, the exhibition of 'Treasures from the Royal Collections' was more interesting. I was impressed with the variety of objects which had been crafted in a richly ornamental fashion – clocks, barometers, cabinets, tables, vases, candelabra, salts, swords and daggers and so on – though the 1990 exhibition, based on items in the Royal Library, lacked the same quality.

In the gift shop, however, one could buy videos of the Queen and innumerable items bearing a likeness of Buckingham Palace, including tea towels at £2.95 or trays at £40. The till receipts are inscribed with 'Buckingham Palace' at the top.

Millar states that the British royal paintings are the sole survivors of their type. Other royal collections in Europe 'have become state property, the foundation of national collections in Paris, Madrid, Vienna, The Hague, Leningrad or Dresden'.[22] Why does the Queen not go the whole hog and hand over the paintings, etc., more of which could then be on permanent public display?

Perhaps there is the 'intensely proprietary attitude' which Edward VII and George V showed. Also, for most very wealthy owners of valuable art, such possessions are part of the project of legitimizing their wealth and position. This emphatically applies to the Queen. The whole idea of monarchy requires the sovereign to be surrounded by beautiful objects. One can't act out the role convincingly without the appropriate stage-setting. If you live in palaces, you need something grand to hang on the wall; copies or reproductions (or, at least, paintings known to be copies or reproductions) would hardly fit the ancient image of the monarchy.

Thus the Queen is not simply the caretaker of the Royal Collection. If a monarch did not possess such works of art, she would have to go out and buy them, as did her predecessors. The authenticity of the Old Masters are there to confirm the authenticity of their owner as the rightful sovereign. Of course, there are many more paintings than can be hung on the wall at the official residences of Buckingham Palace, Windsor and Holyroodhouse. Yet handing over the 'surplus' paintings and other works to the state would create an awkward precedent, leading perhaps to requests that other items of royal wealth be surrendered. And if the collection came to be divided between those items transferred to the state and those retained, no doubt some would make invidious comparisons and say that the Queen retained too many of the best items, as perhaps she might be tempted to do.

By retaining ownership, even with the self-imposed denial of the right to sell, the monarchy retains control over the paintings and other works. Thus it is not just a question of the amount of public access to them. Just as important is the type of access. The Queen and her advisers ensure that the art treasures are used to show the monarchy in a good light. For instance, at the lowest level, there is the conventional acknowledgment given by galleries when paintings are lent to them 'by gracious permission of Her Majesty the Queen'. Much more significantly, the paintings in the State Apartments at Windsor, which are on public display for most of the year (entrance £2.50), are a vital ingredient in the grandeur of that part of the Castle. They help project an image of splendour as a natural part of the monarchy's past.

However, in a more active way, the works of art can be used to enshrine the desired image of the royal family. For instance, one exhibition at the Queen's Gallery was devoted to pieces associated with George III. Plumb and Wheldon in their best-seller, *Royal Heritage*, claim that this display 'came as a great surprise to many who thought of George III as obstinate, stupid and, finally, mad. He was shown to be a man of great taste, wide intellectual interests, including science and astronomy, and a collector of discernment.'[23] George III's revolting support for the slave trade, his prejudice against the Irish and the determination to keep America as a colony featured less in the exhibition.

Similarly, the various works of art were pressed into service for the TV series *Royal Heritage*, of which the above book was a spin-off. The series (repeated several times) was produced to celebrate the Silver Jubilee of the Queen in 1977. Another book and another programme were produced in 1980–81, which more specifically described the Royal Collection in the present reign. Each programme had at least one royal describing some part of the collection. Also, for each programme the cameras were allowed into some royal gathering for 'informal' footage of the Queen and other royals.

It seems a great shame that a serious and interesting historian like J. H. Plumb (now Sir John Plumb) should lend himself to an exercise in sycophancy. The book and TV programmes blend history and artefacts together, such that the merits and sensitivities of the paintings and sculptures etc. seem to become those of the monarch who owned them. The mellifluous tones of Sir Huw Wheldon assure us, as we are shown yet another painting, palace or ornament, that each monarch of whom we have heard anything bad has been much misunderstood and underrated. One of the many monarchs referred to in this way was Charles I, who was defeated by Cromwell's New Model Army and executed in 1649. The great Flemish portrait artist, Van Dyck, is described in Plumb and Wheldon as preserving for us the 'obvious sincerity in his [Charles I's] face and in his carriage that expresses a truth about dedicated kingship that is most moving'.[24]

But was it Charles's face or carriage that appeared on Van Dyck's canvas? Sir Lionel Cust, the Surveyor of the King's Pictures and Works of Art from 1901 to 1927, and a friend of Edward VII, thought not. He contrasts Van Dyck's later portraits with the earlier ones by Daniel Mytens and other painters. In these, 'Charles appears, no doubt, as he was seen, his short stature and other minor defects being in no way disguised. But with Van Dyck the King appears transformed.' We have instead, 'a hero of romance with an indefinable look of destiny and sadness in his eyes'.[25] Cust claims that the artist's portrayal of Charles has influenced historians, who have often ennobled the actions of that King, simply because he looks so noble in Van Dyck's portraits.

Fifty years later, Sir Ellis Waterhouse saw Van Dyck's flattery as not principally achieved by distorting the King's features. Rather, it was accomplished through the use of Baroque accessories in the full-length portraits to make the King and Queen look taller, more graceful and regal. However, he does quote a contemporary to suggest that the features had also been 'improved' somewhat in Van Dyck's portraits. When Sophia of Bavaria saw Charles I's wife, Queen Henrietta Maria, in the flesh, she was 'surprised to find the Queen who looked so fine in painting, was a small woman raised up on her chair, with long skinny arms and teeth like defence works projecting from her mouth'. Waterhouse also described how Van Dyck was knighted and extremely well-rewarded for his 'value as a propagandist in the cause of absolutism'.[26]

At the Queen's Gallery, where Van Dyck's famous triple portrait of

Charles was on display in 1988, it was possible to admire the spectacle of a beautiful painting and to take in the splendour of the 'Treasures from the Royal Collection'. However, another impression altogether would have been given if next to a Van Dyck portrait was hung one by another artist. Even if this was done without comment, the conclusion would be drawn that there was more than one way of presenting this or any monarch on canvas. Or perhaps a portrait of Oliver Cromwell could have been borrowed and hung nearby, remembering that he asked to be painted 'warts and all'. Kings can be flattered or not in their portraits. Those who arrange the exhibition may not wish to make this point.

The costs of repair and restoration of the paintings are met from admission charges at the Queen's Gallery, Windsor Castle and Holyroodhouse, and in some cases by the Department of the Environment.[27] Control lies with the Surveyor of the Queen's Pictures, who is also paid out of the admission money, and remains responsible to the Queen. Had Houghton's proposal of creating a department of the Crown been passed in 1971, then control of the art treasures and much else would have passed in large measure to the minister and civil servants of that department. A major reason why the Queen resisted Houghton's scheme was that she wished to remain the real boss of those who worked for her, and to retain control of her assets, whether they were inalienable or not.

The paintings of Queen Victoria and her family fall within the collection. Idealized paintings of Victoria were common. Franz Xavier Winterhalter was a Court painter throughout Europe and Victoria's favourite portraitist. One of his paintings still plays some small part in creating the image of her as a young woman. It was selected for the front cover of Stanley Weintraub's biography of Victoria, the first full-length biography of that Queen for twenty-three years, which came out in 1987. Later that year, Waldemar Januszczak in the *Guardian* reviewed a Winterhalter exhibition. He saw the German painter as producing individual or family portraits 'set in a kind of historical no-man's land, a Ruritanian court inhabited by fairy princesses, toy soldiers, and children who will grow up to be kings and queens'. A lot of the paintings came from the Royal Collection, and Januszczak argues that Winterhalter 'has been one of the main forces shaping the portraiture taste of all subsequent royals'.[28]

Photography was invented in Queen Victoria's time and the Queen has inherited a vast collection of photos dating back to the early days of photography. As regards the royal image, one may think that the camera cannot lie, but it used to be common for those who sat for posed photographs to have them heavily retouched – especially royalty. Those of Queen Victoria and Queen Alexandra were given this treatment. Thus, in a frequently reproduced jubilee photograph, Victoria 'lost two inches off her waist, a few wrinkles from her face and her hair has been lightly streaked and lightened. Her arms have been trimmed to make them look less podgy.'[29] Alexandra was famous for keeping her looks into middle age, but almost all the photos she sat for were retouched. Nor was this purely a female phenomenon, as pictures of Edward VIII were also considerably altered.[30]

Sir Roy Strong, the former director of the Victoria and Albert Museum, in his recent book on Cecil Beaton's photos of royalty considered Beaton was greatly influenced by Winterhalter and Van Dyck's method of depicting royalty. Yet, at the same time, Strong claims that Beaton gave the royals 'an accessible face more suitable to a democratic age'. Strong argues for the importance of the posed photo-portraits, despite the mass of images in TV footage and photos snapped by waiting press photographers. For the combination of 'art and propaganda' in his work, Strong recommended Beaton in 1971 for a knighthood, which he received in the following year. Beaton's particular achievement, Strong argued, was that 'he re-created a powerful visual mythology for the Crown' after the abdication of Edward VIII.[31]

The Royal Archives and the Art of Royal Storytelling

Royal portraits in print are just as important in shaping the royal image, probably more so, than those in photographs or oil paint. When it comes to past monarchs, the most important are the official biographies, for only those commissioned as official biographers are allowed to draw freely from the Royal Archives. Their books then become the source for other books and countless newspaper and magazine articles. In 1948, Harold Nicolson, author, ex-diplomat and former MP in the Ramsay MacDonald breakaway National Labour Party, was invited to write a biography of King George V. Prophetically, his elder son, Ben, who had until recently been Deputy Surveyor of the King's Pictures, warned him against it. He felt that 'his father would become the equivalent in literature of Sir Gerald

Kelly in paintings'.[32] The latter was a royal portrait painter who produced suitably flattering royal images.

The Royal Archives are not normally thought of in the context of the wealth of the Queen, and it is extremely unlikely that a monarch would even contemplate selling items from the vast historical collection (though in 1984, Princess Diana's father did sell some Spencer archive material to the British Library for more than £100,000[33]). In practice, the Royal Archives are inalienable – but they too have their uses.

Because of the monarch's ownership and control of the archives, the monarch's representatives can choose a suitable official biographer. This is of vital importance to the monarchy, for what the archives may say about past kings and queens bears very much on the presentday monarchy. Such is the way with an hereditary institution. Harold Nicolson's biography of George V was much acclaimed when it came out in 1952 and for many years subsequently. When commissioned by George VI's private secretary to produce the book, the latter discussed the matter with Nicolson, who said he did not like writing biographies where he could not tell the whole truth. Nicolson records how Lascelles, the private secretary, responded: 'But it is not meant to be an ordinary biography. It is something quite different. You will be writing a book on the subject of a myth and will have to be mythological.'[34] Not surprisingly, with this brief, his doubts remained.

Lascelles's statement is quite damning, and it was only in 1980 that this version was published in a new edition of Harold Nicolson's diaries and letters. The previous edition, in 1968, was edited by Nicolson's younger son, Nigel, and quotes Lascelles quite differently. There George VI's secretary is quoted as saying, 'You will be writing a book about a very ancient national institution, and you need not descend to personalities.'[35] The invention of this quote almost certainly occurred in consultation with Lascelles in the late 1960s. It allowed Nigel Nicolson to remain loyal to Lascelles and the monarchy on the one hand, and his father on the other. Nigel Nicolson in his introduction to the 1980 edition states that some new material is included 'which I left out for reasons of discretion which has become less necessary with the passage of time. These new passages are marked by asterisks.' However, in the case of Lascelles's statement, there are no asterisks to mark the substitution of the new for the old version. James Lees-Milne's biography of his old friend actually uses *both* the 1968 and the 1980 versions of what Lascelles said.[36]

Nicolson, as the sole person allowed into the archives to research the biography, gained access to privileged information. George V had died only twelve years before. Government records outside the Royal Archives which related to his reign were not available, because of the fifty-year rule, which was informally observed by most of those in the know, who would make suitably anodyne comments when they wrote about the late King. Thus, whatever Nicolson wrote would be almost impossible to contest. (The fact that since the 1960s the rule has changed to a thirty-year one alters this situation to a degree, but not in its essential features, especially when one remembers that most sensitive material relating to the royal family is covered by a 100-year rule.)

There was a pay-off for Nicolson which undeniably compromised his integrity as a writer. Nicolson's privileged position of access to the Royal Archives protected him not just from criticism, but also from competition.* Rival authors could not provide anything like as much information on a subject of great interest. So Nicolson was guaranteed large sales and recognition. When it came out, Kingsley Martin, despite his republican tendencies, gave it an excellent review in the *New Statesman*.[37] In addition, the Queen in 1953 gave him a knighthood, of the type that is within her personal gift, for having carried out his commission to the stated requirements. Another crucial factor which brought Nicolson into line when he wavered was that discretion was the watchword of his class. The fellow members of the London clubs he enjoyed frequenting would expect him to put discretion, and loyalty to the monarchy, above the truth.

Of course, there are some general dilemmas which confront the biographer of someone who has only recently died. These involve sparing the feelings of the surviving family. For instance, how frank should one be about some of the personal failings of the subject? But Nicolson's book did not simply project a mistaken view of the personal characteristics of his George V. It also misled scores of historians and textbook writers for many years as to certain political events with which the King had been involved. Principally, these were the constitutional crises of Home

---

* There had been an earlier biography of George V by John Gore, who had access to the Royal Archives. However, this was a biography of the King more as a private individual and touched very little on the political issues which George V had been involved in, but with which Nicolson dealt. There is good reason to believe that Gore's opinions of George V diverged greatly from what he wrote, even more than was the case with Harold Nicolson.

Rule, just before the First World War, and the formation of the National Government in 1931.

Nowadays, few historians accept Nicolson's version of many of the events described in his book, not just these two episodes. This is partly because of changes in historical perspective over the past forty years, and the accessibility to modern historians of sources unavailable when Nicolson was writing. But also we can note how he altered the original wording of a crucial memorandum in February 1914, drawn up by the King's private secretary and showing the King in effect threatening the Prime Minister with refusal of Royal Assent to the Irish Home Rule Bill. Nicolson's version removed almost all suggestion of a direct threat, thus preserving the reputation of the neutral and constitutional monarch.[38] Similarly, he gave a less than honest account of George V's relationship with his private financial adviser just before the National Government was formed in 1931 (see Chapter 5, above). However, more than this or that particular deceit, it is the basic apologetic nature of Nicolson's project which made his book an exercise in distortion. In defining George V in the public mind, it was extremely successful for a very long time. Roy Jenkins in 1964 thought it 'incomparable', and the late A. J. P. Taylor, writing as recently as 1981, judged it to be 'one of the outstanding biographical and historical studies of our time'.[39]

In the case of Sir John Wheeler-Bennett's 1958 biography of George VI, we do not have the evidence of his diaries and letters, as with Nicolson. Therefore we do not know if Wheeler-Bennett had any misgivings over his task, or how he was given his brief. However, of the final result his predecessor, Nicolson, in private 'regretfully admitted that his friend's [Wheeler-Bennett's] biography was dull and toadying'.[40] In his *Observer* review of the book, however, Nicolson found that Wheeler-Bennett had 'triumphed over all the difficulties'.[41] Thus did Nicolson stay loyal to the monarchy as well as to his friend.

The Jewels

The paintings provide part of the stage-setting of monarchy. The trusted royal biographers have scripted the parts earlier monarchs have supposedly performed, which go to provide the backdrop against which the present monarch plays her role. And the jewellery is necessary for the costumes that the Queen and princesses must wear on grand occasions when appearing on the royal stage. (A King, too, requires jewels in his crowns.) Jewellery may nowadays be less to the forefront in staging the royal image of the modern 'ordinary family' than in former times, but it is still an essential ingredient of royalty.

For early European monarchs, jewels could serve another function. They could be 'pawned' to help finance wars.[42] As late as the 1640s Charles I sold royal jewels to help raise money for his struggle against the Parliamentary army. The relatives of the Tsar, when fleeing the Bolsheviks, found that jewels were a transportable and international currency.

The most famous of the British royal jewels are the Crown Jewels, on public display at the Jewel House within the Tower of London. Of these, the most fabulous pieces came into royal hands at the height of the British Empire. Previously, the Hanoverians had their own collections of jewels, but to adorn their crowns and project the majesty of the monarchy at their coronations, they had to hire jewels from commercial jewellers.

The jewels seized from the Treasury at Lahore after the defeat of the Maharajah of the Punjab were presented by the Honourable East India Company to Queen Victoria in 1851. The gigantic Koh-i-noor diamond, which was regarded as the greatest treasure of India, was the size of a pigeon's egg and the largest diamond in the world at the time. In 1854, in a singular lapse of taste, Victoria proudly displayed the diamond to the dispossessed young Maharajah at Buckingham Palace. For years he bottled up this insult, but he later referred to the Queen as 'Mrs Fagin' – a reference to her as a receiver of stolen goods.[43] Since 1937, the Koh-i-noor has stayed in the Queen Mother's crown at the Tower.

One of the officials of the Jewel House, whom I spoke to in 1987, told me that some visitors from Pakistan and India were upset that the Koh-i-noor remained in Britain. He generally felt that my enquiries on the diamond were treading on dangerous ground. In 1985 members of India's Janata Party were still demanding the return of the Koh-i-noor. They claimed that it was a national treasure of India, not Britain (though Pakistan too would have a claim, as part of the Punjab is in Pakistan).[44]

In the Tower there is also the Sceptre with the Cross. At its head is the largest cut diamond in the world, the First Star of Africa, weighing 530 carats. The second largest, of 317 carats, is in the Imperial State Crown. Both were cut from the immense Cullinan diamond (3,106 carats) presented by the Transvaal government in 1907 as a peace offering after the Boer War. 'They are both of the highest possible quality', says the Deputy Governor of the Tower of London, Brigadier Mears.[45] Some of the outstanding diamonds in the Crowns have, however, according to Mears, been replaced by crystals so that they can be worn by the Queen.[46]

Mears understandably says the value of the Crown Jewels, regalia and the varied plate is 'impossible to assess', but he does give a 'guess estimate' for the First Star of Africa of £80 million. The jewels at the Tower are Legally Inalienable (category 2). Between one Coronation and the next, they generally stay in the Tower, except for the most imposing crown, the Imperial State Crown, which the Queen wears every year to open Parliament.

There are, however, far more jewels in the hands of the Queen herself. In each of the royal homes there is a specially constructed strongroom where jewels and other valuables can be kept. Buckingham Palace's vault is well below ground level and has a burglar alarm connected to the Palace police station.[47] Other jewels are kept with Garrard, the Crown jewellers.

Leslie Field says that 'there is no complete inventory, either official or unofficial', of the Queen's jewellery. From her own researches, she has made a list of what 'the Queen owns or has worn – and these are not quite the same things as some pieces have never been worn, while others were loaned to her when she was young' by the Queen Mother. Field's list comprises '14 tiaras, 34 pairs of earrings, 98 brooches, 46 necklaces, 37 bracelets, 5 pendants, 14 watches and 15 rings'. Suzy Menkes's earlier estimate in her book *The Royal Jewels* thought the Queen owned as many as twenty-two tiaras.[48] Of course, these bare quantities do not indicate the magnificence of many of these items. If it does not constitute the most valuable personal jewel collection in the world, it is not far off. Also, there is the Queen Mother's enormous collection of jewellery in the vault at Clarence House (a minority of which, because it was lent to Elizabeth II when she was still a princess, would be included in Field's list). Where did it all come from?

Many important pieces have precisely the same imperial origin as some of the Crown Jewels. Not just the Koh-i-noor was seized from the Punjab. There was also the 352-carat Timur ruby, the second largest known ruby in existence. Menkes would like to see this and other famous royal jewels put on public display. The Queen was shown in 1969 in the 'informal'

TV documentary *Royal Family* caressing the Indian ruby and discussing its provenance: 'The history of course is very fascinating. That it belonged to so many of the Kings of Persia and Moghul Emperors' until, as the Queen delicately put it, 'Queen Victoria was sent it from India.'[49]

When India was fully conquered, there was no need for British royals to depend on the activities of British armies to provide Indian jewellery. Pathetically, the maharajahs, to increase their standing in the eyes of British royalty (i.e. to overcome the effects of their subordination to the British Raj and the accompanying racism), showered Victoria and her eldest son with jewels, as on the Prince of Wales's trip to India in 1875–6. The Prince, out of his massive budget for the tour of over £200,000 (or £10 million in presentday terms) provided by the British and Indian governments,[50] gave items like riding whips, flagons and field glasses. Because of the embarrassing disparity in the gifts, British newspaper reporters simply stopped specifying the gifts from the Indian side.[51]

More were heaped on the Queen in May 1876 when, after successfully and determinedly lobbying for the title,[52] she was declared Empress of India; they would have helped her somewhat to put aside the Widow of Windsor role. When Disraeli admired the jewelled gifts she was wearing at dinner, he asked her if she had any more. She sent for three large portmanteaux. The Queen did not think of donating some of her Indian jewels for famine relief when it was needed during the great famine of 1876–88 (in Bombay state, during 1877–8, deaths were 800,000 above the normal figure).[53] Nor did she consider whether it was right in view of the poverty of the country to accept the jewels in the first place.

Victoria was also flooded with jewels on the occasions of her jubilees in 1887 and 1897. In addition, during her long reign, Victoria bought from Garrard £158,887 of jewellery, the vast bulk of which was for herself.[54] Victoria simply loved jewellery.

The next Prince of Wales, the future George V, went off to India in 1905, but the Indian colonial government, feeling it would be embarrassing to have a repetition of the previous orgy of present-giving from the rulers of a poor country to the royalty of a rich nation, 'advised' the Prince that he could not accept presents from the Indian princes. George wanted it known that this was a government decision 'and not due to any fad or peculiarity' of his or his wife's.[55] George's wife, later Queen Mary, whom Menkes describes as 'avaricious' in her acquisition of jewels, could not have been pleased.

However, the Delhi Durbar in 1911, at which George V and Queen Mary were crowned as Emperor and Empress of India, made up for any earlier disappointments. It was a 'banquet of jewels'.[56] The new King had been adamant that he wanted to go off to India, whereas the Cabinet were most unsure of the project, which had no precedent.[57] Without wishing to be so crass as to put the motivation of the King and Queen in some degree down to a desire to partake of an Indian Eldorado, it might nevertheless be said that the King's mystical notions of his role as Emperor might not have seemed quite so powerful without the splendid gifts that he and his wife bore home. The Crown Jeweller, William Bell of Garrard, accompanied the royal party and wrote an account of the Durbar, but even in the 1980s Buckingham Palace would not allow Menkes to see it. In general, she notes the obsessive royal secrecy about the jewels received in India, though some information is available from other sources.[58]

In 1881, a notable sample of South Africa's newly discovered diamond mines was presented to Queen Victoria. Many more were to follow. We have already mentioned the largest stones from the immense Cullinan diamond, which are in the Tower. The rest of the Cullinan is in the Queen's possession. In fact, the most valuable piece amongst the Queen's jewels is the Cullinan brooch. This consists of the third and fourth largest stones cut from the Cullinan diamond. They are respectively 94.4 and 63.6 carats.

In 1947, during an official visit by the royal family to South Africa, Princess Elizabeth (as she was then) was presented by the government with a splendid necklace of twenty-one diamonds for her 21st birthday. According to the books on the royal jewels, the Queen refers to these as her 'best' diamonds. With the South African government anxious to revive the diamond trade, which had not fully recovered from the Second World War, the royal tour was, as Leslie Field says, 'a heaven-sent opportunity to publicize the royal family's interest in diamonds. When this was suggested to the King and Queen they agreed to spend a day ... at the Big Hole mine [Kimberley], hoping that the publicity attached to their visit would have useful sales results.' Whilst there, the young Miss Mary Oppenheimer, of the family which owned the mine and which still controls De Beers diamond company, presented the future Queen with a superb 6-carat blue-white diamond. Like her mother, Princess Anne received a present from De Beers in the year of her 21st birthday. The occasion was a visit to the South African company's London HQ, where she received 'a unique gift of coloured diamonds'. Amongst the Princess's other jewelled gifts has been a pair of pearl and diamond earrings from Madame Imelda Marcos.[59]

Probably the first De Beers gift was in 1901, when the company had presented the Queen's grandmother (later Queen Mary) with a casket of diamonds. One might have thought that the tribute of Empire would have been sufficient for Queen Mary. But the overthrow of the Russian monarchy provided an opportunity to snap up some of the jewellery from the deposed imperial family. In the same way, George IV had bought at a knockdown price the magnificent Sèvres porcelain of the executed Louis XVI (and the Queen Mother owns the diamond necklace of his wife, Marie Antoinette, which Mrs Ronnie Greville left her in 1942).[60] In 1921, Queen Mary bought the Grand Duchess Vladimir's most valued possession, a magnificent diamond tiara.[61] In 1928, the Empress Marie Feodorovna died. She had been George V's aunt as well as the mother of the last Tsar, Nicholas II, who was killed by the Bolsheviks. She had managed to escape Russia, but with only a fraction of her jewellery, which nevertheless was valued at about £350,000 (£10 million at 1991 prices). It seemed that Queen Mary 'bagged all the best'[62] and did not pay the full price for them, though the King had been paying sizeable sums for the upkeep of the Empress. Nevertheless, according to Suzy Menkes, the Queen's lawyers thought it necessary in 1968 for the Queen finally to settle the matter by paying an additional sum to the Empress's grandson.[63]

Despite such purchases, by far the greatest source of royal jewels has been presents. Even when the Queen orders new pieces to be made up, she rarely buys new jewels, for the most part dipping into her pool of unset gems or taking them from existing pieces. In 1973, for example, she commissioned Garrard to make a new tiara, using some or all of the ninety-six rubies in a necklace which had been a wedding present from Burma.

The first wave of presents came to the Queen whilst she was still a princess. There were gifts from her parents, a platinum and diamond watch from the French President when she was 12, an antique diamond bow brooch given her in 1944 by the shipbuilding company, John Brown, when she launched her first ship, HMS *Vanguard*, during the Second

World War (it was traditional when a female royal launched a ship to give her a piece of jewellery). There were also her much-prized South African presents of 1947 and, later in the year, her many wedding presents.

The second wave came with her Coronation in 1953, which was also the year that she inherited most of Queen Mary's fabulous collection,[64] which in turn included most of what had been accumulated earlier. The third wave is still depositing more jewels into her possession as the Queen travels the world and receives other heads of state in Britain. Some magnificent gifts have come from the Saudi kings.[65]

The Gulf rulers now perform the role that the Indian princes once did. In 1979, during an eighteen-day visit to the Middle East, the *Sunday Times* described her receiving from the Amir of Qatar alone, 'a pearl, shaped like a pear, and mounted on natural oyster; a necklace of gold discs studded with gems; a multiple-ring pearl choker; a handbag and watch, likewise of gold, and a bowl of lapis lazuli, mounted on two prancing gold horses, themselves being diamond encrusted'. The Queen responded by giving to the emirs and sultans she visited a silver tray engraved with a picture of the Royal yacht *Britannia* and, for the wives, a *book* about Bedouin jewellery.[66]

What is Crown and What is Private?

Gifts from the Queen to foreign heads of state are paid for from public money, from either the Civil List (which pays for presents to foreign heads of state) or the Foreign and Commonwealth Office (which pays for all other presents connected with official visits). The latter pay such additional expenses of state visits abroad and the costs incurred by the Queen during visits to Britain by foreign heads of state.[67]

The presents from foreign heads of state and foreign governments are received by the Queen in her capacity as head of state, not as a private person. One would expect therefore that these gifts might be said to belong to the government, as is the case with presents given to the United States President from any representative of a foreign government. In her memoirs, Nancy Reagan complains that the engraved silver box given by the Queen for the Reagans' wedding anniversary automatically belonged to the American government. In order to keep the silver box, or any gifts from a foreign government, the Reagans had to buy them back from their own government.[68]

If jewellery presents to the Queen were not actually turned over to the State, one would then think that they would at least fall into one of the inalienable categories (Legally Inalienable or Inalienable by Custom, categories 2 and 3 respectively). In fact, they are absorbed into Private and Personal Wealth (category 8), as Menkes, by a combination of deduction and detective work, established in her book. This was confirmed by Leslie Field, who for her 1987 book had access to more royal records than did Menkes.[69]

However, there is a form of jewellery ownership 'in right of the Crown' which is inalienable, even though the relevant gems are not lodged in the Tower of London. Menkes devised the term 'Crown Jewellery' so as not to confuse them with the Crown Jewels in the Tower. Crown Jewellery consists of those jewels left to the Crown by successive monarchs, but mostly by Queen Victoria, who left a minority of her jewels in this way (including the jewels seized from Lahore).[70] Very little was left to the Crown by Queen Alexandra and Queen Mary. Because of this, and the fact that presents to the Queen become private possessions, Menkes argues that the Crown Jewellery comprises only a minority of the jewels in the Queen's possession.* She says, 'if any of these gifts has been made over to the Crown, I have not been able to find out who holds this information'.[71]

It is interesting to see what is said about jewels in Lord Cobbold's statement to the 1971 Select Committee, describing the different forms of royal ownership of all the Queen's worldly goods. He groups 'The Crown Jewels', together with the Palaces, as being 'similarly vested in the Sovereign and inalienable' (category 2, Legally Inalienable). Midway in his 1,400-word statement, he refers to another set of jewels:

> There are other items of jewellery, etc., which, although they do not fall under any of the above heads, are regarded by Her Majesty as Heirlooms. In no practical sense does the Queen regard any of these as being at her free personal disposal.

---

* Even though Menkes, on one occasion in her book (p. 150), somewhat goes back on this statement, Leslie Field does not seek to dispute the private status of the majority of the jewels. This is the case despite the fact that Field's book, throughout, defends the royal image, whereas the tone of Menkes's book sometimes takes a critical turn when discussing royal gem acquisition.

Further on, under the heading of 'Other Private Possessions', it is acknowledged that 'the Queen and Prince Philip obviously own a considerable amount of furniture, pictures, jewellery, etc., acquired by inheritance, gift or purchase'.[72]

Describing privately owned jewels as somehow not really private possessions, but 'heirlooms', was part of the strategy of asserting that estimates of the Queen's private wealth were greatly exaggerated. Of course, it rings true that the Queen would regard many of the older items as heirlooms and, because of tradition and sentiment, not feel they should be at her free disposal. But this is her own choice about her own private property. It is not like the items of Crown Jewellery, which have explicitly been left to the Crown in Victoria's will or subsequently.

Cobbold makes no separate mention of Crown items kept outside the Tower of London. So if his statement is correct, it suggests there can be only one form of Crown ownership, the jewels in the Queen's possession that are designated Crown being owned in the same way as jewels inside the Tower (Legally Inalienable, category 2). In fact, both the Crown Jewels at the Tower and what Menkes calls the Crown Jewellery are 'the responsibility of the Lord Chamberlain' and 'are cared for and looked after by Garrard', the jewellers.*

Why did Cobbold not mention that some of the jewels held by the Queen are classed as belonging to the Crown? Perhaps it was felt that this was unnecessary detail in the statement to the Select Committee. But Menkes in the early 1980s found that there was practically a denial of the category by the Lord Chamberlain's department.[74] Perhaps it was felt that, if it were realized that the Queen held Crown Jewellery, some might wonder how much jewellery was Crown and how much private, which is the question that Menkes's book set out to answer. They might also feel that gifts received as Head of State should be placed in this class. And worst of all, that if such jewels were owned by 'the Crown', not privately, they should go to the Tower or some other public use should be made of them.

---

* Lord Twining's book, though published in 1960, is probably still the best authority in understanding the issue. Unlike Menkes, he uses the term 'Crown Jewels' to refer to all jewels owned by the 'Crown', whether in the Tower or not. He refers to a list drawn up in Victoria's reign, which was headed 'Regalia in the Tower. Also *Crown Jewels* in the possession of HM the Queen' (my emphasis).

It is said by those who speak for the Queen to authors such as Menkes and Field that the Queen, if left to her own devices, would wear very little jewellery, and that it is her loyal subjects who expect her to be decked out in fine jewels for certain occasions.[75] On the other hand, Menkes also quotes a former lady-in-waiting who says that 'she really does enjoy her jewels now'.[76] Whichever view is correct, the Queen clearly has more than enough jewels, for some are never even worn.

Queen Alexandra, whilst still Princess of Wales at the end of the nineteenth century, pioneered a policy of gaudy display, and her successor Queen Mary liked to be weighed down with jewels. In 1913, when she attended the wedding of the Kaiser's daughter in Berlin, she wore at the same time *nine* diamond necklaces, with Cullinan 3 and 4 as a pendant, six diamond brooches, diamond earrings and two diamond bracelets. Even when she and the King dined privately, she would wear a tiara. Today, it is still very much in keeping with the idea of monarchy for royals to wear jewellery at least on formal occasions. Wearing a lot on other occasions, or seeming to have an endless supply of different items, would be considered ostentatious, especially by the 40 per cent who already feel that the Queen has too much money from the state.[77] But still the jewellery, mostly in the form of presents, accumulates. When the Marchioness of Cambridge raised with the Queen the fact that the Duchess of Windsor's jewels were unlikely to be left to her, the Queen replied, 'Jolly good thing, we've got too much already.'[78] Menkes considers that Her Majesty resolves the problem of over-accumulation by wearing certain of her jewels in public and keeping the rest out of the public eye.[79]

In recent years, a use for some of the jewellery has been found by loaning it to Princess Diana or the Duchess of York for special occasions. Though their image in some respects is often fairly 'ordinary', they nevertheless wear their tiaras, when necessary. However, Princess Diana does not have to depend on the Queen alone. She is acquiring presents of her own. There was the magnificent matching diamond set from the Sultan of Oman, whose continued rule has owed much to British military assistance over the years.[80] The Sultan added a lovely new sapphire and diamond collection during Charles and Diana's Gulf tour of 1986. Menkes, in the third edition of her book, says that the Palace was coy about revealing the extent of the jewelled gifts from the Gulf rulers. On the same tour, the Emir of Bahrein ordered for Charles an £80,000 Aston Martin, delivered the following year. When she eventually becomes Queen, Diana too will have to wrestle with the problem of having more jewellery than any one individual, even a queen, could conceivably 'need'. Her difficulty will be increased by the jewels she is given in the meantime, like the flawless diamond given in 1984 by the government of Botswana, a country which then had less than a tenth the per capita income of Britain.[81]

Another royal wedding, that of Prince Andrew and Sarah Ferguson in 1986, meant more jewelled gifts. The Duchess of York received from the Queen a number of diamond items, costing £60,000, from Garrard. This was the first royal wedding this century when the presents were not put on display, in aid of charity.[82] Generally, whilst the royals are appearing less distant and more modern, there is an increasing sensitivity to knowledge about their possessions.

10

The Duchy of Lancaster

The Duchy of Lancaster in 1987 owned 36,456 acres of mainly agricultural estates, divided into 175 agricultural tenancies. There are also 15,000 acres of moorland in North Yorkshire and South Wales, plus a variety of urban land, mostly in London and Harrogate.[1] The Duchy is still today generally thought of as a collection of landed estates, but in fact other forms of revenue have been just as important in contributing to Duchy profits, which were given in the accounts for 1990 as £3.7 million, from which the Queen drew £3 million for her Privy Purse.

There have been queries about the ownership of the Duchy ever since the late eighteenth century, whenever the Civil List is discussed in the Commons. The main issue has always been whether the monarch should continue to receive its revenues, or whether they should have been surrendered to Parliament in 1760, along with the Crown Lands and other hereditary revenues of the Crown.

The origins of the Duchy lands go back more than 700 years, to the youngest son of Henry III, Edmund Crouchback, and his acquisition of the lands of Simon de Montfort. Simon, the leader of the barons who had rebelled against the arbitrary power of Henry, is generally acknowledged as the founder of the House of Commons, during the brief period in which he was king in all but name. In order more effectively to establish his rule in place of Henry's, he called together representatives of the towns as well as of the shires and the nobility to meet at Westminster, thus greatly extending the basis of representation to Parliament, as it came to be known.

The Queen in June 1965 attended the Westminster celebration of 700 years of Parliament. She stated in her speech that the significance of 'the Parliament of 1265 to us today is that it stumbled upon and gave expression to ideas and principles which have been recognized and maintained with growing conviction ever since.'[2] Despite his constitutional innovation, Simon failed to hold power, and he died in battle, his body dismembered;[3] his broad-based 'Parliament' was abandoned under Henry III and in October 1265 his lands were seized and given to his son Edmund, who was made Earl of Lancaster. The 700th anniversary of these ignoble events was also celebrated by the Queen, just four months after her speech praising Simon's Parliament, when she attended a church service and evening reception commemorating the birth of the Lancaster estates.

In 1266, Edmund was able to lay his hands on the estates of another rebel against the King, Robert Ferrers, Earl of Derby. The Duchy's official history describes this episode as 'little to Edmund's credit'.[4] In fact, the origins of the Duchy of Lancaster are no more worthy of ceremony or celebration than the seizure of monastery land for the Duchy by Henry VIII.

There was a setback to the steady expansion of the Earldom of Lancaster when Edmund's son, Thomas, was executed with thirty of his followers for opposing his cousin, Edward II, who in turn was gruesomely murdered at the behest of his wife. These were lawless times. Thomas's brother, who came out on the winning side in the next round of struggle for the throne, got back the Lancaster estates and the Earldom (it was not promoted to the higher status of Duchy until 1351).

After further vicissitudes, which were similarly survived, and one more very profitable marriage, the holder of the Lancaster estates was by the mid-fourteenth century easily the next biggest feudal landowner after the King.[5] John of Gaunt, Richard II's uncle, was the Duke of Lancaster at the end of that century. His magnificent palace, which symbolized his great wealth and powerful political position, was burnt down during the Peasants' Revolt of 1381.

In 1399, on John of Gaunt's death, Richard II seized the Duchy lands, whilst John's son, Henry, was in exile. The latter returned, and not only raised an army to claim his inheritance of the Duchy, but usurped the throne as well. It is at this point that the history of the Duchy becomes tied to that of the monarchy. Yet at the same time, Henry IV, as he now became, sought to keep the very extensive and 'rightful' Lancaster inheritance separate from the usurped Crown Lands,[6] hoping the former would pass to his heirs whether they managed to hold on to the Crown or not.

It is from this arrangement that the presentday official line derives, that the revenues of the Duchy should be for the private enjoyment of the present and subsequent monarchs. Henry IV's 1399 design is thus used to counter the argument that the Duchy was like other forms of the King's revenues and should have been similarly surrendered in 1760, in exchange for the first fixed Civil List.

Unsurprisingly, though, in a period when winner took all, Henry's attempt to keep the Duchy as a sort of insurance policy for a deposed successor did not work. There were in all three seizures of the throne during the late fifteenth century, and in each case, instead of being treated as a private possession which could be kept by the deposed King and his heirs, the Duchy was an added prize which went together with the throne. Similarly, when James II fled to France in 1688, he lost the Duchy as well as his crown to William and Mary. The Charters drawn up by Henry IV in 1399, and a similar one by Henry VII in 1485, to ensure that the Duchy could be inherited privately and separately from the Crown, had little effect. As Sir Robert Somerville's official history of the Duchy puts it, 'the succession to the Duchy . . . was [by the early eighteenth century] governed less by the early charters than by custom and usage, which had established that the Duchy followed the Crown'.[7] Yet in 1971 the Duchy's written memorandum to the Select Committee placed great stress on the importance of these Charters,[8] Somerville's informed, historical summing-up not being used, because it would lead to an undesirable conclusion: that is, if the Duchy follows the Crown, so it should follow the other revenues of the Crown and be given up to Parliament. So the modern Duchy pinned its case to the Charters to explain why the Duchy was not surrendered in 1760.

However, there is a more fundamental objection to the claim that the Duchy was established as a form of private property in 1399 or in the subsequent Duchy Charter of Henry VII. In those times, private landed property as regards the King did not exist in any modern sense at all. As discussed in Chapter 1, it took a special Act, in 1800, to begin to distinguish the King's private lands from that which he held as head of the government. The argument that the origins of the Duchy, 400 years before that Act, tell us that it has always been private property just cannot be correct.[9]

Moreover, the Duchy Charters of 1399 and 1485 did not talk of the King's owning the Duchy in a private capacity, but as Duke of Lancaster. Yet, as we have noted, the inheritance of this dukedom did not follow the course the Charters laid down, making them long since defunct.

Separate from Crown Lands, but not from Government

The Duchy was administered separately from the Crown Lands, but it was nevertheless very much part of government, and Somerville's book gives example after example of the Duchy's financing government expenditure. Under Elizabeth I, Duchy money was drawn on more heavily than usual for government purposes when the Exchequer's funds were strained by the ignoble and costly task of quelling an Irish rebellion.[10]

In the seventeenth century, the Duchy was an integral part of the Stuart kings' scheme of government, which was to try and rule without Parliament. Rather than submit to Parliament's conditions for granting finance to them, James I and Charles I sought independent sources of revenue. Duchy estates (and Crown Lands) were sold to this end. Under Charles I, the proceeds nearly always went straight to the Exchequer,[11] without even passing through the Duchy accounts. From the Duchy these two kings sold about 230 manors, plus other assets. Under the Commonwealth, in the 1650s, the remaining Duchy estates were sold and not all were recovered after the Restoration. By that time, Charles II did not press his absolutist pretensions as far as his father and grandfather, but still sold off Duchy estates for the same reasons. Even after the Glorious Revolution of 1688, William III used the Duchy in a similar way, rewarding his favourites and followers with grants and long leases of Duchy lands, which likewise gave him a basis of support outside of Parliament.

Because Parliament disapproved of this, it forbade further depletions of royal lands with the Crown Lands Act of 1702. This applied to the Duchy because, like the Crown Lands, it too had been used and misused by monarchs, and in much the same way.[12]

The earlier disposal of Duchy lands on such a vast scale meant that the Duchy revenues became virtually negligible by about 1700 and remained so for a long time, so that from 1700 to 1760 absolutely nothing was paid over to the Privy Purse.[13] It is thus not possible to agree with the Duchy's claim to the Select Committee that by 1760 the Duchy profits were 'earmarked already for the personal enjoyment of the Sovereign of the day'.

The Duchy operated not just as a landlord. Through its control of the courts in Lancashire, it had considerable patronage with regard to appointments of court officials. It used its powers of patronage in Lancashire and elsewhere to help get its own officers elected to Parliament (though this power had much diminished by the late eighteenth century). 'Places', often in the form of sinecures, in the Duchy were also one of the inducements given to existing MPs to secure or reward loyalty to the government. Any government in power wanted as many places at its disposal as possible by which to control the House of Commons. Apart from Chancellors of the Duchy, there were, during the eighteenth century as a whole, about seventy members of Parliament who were officials of the Duchy.[14] Therefore the Duchy was still part of the process of government, albeit a rather tawdry form of government. This was recognized officially in a 1706 Act, which classified a number of positions in the Duchy as being like other government positions, 'offices of profit under the Crown'.

In 1760, the net revenues of the Duchy were a mere £16.[15] Legalities aside, this fact probably contributed to the government's agreeing that the Duchy should not be surrendered at that time. This was also the case with the other very minor revenues known collectively as the Smaller Branches of the Hereditary Revenue.

In the decades after 1760, the fact that the Duchy stayed with the King did not in practice distinguish it from those revenues, like the Crown Lands, which had been surrendered. Both were still managed in much the same fashion as previously, and both were still very much part of government and its patronage system.[16] When the 1800 Crown Private Estate Act did allow the King to own land privately for the first time, the Duchy of Lancaster was not brought within the meaning of a private estate because it was not private. It still had a political significance, even though the system of government as a whole was slowly becoming less dependent on patronage.

In 1830, William IV surrendered the Smaller Branches of the Hereditary Revenue to Parliament. Why was the Duchy not surrendered also? The Chancellor of the Duchy in the new Whig government of 1830 was not unsympathetic, but now the many long leases at absurdly low rents had expired, the Duchy could pay £15,500 a year to William IV. He kicked up a fuss, saying that he should not be dispossessed of his last 'remaining pittance' of an independent income.[17] With the impending issue of reforming Parliament, Lord Grey's government would not have wished to unduly offend the King, on whose support they were then counting.

In the 1860s the Whigs/Liberals took their consideration of abolishing the Duchy much further and set up a committee to look into the matter.[18] We do not know why it left the Duchy as it was, but one very likely reason was the known opposition of Victoria to any interference with the Duchy, and in particular her receipt of its revenues.[19] On matters relating to the monarchy, governments deferred to Victoria unless there was some wider issue involved.

After 1830, the Civil List becomes that of a constitutional monarch. It is explicitly disconnected from government and is intended only for the 'dignity' and personal comfort of the King and Queen. The Duchy revenues served the same purpose. So now, for the first time, the monarch became interested in maximizing its profits. Victoria and Albert played some part in overseeing this transition. Moreover, the industrial revolution provided expanding opportunities to exploit the Duchy's mineral rights, sell land to the new railway companies and benefit from the rising value of urban property. During a period of stable or falling prices, payments to Victoria from the Duchy of Lancaster increased from between £5,000 and £15,000 in the early years of her reign to £61,000 in 1900. Various chancellors had told the Duchy, bearing in mind Queen Victoria's need to accumulate, 'to observe the utmost economy in repairs so as to give the Queen the largest income possible'.[20]

After 1830, governments may have found it expedient to allow the monarch to annex the Duchy revenues for his or her private use, but this was and continues to be an anomaly. Other assets that the King gave up in 1760, like the Crown Lands, or in 1830 like *Bona Vacantia*, had been in much the same category as the Duchy. They were really part of the operation of government in the eighteenth century, but owned by the King as head of that government.

More recently, in 1987, Kenneth Clarke, who was Chancellor of the Duchy before tackling the National Health Service and then education, defined the Duchy as an 'essentially private' possession of the Queen.[21] In January 1988, a few weeks after this statement, Clarke assured Labour's Frank Dobson in the Commons that the accounting practices of the Duchy were wholly above board. If they should stray from such proper standards, the Treasury had confirmed that it would issue a directive to the Duchy enforcing proper accounting practices.[22] How can the Treasury do this to the Duchy if it is, as Clarke himself had stated two months earlier, an 'essentially private' estate?

Clarke did, though, admit that there was more than one aspect of the public–private dimension that 'puzzles me', including why it was that the Duchy had to submit accounts to Parliament.[23] Nor would an essentially private estate, in 1988, find itself with a government minister at its head, having to get a new Act of Parliament specially passed to remove the remaining restrictions imposed by the 1702 Crown Lands Act.

There is another respect in which the insistence on the Duchy's being a private estate is not absolute. When it came to outlining the different forms of the Queen's wealth for the Select Committee, Lord Cobbold did not class the Duchy as one of Her Majesty's 'private possessions'. This enabled him somewhat more easily to talk about the 'wildly exaggerated' estimates of the Queen's private wealth.[24] As with Crown immunity and the tax exemption, discussed in Chapter 7, a different face is presented according to the question raised. When the monarch's ownership is queried, it is primarily a private estate; when the total of the monarch's private wealth is discussed, then the Duchy somehow takes on a more public status.

The Official History of the Duchy of Lancaster

Critics of the monarchy are aware that many notable politicians have stated in the last 200 years that the Duchy revenues should go to the state. These include Edmund Burke, Lord Palmerston, Lord Brougham, Sir Charles Dilke, Clement Attlee and many more. But they are unaware of the past threats to the separate existence of the Duchy from within the government machine, or of the frictions between the Duchy and government departments caused by the Duchy's time-consuming insistence on various ancient rights. These are recounted in the second volume of Sir Robert Somerville's history of the Duchy.[25] This volume also mentions, albeit very briefly, the successful removal of income tax in 1933 (see Chapter 4, above) and, more firmly than the first volume, establishes the case that the early Charters, which the Duchy claimed established the present Queen's ownership, were a dead letter.

The second volume of the official history was *privately* printed in 1970 with the inscription, 'Confidential, for the use of the Duchy of Lancaster only'. Only the first volume is mentioned in the British Library Catalogue or in any other place one would ordinarily look. I knew of the existence of a second volume only because it is mentioned in the author's *Who's Who* entry. When I asked Sir Robert why it was not published in the normal way, he gave a slight chuckle and explained that there were 'certain people in the House of Commons who were rather agin the Queen'.[26] The book would give them 'ammunition'. There was 'no point in creating difficulties if you can avoid them'. Had it appeared publicly in 1970, just one year before the parliamentary debates on the Civil List, then it certainly would have provided ammunition, as Sir Robert suggested. Several Labour MPs would have produced some more effective salvoes if they had been better informed.* On the whole, though, the book itself is written very much as a justification of the Duchy. Despite this fact, like the first volume, it represents a very considerable piece of scholarship which summarizes a vast mass of material.

The Chancellor of the Duchy of Lancaster

It is usually stated that the survival of the post of Chancellor of the Duchy of Lancaster, which dates back to 1377, allows the Prime Minister to appoint a colleague to a position that leaves him or her free of onerous departmental and parliamentary responsibilities. Thus this minister, whether made a member of the Cabinet or not, can be given sundry tasks as and when needed (currently it is Chris Patten, Chairman of the Conservative Party). Though other countries manage to have such ministers 'without portfolio', even when they have no such ancient posts. The Duchy pays the Chancellor approximately £2,000 a year from its own funds, and since the 1930s the government foots the bill to bring the salary up to the going ministerial rate.

The Duchy's representative made loud protestations to the 1971

---

* However, Sir Robert was good enough to tell me that a copy was available at the Institute of Historical Research and another at the Public Records Office, Chancery Lane. Until recently, the one held at the Institute had the last two chapters, dealing with the twentieth century and including the removal of income tax, physically excised. It does now have a full copy, with the 'Confidential' inscription crossed out and initialled by the author. The copy at Chancery Lane is still minus these chapters. Sir Robert thought that a copy had already been deposited at the British Library, but at the time of writing (June 1991) it was not yet available.

Select Committee to the effect that, because of the £2,000 payment, the Chancellor was responsible to the Queen and not the Commons for the running of the Duchy.[27] However, in 1988, the then Chancellor, Kenneth Clarke, correctly described the Chancellor of the Duchy as being 'answerable to Parliament' for the running of the Duchy, echoing Gladstone's comments on the Duchy of over a hundred years earlier.[28]

Moreover, the Chancellor is appointed in the same way as any other 'responsible minister'. As such, the monarch has to accept whoever the Prime Minister chooses for this post. George V had objected to Lord Beaverbrook's becoming the Chancellor of the Duchy in 1918, but had to accept Lloyd George's choice despite his contention that the Duchy was 'the personal property of the Sovereign'.[29] In 1948, George VI resisted Hugh Dalton's appointment in vain, the Prime Minister, Attlee, threatening a constitutional crisis if the King were to persist.[30]

It is the Chancellor who has final authority over the affairs of the Duchy, not the monarch. Thus it was the Chancellor in the 1930s who gave the go-ahead to Somerville's official history of the Duchy. Even when deciding exactly how much is to be paid annually from Duchy profits to the Queen's Privy Purse, it is the Chancellor who has the final say.[31]

Bona Vacantia or Devolutions

In addition to mentioning the ties of the Duchy with government, there is the fact that the Duchy itself was, and still is in some ways, a form of government itself. As a 'County Palatine' it has since 1351 exercised many of the rights of government in Lancashire. We have seen, for instance, that it still collects Bona Vacantia (literally 'vacant' or ownerless goods) in the county of Lancashire, including Merseyside and Manchester. The Duchy of Cornwall has a similar right in its county.[32]

'Devolutions', as the Duchy refers to Bona Vacantia, came to be a mainstay of Duchy profits. Of course, wars tended to increase the proceeds, and Somerville noted that Duchy revenue during the Second World War 'had done surprisingly well'.[33] An 'annual payment of £85,000 [at 1991 prices, £1.97 million] to the Privy Purse was maintained'. Of course, it was of assistance that the Duchy did not have to pay income tax, especially when rates of taxation had spiralled to meet the cost of the war.

The accounts show a sharp rise towards the end of the war and just after for 'devolutions and forfeitures', only a small part of which can be explained by inflation. Forfeitures referred to income from fines collected by the Duchy's courts of Quarter Sessions. The war generated extra income for the Duchy from this source, through the considerable penalties for black-market and other war-time offences, but forfeitures were only a minor proportion of the combined category of devolutions and forfeitures in the years 1944–6.

In the 1930s, the average in the Duchy accounts for devolutions and forfeitures was just under £7,000. In 1943, the figure is £13,733, in 1944, £23,464, and in 1945, £41,495 (or about £800,000 in current prices). After the war, the figures decline sharply. Unless this can be explained by some other circumstance, the conclusion must be that George VI, through the Duchy, benefited from the increasing number of deaths during the war, which produced more intestates. That there was a connection between the war and the Duchy's rising income from intestacies is further suggested by the way in which the link occurs in the country as a whole and for the Duchy of Cornwall.[34]

In 1988, the figure for devolutions came to £1.22 million, which was over 30 per cent of the total net revenues of the Duchy. Prince Charles, since the time of the enquiries into, and publicity over, the Civil List in 1971–2, has employed all this money for charitable purposes in Cornwall. The Duchy of Lancaster, covering a more populous area, gains much more from *Bona Vacantia*, but waited until 1983 before setting up a Benevolent Fund along the same lines. But from 1983 to 1988, only a quarter of the *Bona Vacantia* income (£1.3 million) was handed over to the fund. Some of the remaining £3.9 million will have been expended in related administration expenses. But after allowing for that, the residue will have formed at least a third of the £9.97 million withdrawn by the Queen in the years 1983–8.

The Duchy in its governmental role still appoints magistrates in Lancashire. But the Criminal Justice Act of 1967 had the effect of removing the right of the Duchy to receive the fines imposed by magistrates in courts of Quarter Sessions. The government felt it necessary to pay just under £200,000 in compensation to the Duchy (at 1991 prices, £1.5 million). In 1971, all courts of Quarter Sessions were abolished anyway; the compensation came just in time.

Old privileges relating to feudal rights or governmental functions have usually been cashed in rather than simply relinquished. A more modest earner was the Duchy's right to an annuity of £803 a year, compensating the Duchy for no longer being able to charge certain long since defunct wine duties. In 1984, the ever willing Treasury paid Her Majesty's Duchy of Lancaster £8,375 compensation for ending the annuity after nearly 200 years.

However, in 1989, the Duchy actually decided for the first time to pay over all the devolution income to the Duchy Benevolent Fund, or at least to do so after deducting a raft of expenses, which do not all relate to administering devolutions. Thus, the 1989 income for devolutions was £839,845, less various expenses of the Duchy of £345,144 (Palatinate administration, Castles and Historic Monuments, Savoy Chapel in London and Ceremonial Expenses). This left £494,701 to be handed over to the Benevolent Fund.[35] Whatever inspired the change, it involves a recognition of the anomaly behind the Queen's previously laying hold of this money. Therefore, it is proper to suggest that she should repay the millions of pounds that have come to her from this source. This would do a power of good to the Duchy's Benevolent Fund.

Her Majesty and the Property Developers

Per acre, by far the most potentially valuable urban land owned by the Duchy is the freehold of 2.25 acres in the Strand area of central London.[36] Most of it lies between the Savoy Hotel and Somerset House and is part of the old manor of the Savoy. Kenneth Clarke, when he was Chancellor of the Duchy, steered a Bill through the House of Commons whose purpose was to loosen certain statutory restrictions on the Duchy, mainly those imposed by the 1702 Crown Lands Act. Clarke stated the problem was that certain Acts 'inhibit the Duchy's ability to contemplate some of the more ambitious development schemes that we would like to have a look at, in particular for parts of the Savoy estate'.[37]

The Duchy of Lancaster Act 1988 also places a general duty on the Duchy to seek 'the best consideration in money or money's worth which can be obtained', unless the lease is for public or charitable purposes, something that is definitely not envisaged for the Savoy. However, in the early sixteenth century, on Henry VII's orders, the same Savoy land was handed over for the use of a hostel to provide accommodation for the poor and infirm.* The property in the Savoy not occupied by the hostel was rented out to help pay for its expenses.[38] Thus it was a royally financed project to ameliorate the problem of homelessness in London, a problem which still afflicts the capital and in recent years has grown to alarming proportions, attracting contemporary royal concern from Prince Charles.

Even though much of the Savoy property is already let and thus not available for London's homeless, the income it yields could be so employed – together with any future bonanza that comes to the Duchy from any new development made possible by the 1988 Act. As described earlier, the Duchy evidence to the Select Committee set great store on Henry VII's Charter of 1485, arguing (wrongly) that the Charter established the present Queen's private ownership of the Duchy. Henry VII's intention to provide the Savoy precinct for charitable purposes is, however, long forgotten. If tradition counts so much for the monarchy, surely this is one example from the past worth copying.

Generally, though, the Duchy seems to be significantly reducing its interest in land, whether it be urban or rural. From 1982 to 1990, sales of land totalled £16.3 million compared to purchases of land of £7.6 million.[39] This allowed resources to be switched to more liquid assets. The market value of the stocks and shares held thus increased from £2.38 million in 1982 to a peak of £16.82 million in 1987. The Duchy has a distinct advantage over other investors when selling its land or its shares at a profit: it is not liable to capital gains tax. Not having even to consider the heavy tax liabilities that would be involved if capital gains tax did apply allows a much greater flexibility to wheel and deal when the Duchy so chooses.

Similarly, there was an increase in money lent by the Duchy on deposit, which led to a quadrupling in income from this source from £275,803 in 1982 to £1,097,985 in 1990. This latter figure plus the dividends on government securities (£85,983) and from company shares (£359,876) yielded a total investment income of over £1.54 million in 1990. In fact, this income nearly rivals that from the landed property of £2.26 million, and if the recent trend continues it will overtake it. So the old image

---

* The Tudor monarch's charitable intentions did not take root in the long run. Due to corruption and neglect, the Savoy hostel (or 'hospital' as such institutions were called at the time) eventually ceased to fulfil its intended role and was dissolved in 1702.

of the Duchy as a rural landlord is only part of the picture, especially bearing in mind the move away from agricultural land. The Duchy is in fact part landlord and part investment company.

In all, the Duchy, which employs sixty-one people,[40] is worth nearly £70 million. Its 1990 accounts show investments in stocks, shares and unit trusts with a market value of £9.4 million plus £7.1 million in bank deposits. The value of the landed property, mineral rights, reserves and other assets is approximately £50 million. (If one capitalized the devolution income, which the Duchy collects and which it could revert to treating as profits, this would add another £10 million or so.)

The Duchy survived Willie Hamilton's attempt in 1972 to bring both it and the Duchy of Cornwall into public ownership, without compensation. His bill did, though, get as many as 104 supporters (with 233 Conservatives against). As well as those on the left of the Labour Party, many firmly on the right of the party voted for it, including the former Foreign Secretary Michael Stewart, the Labour Chief Whip Bob Mellish, plus two Liberals, Jo Grimond and John Pardoe.[41] The case for public ownership of the Duchy does not depend solely on its legal/constitutional status, which has been discussed in this chapter. Even if the Duchy's case was correct, and there proved to be some uninterrupted personal, royal ownership going back to 1399, it would mean only that the Queen was the beneficiary of the series of acts of feudal violence that had put together the Duchy by that date. Such hereditary privilege can be questioned by itself. Similarly with many of the uses to which the Duchy revenues are put.

From the £3 million made over to the Queen's Privy Purse by the Duchy in 1990, the Queen paid out £435,000 to her three cousins (the Duke of Gloucester, £119,500; the Duke of Kent, £161,500; and Princess Alexandra, £154,000).[42] These are three of the grandchildren for whom George V accumulated money from his savings on his Civil List, and as such are not in great need. There is also the valuable jewellery which they have inherited from Queen Mary and other sources.[43] The above sums, received from the Duchy via the Queen, are tax-free, as the Treasury conveniently considers them gifts from Her Majesty and not a form of income.

The remaining £2.56 million is for the Queen's personal use, and is also of course tax-free. In 1971 Lord Cobbold told the Select Committee that such sums were used for 'current personal expenditure', and assured the Committee that they were not used to build up the Queen's personal fortune. Probably, up to that time, most of the surplus Duchy revenue was spent on Balmoral and Sandringham.[44] Nowadays, they should have little or no need of Duchy funds. Certainly the image projected is that Sandringham is entirely self-financing, and that no money is wasted at Balmoral. As we shall see in the next chapter, though, these changes have occurred without interfering with what the Duke of Windsor called 'the tradition of Royal abundance'.[45]

11

Private Estates and Racehorses

Balmoral and Sandringham

In 1988 the *Mail on Sunday* did a feature on Balmoral in which they positively drooled over the luxury of the Queen's 50,000-acre estate in Aberdeenshire.[1] Many wheels are set in motion in preparation for the arrival of the royals for their main visit, which starts around mid-August each year. The Queen usually remains for about eight weeks, taking her stay into October, leaving for the occasional official visit. During this period her public engagements are greatly reduced. In fact, in 1988 between her arrival at Balmoral on the afternoon of 15 August and her return to Buckingham Palace on 11 October, the Court Circular revealed that she did not leave Balmoral to fulfil a single public engagement. During her 1989 stay she had two public engagements outside Balmoral. Prince Philip comes and goes more frequently, and other royals do not generally stay the whole period.

The horses are groomed ahead of the royal arrival. Two thoroughbreds are transported by horse-box from Windsor. The various gardens around the castle have been maintained so as to be in full flower in August and September. The flowers which decorate the castle are arranged and distributed through the rooms by a special servant known as 'the flower girl'. Leeks are specially grown out of season for Her Majesty, who has a particular liking for them. The gardens also provide abundant raspberries and strawberries. Apart from horse-riding, activities include salmon-fishing, deer-stalking (the Queen is an excellent shot), first-rate grouse-shooting and a round of golf on the private nine-hole golf course. There is even a cricket pitch.

A long walk need not involve leaving the estate, as it is about 12 miles long by about 14–16 miles wide.[2] Within this large irregular rectangular area, one can cover five glens, each with its own lodge where one can take a rest. The scenery is some of the most spectacular in Scotland and includes Lochnagar, which rises to a height of 3,786 feet and is the third highest point in Scotland. Guests may find themselves taken to this part of the estate and shown what is being done for the cause of conservation by the Scottish Wildlife Trust, with encouragement from Prince Philip. The young children of the royals are usually accompanied by their nannies, so they need not interfere with their parents' enjoyment of such outings. In the event that any of the royals or their guests should wish to do a spot of reading, Book Trust, a charity which promotes the reading of books, makes a selection of new publications, which are dispatched to Balmoral. They are asked to provide suitable reading for all four royal generations, and in 1990, thirty-four books, with a retail value of £500, were sent free of charge.[3]

The Queen and Prince Philip can travel to Balmoral by the Royal Train, a plane of the Royal Flight or by sailing to nearby Aberdeen in the Royal Yacht, all paid for from government funds. Once at Balmoral, the royals do not all have to cram into the one castle. The Queen Mother has Birkhall, which stands nearby. In 1987, she lent it to Charles and Diana, leaving Craigowan House, where they used to stay, free for other royals, guests and courtiers.

Before the Second World War, the richest of the old and the new aristocracy also lived in great houses. Both their country homes and their London residences were maintained by masses of servants. Lords Astor, Londonderry, Derby and so on lived on the grand scale, if not up to the standard of the King. Now Her Majesty is left alone on her lofty royal eminence. After the war, when wages rose sharply, the 'servant problem' was greater for the aristocracy than for the monarch. Another difficulty in finding servants was due to full employment, and also a general desire by working-class people to be something better than someone else's servant.

In maintaining a supply of servants, the Household has had its problems. As already remarked in Chapter 6, there have been difficulties recruiting and keeping staff because of the level of pay. It has certainly not been able to find an adequate supply of the 'old retainer' type. Yet even during the long period of full employment after the war, curiosity about the royals has always prevented the stream of recruits from drying up, even if many did not stay very long.[4] The post-war 'servant problem' has been less difficult for the monarch in another respect also. Through the Civil List, the vast majority of servants are paid by the government, which has footed the bill for wage increases and directly provides the occupational pensions of those paid from the Civil List.[5] This is why the Queen, not only at her official residences, Buckingham Palace and Windsor, but also at her private estates of Sandringham and Balmoral, can easily keep up the old, grand style.

On the tax front, we know only too well that the monarch enjoys a tax loophole greater than any the aristocracy could contrive. The Queen has come to pay only the Uniform Business Rates, and is considered by the Inland Revenue no longer liable for tax on farm rents from her private estates. We have not considered death duties, the tax most associated with hitting the aristocracy in any detail, having concentrated mostly on the taxes that the monarch once paid but has more recently managed to avoid.

When the Liberal government introduced Estate Duty in 1894, Victoria certainly did not repeat her gesture of 1842 when she volunteered to pay income tax. She deplored the new tax, which was fixed at 8 per cent. From Balmoral, she raged at its instigator, the Chancellor of the Exchequer, Sir William Harcourt. It 'cannot fail to cripple all landowners', while many of the poorer classes would be thrown out of work and 'charities denuded of support'.[6]

The Solicitor-General in 1910, on behalf of the government, considered that the monarch was one of those landowners who were liable to be 'crippled'. Sir Rufus Isaacs drew up a confidential memorandum which he submitted to the Prime Minister, Asquith, and which can be found in Asquith's Papers at the Bodleian Library in Oxford. Isaacs generally accepted that the monarch should enjoy Crown immunity from taxation, but made the one exception as regards Estate Duty on the Sovereign's private landed property. The latter was covered by the Crown Estates Acts of 1800 and 1862, which laid down that landed property such as Balmoral and Sandringham were 'subject and liable to all such taxes, rates, duties' etc. 'as the same had been the property of any subject of this realm'. Isaacs reasoned that it did not matter that these Acts were passed long before Estate Duty was introduced in 1894. 'The words of the Acts are wide enough', Isaacs contended, 'to include this tax within their meaning and consequently to render the King liable to it in respect of his private real estate.'[7]

Isaacs's opinion on Estate Duty has never before been mentioned publicly, the Treasury memorandum to the 1971 Select Committee explicitly denying that 'any of her [the Queen's] property is liable to estate duty'.[8] If Isaacs's opinion had been put into practice in 1952, when George VI died, the estates would have been liable to estate duty of 80 per cent for any amount over and above £1 million, plus a sizeable chunk of the first million. In an article in *British Tax Review*, Roy Bartlett concluded, even without knowing about Isaacs's opinion, that estate duty was applicable to the private estates. And similarly, he has since claimed that, under the 1862 Act, the Queen's successor should be liable to Inheritance Tax, the present form of the old estate duty.[9]

Of course, in practice, the impact of the tax could be minimized quite simply and legally by the landowners making transfers of property before they died. It was said that those whose estates suffered substantial death duties were only 'those who dislike the Revenue less than they dislike their heirs'. This explains the low yield from this type of tax, even when its rates were very high on large estates. Such methods have, it seems, been used by other royals who have been and still are liable to death duties. One comes across authoritative references to trusts set up by George V's younger sons, the Dukes of Kent and Gloucester. And in 1989, during the public row between Marina Ogilvy and her parents Angus Ogilvy and Princess Alexandra of Kent, Ms Ogilvy made reference to her trust fund.[10]

Balmoral and Sandringham not only escape taxation, but also receive state subsidy. They are not official residences, like Buckingham Palace and Windsor Castle, which are maintained from the Civil List and government, but both these sources of revenue also go some way to maintain Sandringham during the Queen's six-week break after Christmas and Balmoral during her eight-week summer–autumn break. Since 1951, the fuel bills incurred when the Queen is in residence at her country estates have been paid by the Department of the Environment. Several of the top civil servants in the Ministry of Works, now part of the DoE, objected to this because these costs 'were part of the Sovereign's private life and nothing to do with her public life'. Moreover, they were concerned that they had no control over this expenditure.[11] It is contended that Her Majesty is somehow there on official business, because she has to read her red and blue boxes containing masses of official government business.

Stephen Barry describes how, when he appeared in the famous 1969 documentary *Royal Family*, made by the BBC, he was shown at Balmoral needing help to push a trolley-load of these heavy-looking boxes, which in fact were all empty. The apparent struggle to push the trolley, Barry claims, was purely for the cameras: 'The idea was to show how hard she works reading state papers, and how this chore never stops even when she is on holiday.' Barry claims that these imposing-looking boxes arrive at Balmoral 'mostly nearly empty'.*[12]

On the 120 staff at Balmoral during the eight-week royal stay, some are specially hired from Edinburgh. 'The Edinburgh women', as they are known, were not well paid according to Barry, but otherwise seem to find the stay a repeatable experience. One sold her story to a Paris magazine, stating the pay to be £2.25 an hour in 1987.[13] But the large majority of the servants are brought up from Buckingham Palace and Windsor, and are paid from the Civil List. The Chancellor of the Exchequer, Anthony Barber, insisting that there is no element of personal expenditure about the Civil List, assured the 1971 Select Committee that at Balmoral (or Sandringham) the Queen merely takes with her 'necessary staff' for carrying out her 'constitutional and official duties' while in residence there.[14]

During the summer–autumn stay at Balmoral, the royal family is guarded by about 120 soldiers from one of the Scottish regiments. The army also organizes the transport of the trailers which carry the luggage from Buckingham Palace. The finer points of security are looked after by Scotland Yard detectives.[15] The army are not generally employed at Sandringham, though they were called in in 1955, when the Queen lost her platinum and diamond watch (the smallest watch in the world, a present from the President of France) whilst walking her dogs there. This was after an intensive search by the police, farm workers and Boy Scouts, but even soldiers deploying mine detectors could not find the watch.[16]

A further service rendered by the significant police presence at San-dringham these days is to back up the gamekeepers in dealing with

* Barry may have exaggerated to add force to his anecdote. In an earlier book (both written with the same journalist), he implies the Queen's official boxes involve more work than is indicated above. Nor does this writer wish to suggest that it is desirable for a monarch to spend a great deal of time absorbing herself in government matters. A high level of such involvement may indicate a desire to politically interfere.

poachers. Large landowners who rear game for shooting have always to be on the lookout. In 1986, two poachers shooting the Queen's pheasants on the royal estate were caught by a police dog-handler. They pleaded guilty and were fined £100 by King's Lynn magistrates.[17]

Despite state help, at the time of the Select Committee in 1971, Sandringham and Balmoral were not self-supporting. Lord Cobbold recorded that Privy Purse money was needed to maintain them as royal residences. This has changed as regards Sandringham. The Sandringham Estate Office has produced several editions of a booklet about the great house, its gardens and the surrounding estates. The booklets contain the usual glossy photos of the royals, but also the most recent edition is positively keen to portray Sandringham Estate as a profitable business, which is constantly modernizing. It states that the estate 'provides the income to maintain the house and its beautiful surroundings'.

The profits which support the royal lifestyle in Norfolk derive from renting out about 12,000 of the total 20,456 acres to tenant-farmers. A further 3,310 acres, on which are grown wheat, barley, sugar beet, peas, beans, cress, apples and blackcurrants, are retained and farmed under the control of the Queen. Another 2,000 acres are given over to forestry. To better deal with the timber, the estate's sawmill was greatly expanded in 1988. Similarly, the purchase of new machines has greatly reduced the problems associated with harvesting the blackcurrants on the fruit farm. The workshop on the estate now contains the necessary modern welding, pressing and cutting equipment to keep the 150-plus tractors, lorries, etc. functioning. Edward VII's glasshouses have been replaced by ones with the 'latest automatic heating, ventilation and watering systems'. The flowers and pot plants produced under glass are sold, with the exception of those used to decorate the house.

The gardens of Sandringham House (there are 85 acres of grounds) are open to the public, and since 1977 the house also, for most of the time from Easter to September, except when the Queen or another royal is staying. The £2.20 admission fee 'helps to pay for maintaining and improving the gardens as well as providing a substantial contribution to local charities'. The Souvenir Shop did brisk business at the time of the royal weddings,[18] and the restaurant and cafeteria built in the 1980s also provides an income. Thus a more businesslike Sandringham no longer needs Duchy of Lancaster money to maintain the huge house and staff not brought in from Buckingham Palace. It is all very different from the profligacy at Sandringham during Edward VII and George V's reign. Game is not reared on the same astounding scale, and the thousands of game birds shot each season are sold, whereas the Marquis of Lincolnshire records in 1913 that the massive bags then were not.

Her Majesty's Land Agent at Sandringham did not let slip the chance, in 1973, to apply for and obtain, from the tiny Freebridge Lynn Rural District Council, an improvement grant of £1,000 to convert two labourers' cottages into one. The council's clerk told the press that the Queen had been receiving such grants for some time. The council's successor, the West Norfolk District Council, continued the practice. A Palace spokesman said that there was a continuous programme of modernization going on at Sandringham and that the estate was run as a business and was eligible for the grants like any other business.[19]

Also, many cottages on the estate have been sold – none, one trusts, which have attracted an improvement grant, for in 1974 the Keeper of the Privy Purse assured Willie Hamilton that 'it has never been the policy to sell properties where a Local Authority grant had been received'.[20] The estate in the mid-1970s had about 350 cottages for farm workers of the Queen and her tenant-farmers. But as modern farming uses less and less labour, many cottages are not needed.[21] Some have been used as retirement homes for Palace staff and estate workers at Sandringham. Those that are sold fetch good prices, because buyers can boast that they bought their home from the Queen.[22]

Still, it's not all business, or at least not always all-out, profit-maximizing business. The Queen, because she is the Queen, has to make the odd gesture. For instance, in 1988 some old barns were renovated so that they could be let out to local business. A local shed-maker, David Crane, wrote to Prince Charles urging that the barns be converted, and rented the first 1,200-square-foot barn for £57.50 a week.[23] In 1989, again at Prince Charles's behest, if the papers are to be believed, the Queen leased some land on a disused dairy farm to a housing association which planned to build seven houses to let at 'reasonable rents'. Because of this, one assumes that the lease was sold at something below the market rate (though this claim was not actually made). Even if this is the case, it may not all be down to Charles and charitable motives. Julian Lloyd, the Queen's Sandringham agent, said, 'we want young families to come in to keep the school, the church and village shop going'.[24]

The Queen also farms at Windsor, though this is not a private estate.

Plumb and Wheldon describe this enterprise as including 'a highly productive and profitable mushroom farm'. The Minister of Works in 1958 anticipated that the Duke of Edinburgh would tackle him on 'the question of the piggeries and mushroom sheds at Windsor'. The minister was unhappy about the use of government money for this purpose, as it had nothing to do with the maintenance of Royal Palaces as official residences. There are clear indications that public money was in fact used.[25]

Balmoral is financially a very different proposition from Sandringham and Windsor. The climate and the terrain, of hills and moorland, mean that it is relatively little farmed, though several thousand acres are given over to commercial forestry. And as at Sandringham there are the gardeners, gamekeepers, some of the servants to pay, and so on. So perhaps a certain amount of Duchy of Lancaster money is still necessary for the Aberdeenshire home.

An eye is still turned to reducing costs where royal comfort is not affected. Any 'sportings' (shooting and fishing rights) not wanted by the royal family 'are let on the open market' says the Balmoral official guide booklet. The ponies used by the royals to recover the red deer shot by them in the stalking season are put to work from the beginning of May to the end of July. For £14 a day (bring your own packed lunch) one can go pony-trekking; a two-hour session costs £8. This is also a means of exercising the ponies, a task often given to the soldiers who form the Queen's Guard when the royals are in residence.

The pony-trekking is part of a somewhat greater public access to the estates. Balmoral Castle Gardens were opened to the public as long ago as 1931, and visitors are allowed during the May–July period into a limited section of the grounds, before the main royal visit in mid-August. A refreshment room was added in 1968 and there are now also souvenir shops. An exhibition has been provided in the Ballroom of the Castle, which is otherwise closed to the public. Ralph Whitlock's book on the royal estates tells us that much of the money (but not, it seems, all) goes to charity. In a response to a request in the mid-1960s from Lord Hunt, the Rector of Aberdeen University and also then the Director of the Duke of Edinburgh's Award Scheme, a hut at Alltnaguibhsaich Lodge was leased to the University Mountaineering Club. They and others have access to Lochnagar and Loch Muick except in the deer-stalking season, which is when the royals are there.

As noted earlier, the Queen has acquired extra land at Balmoral, a 6,700-acre grouse moor at Balmoral upon which stood the twelve-bedroom Delnadamph Lodge. Not only was the latter demolished as surplus to requirements, but so were ninety-one rooms of Sandringham House in the mid-1970s.[26] Sandringham House still contains 274 rooms and is perhaps still too big.* It is an unusual form of housing problem, having too much.

The Queen and other royals go to Sandringham directly after Christmas, and Her Majesty takes a six-week break there. Generally the Queen and the royal family have been spending more time at Sandringham, according to figures produced by the Chief Constable of Norfolk. In 1984 they spent eighty-eight days there, rising to ninety-five in 1985 and 115 in 1986 before falling back somewhat to 102 in 1987. In 1985 it took Norfolk police '5,000 man days' to ensure the safety of the royals at Sandringham. And in 1987 a £2 million 'electronic moat' was installed.[27] This is a reference to the video cameras, with night vision, installed around Sandringham House and the microwave beams that would be tripped by intruders.[28]

There is much to take the Queen to Sandringham. There is her labrador stud to breed and train gundogs, which are used by the royals during their shoots. In nearby King's Lynn there are the 200 racing pigeons of the 'Queen's Flight'.[29] But Her Majesty's principal passion is the breeding of racehorses. The Queen's studs at Sandringham have yet to produce a Derby winner, but this has not diminished her enthusiasm for the sport of kings and queens.

Racehorses

From very early in her life, horses have been a passion of the Queen. But that interest has long since centred on racehorses which run on the Flat.[30] Moreover, one former Prime Minister, Lord Callaghan, described the Queen's involvement in the racehorse business as having more significance than just being a pastime. It is in many ways her only direct door on to the world. Callaghan remarked, about her ability to

---

* As regards the official residence of Windsor Castle, the problem of size seems too much for guests staying with the royals. Stephen Barry said that the Castle is truly enormous. When he stayed there as valet to Prince Charles, he 'was forever finding lost souls wandering about trying to discover the way back to their rooms'.

make judgments on political matters, 'All her experiences are received' – depending upon what someone has told her. Talking just a little more frankly about the monarch than is usual for an ex-Prime Minister, he continued, 'she has very little direct experience except in one field – horse-racing and breeding'.[31]

The Queen's attendance in June and July at Ascot, Epsom (for the Derby), Goodwood or Newmarket forms part of her regular yearly round (the Badminton Horse Trials in April/May and the Royal Windsor Horseshow in May have also been favourites with the Queen). Indeed, earlier in her reign, at least up until 1969, government ministers had to adjust to the Queen's presence at Goodwood during racing week at the end of July. To hold vital Privy Council meetings, to ratify all kinds of government measures, they had to travel to the Duke of Richmond's or the Duke of Norfolk's country home, where the Queen generally stayed during 'Glorious Goodwood'. In 1956, the proclamation to call out the army reserves, in preparation for the Suez invasion, was brought to the Queen's private room in the Duke of Richmond's private box at Goodwood. The next day, 3 August, a hastily arranged Privy Council was held at Arundel Castle (the Duke of Norfolk's home), where the Queen signed the proclamation.[32]

Andrew Duncan, who followed in the Queen's footsteps for nearly a year in 1968–9, spoke to one unnamed Privy Councillor who was not happy about the trip to Goodwood in 1969:

You can't get it into her head that she's supposed to be working, poor thing. She finds it a bore, and I don't blame her. We barge in on her privacy. She can't see how royalty can travel up to London for the sake of meeting with politicians.[33]

Horses and equestrian sports abound in royal life, generally. Horses are an essential ingredient of royal ceremonial, like Trooping the Colour. The Royal Mews at Buckingham Palace houses the horses which perform that function. Horses are also creatures for riding around on one's estates. There are Prince Charles's polo ponies, polo being another expensive pastime. Prince Philip needs another type of horse to form teams for competitive carriage driving. Princess Anne has showjumping and eventing horses and occasionally rides in Flat and National Hunt races. The Queen Mother has nine horses in training for National

Hunt Racing and Charles and Anne have the odd racehorse. But it is the Queen's racehorses which are the most valuable.

In financial terms, the Queen's whole horseracing enterprise is worth many millions. Her approximately quarter share in just one horse, Shirley Heights, the stallion at the Sandringham Stud, is worth over £1 million.[34] But this does not mean that the racing and breeding business makes a profit – probably the reverse. The Queen will have made money in some of the successful years during her long reign, but not in recent years.*

The Queen decides which stallions her twenty-three broodmares go to, in order to be covered. She is assisted in such matters mainly by her racing manager, the Earl of Carnarvon (until 1987, Lord Porchester, and still known as 'Porchie'). Such decisions are attempts to solve the extremely tricky question of precisely what combination of bloodstock goes to make a top-class horse.

Another indication of the Queen's desire to be involved as much as possible was the leasing of Polhampton Lodge Stud in the late 1960s, and its purchase in 1971.[35] Before then, her yearlings had been sent to the Republic of Ireland until they were put into training. This meant the Queen could not follow their development, and thus lost some of the satisfaction of being an owner. Now at Polhampton, on the Hampshire Downs, they are within driving distance of Windsor and London. This was probably decided before the onset of the Troubles in Northern Ireland from the late 1960s. Since then, it seems that the Queen has very rarely, if ever, sent her horses to race in the Republic of Ireland, which other comparable owners do. She has also limited her breeding options by not sending, since 1972, any of her mares to Ireland to visit a stallion.[36] The royals themselves do not set foot in the Republic, for probably the same security reasons, though again this policy seems to pre-date the recent Troubles.

In 1982 came another property acquisition, West Ilsley stables in Berkshire, bought from Sir Michael Sobell and Lord Weinstock for about £750,000.[37] This was where many of her horses were already being trained, by Major Dick Hern, the most senior of the Queen's three trainers. Its purchase exhibited the Queen's desire for more control on the

---

* Oddly enough, that most extravagant of monarchs, Edward VII, did make money from horseracing and breeding. It was he, when Prince of Wales, who founded the Sandringham Stud in 1886. He enjoyed great fortune on the Turf with three Derby winners.

training side. As Dorothy Laird commented some twenty years earlier, the Queen was spending more time 'in visiting studs and stables, and less in going to the actual race meetings, as it is breeding and stable management which interest her most'.[38] It is a bit unusual for a racehorse owner to go on to buy an already existing stable. Lord Porchester, as her racing manager was still called, commented at the time, 'the idea originated with the Queen herself. She thought she would like to own a racing stable.'[39] He has also confirmed that she is 'very very interested' in the details of stable management, including the conditions in which the staff worked.

The Low Pay of Stable Staff

It is universally recognized within racing that stable staff are generally underpaid. Also, it is necessary to make it clear that the Queen did not employ the fifty people working at West Ilsley; Hern, as the trainer, did. Nevertheless, the Queen is not a distant and passive owner of her stables. Similarly, where her horses are in stables which she does not own, she has still taken a great interest in the organization of those establishments. So the question arises of whether she should apply a little regal pressure on her trainers to get them to increase the pay of their stable staff. Or, at West Ilsley, she could reduce the rent she charged the trainer, to encourage him to raise wages.

Hern's skill as a trainer of top-class horses won him 'the esteem of his workforce', but 'Hern is not regarded as a good payer' compared with other top-flight trainers. In 1989, the stable staff received a basic wage of only £123 per week, plus free accommodation,[40] for training the horses of the Queen and those of other mega-rich owners like Sheikh Hamdan Al Maktoum, Lord Weinstock and Sir Jakie Astor.

As was stated generally about stable staff in the horseracing daily the *Sporting Life*, in January 1990, 'beneath the glittering surface of a seemingly prosperous industry . . . has lain the unacceptable wages and conditions of a workforce which despite recent major increases remains among the lower paid in the country'.[41] The increases referred to brought basic minimum wages up to £117.35 (not including accommodation) and introduced a new grade covering experienced 'lads', giving them a basic minimum of £131.[42] Top trainers like Hern pay above these rates, but not enough to lift their staff out of the lower-paid category for what is a very hard and demanding job. The agreed increase was, it seems, brought about less by what the *Racing Post* termed the 'mounting public scorn' about poor pay for stable staff than by the increasing difficulty of getting and keeping staff.[43] The pay increase has only reduced that difficulty somewhat and is far from having removed it.[44]

The concession was seriously marred by the previous withdrawal of recognition, in the autumn of 1989, from the Transport and General Workers' Union by the employers' side, the National Trainers Federation. Ian Balding, who also trains some of the Queen's horses, at Kingsclere Stables on the North Hampshire Downs, was one of the Trainers' Federation representatives on the National Joint Council, at least up until 1989.[45]

The stable staff are left with the Stable Lads Association to represent them on the National Joint Council. The TGWU had no doubt slipped in strength in recent years, but as Jack Logan pointed out in the *Sporting Life*, the 'blatant act of discrimination' against the TGWU had hit not just that union, but union organization generally in an industry which is extremely difficult for unions at the best of times. It had already made life difficult for Bill Adams, who runs the Stable Lads Association. He had been refused permission to go to a number of yards to address stable staff on the latter's invitation.[46]

It seems to be the case that those industries which cater to the very rich often involve poor pay. One is reminded of those who work for the Queen herself at Buckingham Palace, and, more generally, employees in luxury hotels, restaurants and the garment industry, including those who produce 'haute couture'. In the 1970s, there were hard-fought attempts in a number of large hotels to establish an effective trade union presence, which were mostly defeated. Also in the 1970s, the TGWU had launched a recruitment drive amongst stable staff and led a dispute with the employers, and in 1975 unofficial action was taken when some stable staff disrupted the start of the 2,000 Guineas. The trainers were obliged to accept collective bargaining, but the dispute created an enduring enmity towards the TGWU.[47]

I asked Lord Carnarvon if the Queen had tried to get the pay of stable staff employed by her trainers increased. He replied that 'the wages are negotiated nationally, there's nothing you can do about it'. I pointed out that trainers were not bound by these rates. He insisted that the matter had nothing to do with the Queen and that it was purely a matter for the trainers. He said that the staff were well-housed at West Ilsley and he had 'never heard any complaints', although he did concede generally that the 'stablemen', as he called them, 'are still underpaid'.[48]

Trials and Tribulations of the 1989 Season

One decision that was down to the Queen herself, in March 1989, concerned Hern, the resident trainer at West Ilsley who rented the stables from her. That year, the Queen refused to grant an extension to his lease, which expired at the end of the 1989 Flat racing season (though he could still remain in his home near the stables). Hern, aged 68, had been suffering the effects of a bad hunting accident in 1984, but had resumed his training duties from a wheelchair. Despite his problems, including heart trouble, he had a good season in 1988, with his assistant, Neil Graham, substituting for him for much of the time. By early 1989, he had made a good recovery from open-heart surgery and had West Ilsley in good shape for the coming Flat season. But in March it was announced that in the autumn, Willie Hastings-Bass, who was already training some of the Queen's horses elsewhere, was to be installed in his place.

Jonathan Foster's article in the *Independent* was quite typical of the reaction in most newspapers. He described how the 'racing community has been offended by the nature of the act and agitated by its apparent lack of rationale. In the sport of Kings, the opinion gaining ground is that the monarch has behaved badly. Or been badly advised by a peer of the realm.'[49] The latter is a not so oblique reference to the 7th Earl of Carnarvon.

Willie Hastings-Bass also has impeccable breeding, and fits easily into the royal circle. A friend of Prince Charles when they were both at Cambridge,[50] he is descended from an earl on both sides of his family – the great-grandson of the 17th Earl of Derby, he has himself since become a 17th Earl (of Huntingdon). His late father trained horses for the Queen,[51] his sister married the Queen's other trainer, Ian Balding, and he is a cousin of one of the Queen's longest serving ladies-in-waiting.

Lord Carnarvon subsequently accused the press of making a scandal out of the transfer of West Ilsley, whereas another peer, Lord Oaksey, replied in the *Racing Post* that there would have been a much greater fuss from the largely royalist racing press had it been any other landlord except the Queen.[52] In fact, one device used by several articles on the affair to shield the Queen from criticism was to imagine that the decision had nothing to do with her. The Queen had merely acted 'constitutionally', as it were, on the 'advice' of her racing manager. This overlooks the fact that Her Majesty's racing affairs are hardly matters of state, and that normally, and especially in relation to her successes, she is credited with taking key decisions.

Willie Carson, five times champion jockey, reacted angrily to Hern's treatment: 'The Major has come a long way through a very dark tunnel since his accident, and now, just when we're beginning to see the light, it's as though someone has dropped a trap-door and shut off that light.'[53] When Nashwan, trained by Hern, won the 2,000 Guineas, the racecourse crowd's 'prolonged cheering' showed their support for the trainer. *The Times* thought that the emotional reception afforded to Hern 'was almost certainly instrumental in persuading the Queen to give the trainer a further year in her stables in 1990'.[54]

During this extra year conceded by the Queen, in a very unusual arrangement, Hern had to share the yard with Hastings-Bass. A Palace official stated that a proposal to share the yard had been put to Hern back in November 1988, but he had turned it down. The *Daily Mail* disputed this version.[55] Nashwan meanwhile romped away with the Derby, three weeks later. In 1990, Hern had another successful season, if not as spectacular as that of 1989, coming eighth amongst trainers in terms of prize money. It is unusual for a trainer who has been rejected by one of the less successful owners to be taken up by the most successful. Sheikh Hamdan Al Maktoum, who topped the owners' league in 1990, has built a brand-new stables for Hern on the outskirts of Lambourn.

The most that Lord Carnarvon would say about not renewing Hern's lease was that racehorse training was a 'young man's life'.[56] But maybe the royal desire for change at West Ilsley had something to do with the Queen's modest horseracing successes in the 1980s. What owners crave are those heady days of triumph when they can savour victory and also future breeding successes with the victorious horse. One such day was enjoyed back in 1974 when the Queen crossed the Channel to see her filly, Highclere, win the French Oaks at Chantilly. Hern and jockey Joe Mercer were invited along with their wives to Windsor Castle for dinner the same night. The Queen met them on a rainy Berkshire evening, umbrella in hand.[57]

When the Queen inherited her position, whose tenure does not require satisfying the type of harsh competitive criteria that exist for trainers and jockeys, the royal horses were very successful. The royal stud was producing a number of top-class horses. In fact, the Queen was leading owner in 1954 and 1957, as measured by prize money won. There have been notable successes since then – Highclere, already mentioned, who has also been a successful dam, and Dunfermline, the winner of the Oaks and St Leger in 1977. But generally speaking, the Queen's horses have not been very successful in the 1980s, and the Queen has not come anywhere near being in the top ten owners for the decade. Some good horses have been bred, but there has been a dearth of top-class horses.

Economics and Image

The last top-class horse the Queen had was the filly Height of Fashion, which she sold in 1982. The great irony of the victories of Nashwan in the 1989 Derby, 2,000 Guineas, Eclipse and King George was not just that he had been trained by someone she felt was no longer up to the job. It was also that he had been bred from Height of Fashion, which the Queen had sold to Sheikh Hamdan Al Maktoum for somewhere between £1 million and £1.8 million. Height of Fashion has also produced two other Group-winners, Alwasmi and Unfuwain. The Queen wanted to buy West Ilsley, but has in some measure always been sensitive about being seen to have vast amounts of money. The preferred image is that her racehorse hobby/business, like Sandringham, is self-financing, and, like Balmoral and the Civil List, is run efficiently, without extravagance. As Tony Morris explained in the *Racing Post*:

> The £2 Tote punter would never credit the notion that an operation owned by one of such immense personal wealth could be failing for lack of finance. But the same fellow, even as a keen royalist, would probably take a dim view if his Sovereign were to indulge in the massive expenditure which others have employed to enable them to achieve better results.[58]

With the benefit of hindsight, one can note, along with the *Guardian* in June 1989, that Height of Fashion was 'the most valuable broodmare in Europe, if not the world'.[59]

The Queen is frequently described as one of the foremost experts on the breeding of thoroughbreds. As we have seen, this expertise has not for

215

some time produced results on the racecourse, although 1990 was a much better year than most in the 1980s, with the Queen coming thirty-second in the owners' list, receiving prize money from winning horses totalling £76,979, plus a bit more for placed horses. Yet the yearly cost of keeping a single horse in training with a leading trainer is between £13,000 and £15,000. As the Queen has thirty-four such horses, the annual cost of training them comes to over £400,000.

Of course, there is the question of luck. Horses with immaculate breeding do not necessarily perform accordingly on the racecourse. The Queen may just have to wait her turn for the top-class horse to come along. One attempt to shorten the odds on producing such a horse has been to produce a three-quarters brother to Nashwan. The Queen had retained Highclere, Height of Fashion's dam, which in 1989 was mated with Blushing Groom, the sire of Nashwan. The charge for a 'nomination' (the stud fee) payable to the owners of Blushing Groom was normally $160,000 in 1989.[60]

In addition to training costs, there is the cost of such nominations when sending her mares to be mated with stallions. In the last couple of years, this has been in the region of half a million pounds a year, if she were to pay for them all. Recently, the Queen has sent some of her broodmares to some of the top sires on both sides of the Atlantic.

She maintains half a dozen mares in Kentucky, where she paid a five-day private visit in each of the years 1984, 1986 and 1989, and a three-day visit in 1991. Kentucky is the centre of the world bloodstock industry and has the finest collection of stallions in the world. On each occasion, she stayed with Will Farish, friend of President Bush, at his vast stud Lane's End Farm, where some of her mares are kept. The *Daily Express* (8 June 1989) suggested that on her 1989 visit to Kentucky 'the American breeders were only too eager' to make a gift of the services of several stallions for the mares she keeps in Kentucky. Lord Carnarvon confirmed to me this generosity of American breeders, which could have saved the Queen hundreds of thousands of pounds a year (but not as much in 1991 because US stud fees have declined sharply).

Even without being in the Bluegrass state, the Queen can, using computer software given to her during an earlier visit to Kentucky, inspect the pedigree of various American stallions.[61] The Queen continues searching for the coupling that will produce the still elusive Derby winner – she has not even managed one Derby runner since 1981.

The Queen has notched up victories in the other four English classic races, but the last was back in 1977, with Dunfermline.

There are also the costs of running the three studs, two on the Sandringham estate and the one at Polhampton for yearlings. But the studs also produce the main income in the whole of the Queen's racing venture. The Queen's quarter share in Shirley Heights is easily the biggest source of income from her whole racing operation. The stallion stands at Sandringham stud and at the time of writing is one of the top three established stallions in England, and as such brought in a nomination fee of £40,000 in 1990 for every successful covering, of which there are about forty or so a year. The Queen, as the major owner, also exercises the right to some free nominations for her own mares.

Travelling three miles from Sandringham stud, but still remaining on the Sandringham estate, one reaches the Queen's Wolferton stud. The stallion there is the less valuable Bustino (£6,000 per successful nomination); the Queen bought a quarter share in him in 1975. Bustino has his own 'day house' which a *Daily Mail* report in 1984 described as 'the size of a cottage for a family of four – except that one side was open to the elements'.[62] This recalls remarks that used to be made at the beginning of the century, that some of Edward VII's horses were better housed than many members of the working class. Belmez, Sheikh Mohammed Al Maktoum's 1990 winner of the King George and Queen Elizabeth Diamond Stakes, has also taken up residence at Wolferton. His stud fee was £18,000 in 1991.

The other stallion which the Queen has a share of (most of the top stallions are syndicated amongst a number of different owners) is Soviet Star. Lord Carnarvon indicated that she has been given a share in other stallions, which he did not name, perhaps including Belmez. She will also get a rent from the trainer at her West Ilsley stables. The sale of her horses does not usually yield much, an exception being Height of Fashion.

An overall look at the Queen's racing activities in the 1980s and 1990s, with the relatively low prize-money income from her horses, would see her as making a loss. Moreover, since the mid-1970s, racing has been transformed. The Queen used to be clearly in the leading rank of owners in Britain, and as late as 1977 she was the second leading owner in terms of prize money and second in the league table of breeders in that year. But first Robert Sangster, then the Maktoum brothers of Dubai and the

Saudi Prince Khaled Abdulla, began to operate on a totally different scale from previous owners.

If the Queen felt able to increase the size of her racing venture, to reduce the gap between her and the Arab owners, it would obviously raise her chances of a Derby winner. Yet, as indicated above, there is much scope for an improvement of the Queen's prospects without changing the scale of operations. Also, to keep more broodmares and more horses in training would make it all a more complex affair for her to stay in touch with. The three studs and one stable, as they are at present, constitute a fairly sizeable business. Lord Carnarvon suggested the Queen welcomes the challenge of breeding a Derby winner with her existing racing set-up. Moreover, unlike a Saudi prince or a Dubai sheikh, she is under the surveillance of her own country's media. As we have already suggested, it would not do to be too obviously extravagant and, say, buy a £1 million yearling at the Kentucky sales. We have observed a similar constraint regarding the royal jewels, much of them remaining in store so as to limit comments about how extensive and valuable they are.

In relation to her public image, horseracing provides a vital component. The pictures, much beloved by the 'quality' as well as the tabloid press, of the Queen cheering on her horse or looking rather glum at a disappointing performance, show natural and spontaneous reactions. As one reads constantly of new ways in which the monarchy comes to appear more human and less distant, it is still the case that some of the most natural images of the Queen are those at the racecourse. The naturalness of the pictures make us less mindful of the inequalities behind the image – the vast wealth of the monarch and the low pay of those who work in the stables.

12

Private Investments

Both the Queen's racehorses and her investments form part of her strictly private possessions. However, though there is no legal difference between the way these two items are owned, one is completely visible and the other shrouded in secrecy. Horseracing is an activity which takes place openly and in public. What horses the Queen owns, which ones are in training and so on, is public knowledge in the racing publications. This openness makes it wise to observe certain constraints which inhibit any too obvious extravagance, on buying horses or nominations. Unlike racing, the joys of shareholding do not have to be shared with the populace.

It will be recalled from Chapter 7 that the official Labour Opposition policy in 1971 was that the Queen should pay tax or disclose her investments. The *Financial Times* took the same line. The suggestion was that only if the Queen paid tax like everyone else should she be entitled to financial privacy, like anyone else. But as long as she received investment income tax-free, the extent of her investment should be revealed. Then it could be seen how much subsidy was given to the Queen in this fashion, and this should be taken into account in determining whether the Queen actually needed an increase in the Civil List at that time. Her Majesty and Her Majesty's government successfully resisted the argument, albeit not with any convincing arguments from their side. Less than two years after this issue, another development loomed. Without appropriate government assistance, this threatened to bring disclosure, not of all the Queen's investments, but at least of those funds invested in British companies.

In 1973, after a series of scandals in the City (*plus ça change*), the Conservative government under Edward Heath had intended to introduce

219

a new Companies Bill. As is the way with such legislation, this Bill did not have many effective teeth, but it did contain a clause giving companies power to force shareholders to identify themselves when they held shares in the name of a nominee company. Such a company exists merely to be the nominal owner of shares, whilst the names of the real owners are not revealed to the public company (ICI, Marks & Spencer, etc) whose shares are bought. The nominee company, not the real owners, appears on the public company's share register, which by law is publicly available. The Queen had always used this perfectly legal dodge, as had others, to conceal the true nature of her shareholdings. But now it would be far from foolproof.

Documents 'leaked' in February 1975 to the Communist Party's paper the *Morning Star* showed that the Queen and her advisers had been alive to the danger and wanted to keep her shareholdings safely hidden.[1] Sir Geoffrey Howe voiced his disapproval that royal concern over disclosure should have been 'quite improperly' revealed.[2] In other words, even the Queen's desire for secrecy should be a secret. The disclosure clause in the 1973 Companies Bill, Howe explained to the Commons, was 'designed to curtail the practice of "warehousing" whereby some people acquired by stealth a dominant position in a company'. Having been involved in the framing of the legislation at the time, Sir Geoffrey was able to inform the House of Commons that:

> the advisers of the Queen, as they do as a matter of routine, examined the Bill to see whether it contained, inadvertently or otherwise, any curtailment of the Royal Prerogative . . . They drew the government's attention to the possibility that the provision might impose an unreasonable and unnecessary burden on the Queen and her advisers, who were hardly likely to practise the mischief at which it was aimed.[3]

Like Sir Geoffrey, one would hope that it is safe to assume that the Queen and her advisers have never been engaged in any nefarious sharedealing. However, the draft Bill did not strictly speaking impinge upon the Royal Prerogative, of which our old friend, Crown immunity, is usually considered one aspect,[4] for the Queen could still have said that, because the legislation did not specifically mention the Crown, she was not covered by its disclosure clause. Yet pleading Crown immunity, though perfect for avoiding income tax, could be self-defeating in trying to

220

escape disclosure. A nominee company laying claim to Crown immunity, in answer to enquiries about ownership of shares, could identify the Queen as the owner. It could then be argued that in practice Crown immunity had been undermined. How concerned Her Majesty was about the constitutional question, if indeed this matter should be elevated into a constitutional matter, one cannot say. It looks rather as if the practical issue at hand dominated. This was the problem of devising a means of drawing a veil over the Queen's shareholdings, one that could conceal the shares of the other royals too.

It is clear from Sir Geoffrey's remarks, and the government documents themselves, that the initiative to amend the Companies Bill came entirely from the Queen's advisers. The leaked papers, whose authenticity was confirmed by the Prime Minister, Harold Wilson,[5] detailed the behind-the-scenes activity. In December 1973, Robert Hird of the Department of Trade received a letter from the private secretary to the Prime Minister, Robert Armstrong (who became Secretary to the Cabinet for the period 1979–88, still retaining his interest in preventing disclosure, e.g. in his testimony to the Australian Courts in the Peter Wright case). According to Armstrong:

> the PM [Mr Heath] has seen your letter. He has asked me to say that he will attach great importance to arrangements which protect the Queen's private shareholdings from disclosure. Since this has been raised with me (though not with the PM) by the Palace, I should be grateful to be kept informed of developments.

On the odd occasion, governments will quietly slip into a much larger piece of legislation a clause specially promoting the privileges of the royals. Another example of this practice was concerned with compensation to the Duchy of Lancaster for removal of its criminal jurisdiction.

The clause in the Companies Bill, drawn up with the assistance of the Bank of England, exempted 'a person' from disclosing their shareholdings 'if he [sic] is for the time being exempted by the Secretary of State' for Trade. No embarrassing mention of the Queen in this clause, and of course it could be used to assist other big fish to swim through the net of disclosure.

Sir Geoffrey Howe, then Minister of Trade and Consumer Affairs, informed Armstrong that the legal advisers of the Queen thought the provisions of the clause offered 'a perfectly reasonable solution to the problem . . . and that they could not ask us to do more . . .'

However, all this good work might have been undone when the Heath government was toppled by the miners in early 1974. And Harold Wilson, in the House of Commons a year later, could not have sounded too reassuring to royal ears. Wilson told a left-wing backbencher that on this question, so far as he knew, companies legislation under Labour was proceeding 'on somewhat different lines' from Tory legislation, which had now lapsed.[6] There was, however, no reason for royal concern: Labour's Companies Act of 1976 maintained the same special clause.[7]

Bank of England Nominees

In answer to a parliamentary question of 21 April 1977, it was discovered who can escape disclosure and how this exemption works in practice. Around this time, a special nominee company, the Bank of England Nominees Ltd, was set up, which could be used by heads of state, their immediate families, governments and official bodies controlled by or closely related to governments. The formal written parliamentary answer naturally avoided mentioning the Queen by name, but obviously she qualifies as a head of state. The mention of 'immediate families' seems tailor-made for the other British royals to enjoy the same privilege as the Queen. Furthermore, it is hard to see that other heads of state and overseas governments would require a British nominee company to act on their behalf 'in any part of the world'. The *Guardian* remarked at the time that 'the wide application of the exemption caught many observers in financial circles by surprise'.[8] There may well have been other motives for exempting the Saudi royals and all the others who would benefit, but clearly, from the evidence cited, the prime moving force in these machinations was concern for the British royals.

Only if one of those for whom Bank of England Nominees (BoEN) held shares owned as much as 5 per cent of a company did BoEN have to reveal who really owned such shares. (The 1989 Companies Act reduced this to 3 per cent.) With other nominee companies, since the 1976 Companies Act, the nominee company has to provide that information should the company they hold shares in, say, Marks & Spencer, request the information. Moreover, Marks & Spencer would have to make available this information to anyone who asked to see it.

Christopher Hird and Richard Belfield have taken advantage of this provision to compile the *Index of Nominees*, which lists various nominee holdings, together with the beneficial (i.e. real) owners. Thanks to the BoEN arrangement, no British royals appear in this directory.

When one sees 'Bank of England Nominees Ltd' in the share register, there is no way of finding out exactly who owns the shares – the Queen or her immediate family, King Fahd of Saudi Arabia, the Sultan of Brunei, King Bhumibol Adulyadej of Thailand, the Kuwaiti Investment Office, various presidents who also qualify as heads of state like Saddam Hussein, members of their family, governments or whoever. Or, of course, the BoEN holding in a particular company could belong to a *combination* of those entitled to use this facility.

BoEN has an obligation to report to the Secretary of State for Trade and Industry. But in fact this involves passing on to the minister only limited information. All that BoEN is committed to do is to pass on 'annually to the Secretary of State . . . the identity of those for whom it holds securities, and, provided that it holds securities for two or more people, the total value of the securities held'.[9] Thus there is no breakdown given, even to the Secretary of State, of who owns what, or what any individual like the Queen may own in total. The minister is not to be trusted with such 'sensitive' information, and the danger is averted of a Labour Trade minister not sufficiently devoted to the Queen spilling the beans. Instead, it is the City folk who run the Bank, and who are more naturally Her Majesty's allies, who are trusted.

The above arrangement appears to be the solution worked out originally in December 1973, as the leaked papers mention the involvement of the Bank of England and other heads of state, overseas governments etc. The whole arrangement secured what the 6th Earl of Limerick, a junior Trade Minister, termed a 'defensible solution to the problem of the nominee holdings provisions for the Queen's private shareholdings'. Not that it was ever meant to be *publicly* defended, or even mentioned.

The idea that the solution is defensible is not shared by everyone. Though the Queen may not practise 'warehousing' of shares, the Kuwaiti Investment Office has on occasion hidden behind BoEN. The KIO, it was discovered later, were involved in spring 1987, when there was a fuss over who really owned a 4.4 per cent holding in Morgan Grenfell, held in the name of BoEN. The *Financial Times* was unhappy about this way of using BoEN and was unable to find 'any satisfactory reason'

223

why those using BoEN 'should be accorded extra special treatment'.[10] The Bank of England was embarrassed, as it had been committed to considerably more disclosure of the real owners behind nominee names, to prevent breaches of the takeover code. Thus a Bank spokesperson, on this occasion, practically disowned the BoEN – 'it is not a Bank of England creature but a government creature for which we act as a vehicle. It is not our idea.'[11] However, the leaked papers do record 'the help of the Bank of England' in formulating the means of allowing the Queen to escape disclosure. One can be sure that the Bank is loyal to the Queen, even if it does not like all the ramifications of the arrangement for disguising her shareholdings.

Moreover, the Queen and her immediate family increasingly stand out as exceptions in wanting to hide behind nominees. Most use of nominees has traditionally been more for convenience than for secrecy. For instance, a stockbroker holding discretionary funds on behalf of many different clients will bundle them together when dealing in the shares of a particular company, in order to cut down on the paperwork. The easiest way to do this is to use his or her firm's nominee company. As Hamish McRae has written in the *Guardian*, this is less necessary now with computerization. Also, it is in theory now possible 'to allow anyone to "see through" nominee names to the beneficial owner, without involving the user of the nominee in any particular administrative burden'.[12]

When BoEN was made ready for the Queen and other Heads of State etc., Stanley Clinton Davis (Labour's successor to the Earl of Limerick as junior Trade Minister) said that only one exemption to the requirements of disclosure had been granted, and that was to BoEN.[13] No more exemptions have since been granted,[14] so this is the only British nominee company which the royals can use which *guarantees* to keep their holdings secret.

Yet after all this trouble to which both Conservative and Labour governments have gone, to help the Queen in hiding her investments, it does not necessarily mean that she uses BoEN. Even back in December 1973 the legal advisers to the Queen,* though pleased with the BoEN idea, stated that they did not commit themselves to using the 'suggested

---

* The Queen's legal advisers were Farrer and Co., Matthew Farrer (now Sir Matthew) being designated 'private solicitor to the Queen'.

new facility'. There are several reasons for thinking that the Queen may not use BoEN, or do so for only a part of her fortune.

First, BoEN was intended to be started with little or no public attention. This was spoiled by the *Morning Star* leak and subsequent publicity. The Queen may therefore wish to avoid such a high-profile nominee company. Second, the amounts, especially recently, invested in UK companies through BoEN are fairly minor, meaning that clearly it is not used very much by the Heads of State and government bodies that are entitled to use it. Perhaps they and the Queen prefer less well-known nominee companies to hide their money. Third, it is possible to use other nominee companies and still avoid disclosure. For instance, a public company is unlikely to try and find out the real owner behind the nominee appearing on its share register if the holding is of long-standing. They will see such a holding as beneficial to the company and leave the owner safe from disclosure, lest he or she sell the shares to avoid revealing their identity.

Fourth, and more importantly, much of the Queen's money may be abroad. For some reason press estimates of the Queen's private wealth tend to assume that it must be patriotically invested in Britain, in blue-chip companies. With the ending, in 1979, of exchange controls much money left the country, and it became an increasing tendency for City institutions like life insurance and pension funds to invest abroad. Even the Church of England Commissioners had, by 1983, one third of their shareholdings out of the country.[15] In countries like the United States, France and Germany there is very little danger of anyone finding out the real owner of shares, if that owner wants to remain anonymous. Hence, BoEN, though it is empowered to act abroad, is not generally needed and buying equities in its name in fact could attract attention.

Fifth, a good deal of the Queen's capital may be invested, whether in Britain or abroad, in bonds, government stock or in bank deposits where there is obviously no share register or equivalent, and therefore no problem of disclosure.

It has to be admitted that the concealment of the Queen's investments has been up to now a complete success. There are no leaks as regards the extent of the Queen's fortune or how it has been invested. The *Guardian* noted in a very general way, in April 1977, 'It has been well known in the City for several years that the Queen is among the nation's largest private shareholders.'[16] 'What is known', said Lindsay Vincent writing in the *Observer* in 1983, 'is that Barings, the oldest merchant bank in London, certainly administers her portfolio of shares, using select stockbrokers to execute the orders'.[17] Also one of Charles's Duchy of Cornwall accounts refers to £1.25 million held at Barings. Barings could assist the Queen in investing abroad, as one of its subsidiaries specializes in handling investments in Japanese shares. Barings are also active throughout South-East Asia, North America, West Europe and Australia. Moreover, the Queen enjoys 'Sovereign immunity' from tax on income reaped abroad in those countries which recognize the convention, as does Britain, that Sovereigns and governments should be immune from tax.[18]

Another merchant bank, Morgan Grenfell, also handled a 'significant portion' of the Queen's wealth. The late Sir William Hill-Wood had done this for George VI and continued to do so for the Queen. This would seem to be the only visible reason for the Queen's giving him, in 1976, the form of knighthood, which is in her gift and not the Prime Minister's. His *Who's Who* entry gives no other clue to why the Queen should decide to honour him. When she knighted him at Buckingham Palace, 'she took the sword from behind the curtain, tapped him, and then whispered slyly, "you can get up now, Willy."[19]

None of the difficulties in finding out about the Queen's private investments has prevented 'estimates' of their value. The lowest I have seen, which admittedly was a minimum guess, without pretending to be otherwise, was in *The Times* in 1987. This put the value of the tax exemption at not less than £500,000 a year. This would suggest investments of about £15 million. At the other extreme is a much bandied about figure of £2,000 million. This seems to have appeared first in the *News of the World*, in 1985, and is attributed to an anonymous stockbroker. The figure was repeated a few months later in *Woman* magazine and the *Daily Express*. In 1987 it appeared in America's prestigious financial magazine *Fortune*.[20] Thus given added credibility, this figure looks as if it has returned back across the Atlantic, to form the basis of some of the most recent estimates of the Queen's investments in British publications,[21] and with inflation swollen to £3,000 million.

There have been other figures in other newspapers and magazines which like to draw up league tables of the world's billionaires or Britain's richest individuals or whatever. For this purpose, they all need 'estimates'.

As Brian Moynahan has pointed out in the *Independent*, 'in the absence of any official guidelines' the press 'is free to pluck headline-hogging figures out of thin air' or to quote those who have employed this method.

Paradoxically, this may suit not only sections of the press, but also the Palace. For this gives them the opportunity to 'seize on the exaggeration', to discredit criticism of the monarchy's financial affairs as ill informed.[22]

In nearly all cases, the basis of these estimates of investment wealth is not revealed. Therefore it is important to lay down clearly the assumptions one is making and equally to be clear they are only assumptions. As indicated earlier, the Queen's investments could be spread all over the world, but for the sake of simplifying the exercise, I've assumed they are all in one country, Britain, invested in UK equities. If one starts in 1971 from a figure of £20 million, bearing in mind Cobbold's strictures before the Select Committee in that year that estimates of between £50 and £100 million were 'wildly exaggerated', and if that £20 million had increased at the same rate as the UK stock market as a whole, and if the dividends have been ploughed back, then today (June 1991), it would be worth £341 million.[23] It is not particularly unreasonable to assume that the income would be reinvested, for three reasons. First, because unlike other members of the super-rich, nearly all the Queen's needs are met by the state, with the exception of buying the odd grouse moor, as in 1978, or Andrew and Fergie's new home more recently. Second, she already has a personal income of over £2 million a year from the Duchy of Lancaster, after the annuities she pays her cousins who don't get an allowance from the state. Third, because one learns from royalists that the Queen is not extravagant and is even, as Lord St John has argued, 'very careful' with her money.[24]

One would expect the Queen as regards investments in shares to have done better than the UK average, if her investment advisers were doing their job; and the financial advice she receives must be some of the best available. Therefore, some withdrawals of dividends should have been possible, without preventing her capital rising faster than the UK market average.

The average dividend on the top 100 companies provides a return of 5.4 per cent, bringing in £18.4 million a year on £341 million. By not paying income tax, virtually all of which would be charged at 40 per cent, the Queen would save £7.3 million a year or £20,000 a day, based on these calculations. She will escape any Capital Gains Tax she might otherwise incur on the profits of buying and selling shares. Nor will inheritance tax be levied on anything left to her successor, to other royals or to anyone else.

Unless the Queen authorizes disclosure of the extent of her private investments, with or without government 'advice' to do so, it will be impossible to know their actual value, as opposed to their estimated value. But one can say that, as long as the nature of the economic system is to reward people for owning capital, then other things being equal the future financial prospects are good. In the past, the steady upward graph of monarchical accumulation was disturbed by Victoria dividing up the first 'considerable' private fortune of a monarch amongst her many younger children. Only part of George V's fortune was passed on to George VI, but the latter had only two children, one of whom is the present Queen. Moreover, she has already had a long reign, during which accumulation has taken place.

Clearly, she has advantages over the person reputed to be the second richest in the country, the Duke of Westminster. He has to pay all the expenses incurred to maintain his lifestyle. He doesn't receive presents from foreign heads of state and he has to find ways to minimize his tax bill. We have the Duke of Westminster's word for it, that the last matter is 'very wearing', though apparently worth the effort.[25]

It's Not Just the Amount that Matters

It should be understood that the secrecy over the Queen's shareholdings is not just to hide the *amount* of her shareholding wealth. The intention is also that the actual companies in which royal wealth is invested remain unknown. Business investments involve particular companies, which make their money in particular places, supporting particular governments, enforcing particular working conditions, wages and so on.

We read in the royal biographies that the royals are scrupulously fussy about which charities and voluntary organizations they lend their names to. We read also that the Duke of Edinburgh's private secretary had to resign his post in 1957 (two years after Margaret decided not to go ahead with marrying the divorced Townsend) because he and his wife were getting divorced. His resignation was required to protect the 'irreproachable moral probity that must surround the Crown'.[26] More recently, Marina Ogilvy described, in October 1989 on BBC's *Kilroy* programme, the clash with her parents, Princess Alexandra of Kent and Sir Angus Ogilvy, who could not tolerate the idea of her having a child outside of marriage and she was cut off from her trust fund. Marina Ogilvy, despite being a distant twenty-fourth in line to the throne, was told by her father that he put the Queen and Church first. Monarchist writers understand such considerations, and are fond of quoting Bagehot's description of the monarch, as 'head of our *morality*'.

One can, then, readily appreciate what a pity it would be to ruin all the time and trouble devoted to the surface image of the monarchy by having the Queen associated, through her various shareholdings, with all the practices that companies may involve themselves in. These can easily include supporting apartheid; paying starvation wages to workers in South Africa and many Third World Commonwealth countries; refusing to change unsafe or unhealthy working conditions; opposition to the unionization of workforces; destruction of the environment; producing armaments, tobacco or asbestos; bribery and corruption and so on.

RTZ, the international mining company, has certainly been a controversial company, not least by its construction of a uranium mine in Namibia in the 1970s and its operation of the mine thereafter. The company ignored United Nations resolutions which outlawed mining in mineral-rich Namibia whilst it remained under South African occupation. The UN repeatedly stated that South African rule, which finally ended in 1990, was illegal.

When this author first examined the company share register of RTZ, for June 1983, there was BoEN doing its job of holding about £25 million of shares for one or more members of that group entitled to use it – British royals, foreign heads of state and their immediate families, government organizations from different countries and so on. Of course, we do not know if the Queen or any of her family owned any of these shares. Though Andrew Morton gives some indication that the Queen owned shares in RTZ in 1977, it is far from conclusive.*

---

* Morton reproduces in his book (p. 84) a transfer form from April 1977, showing the transfer of shares in GEC from one Bank of England company, Houblon Nominees, to the newly set up Bank of England Nominees Ltd, which from that date has been the only company to enjoy exemption from disclosure. In 1977, these GEC shares were worth £1,331,508, and RTZ shares, similarly transferred, £244,500. In addition, Morton says that he had 'private information from the Bank of England' that the Queen held shares in RTZ and GEC in 1977. Even if Morton's private information is accurate, that does not necessarily mean that Houblon Nominees held these shares for her. And even if it did hold shares for the Queen, there is no way of knowing what proportion, if any, of the transferred GEC and RTZ shares belonged to her. Houblon Nominees (LG Account) could easily have been holding shares for others besides the Queen, who were also eligible to transfer their interests to the new BoEN. And the Queen need not have used only one nominee company before 1977. Morton's conclusion, that the Queen held shares in these two companies, has been taken up, it seems to me over-enthusiastically, by Charles Higham and Roy Moseley, in *Elizabeth & Philip* (Sidgwick & Jackson, 1991), pp. 301, 322–4, 334–6.

There was, however, something of a royal connection with RTZ. Lord Charteris is always described as someone very close to the Queen during his twenty-seven years of royal employment. In 1977 'a Palace person' told the *Sunday Times* that Charteris 'has been to Her Majesty what Burleigh was to Elizabeth I'.[27] In 1978, on his retirement as the Queen's private secretary, the latter-day Burleigh joined the RTZ board as a non-executive director, a position he held until 1984.

Direct royal contact with an RTZ company was made by Prince Philip. In 1971 he visited its Panguna mine in Bougainville, an island which is part of Papua New Guinea. Richard West, in his book on RTZ, describes the massive deforestation there, with its apparent adverse effect on rainfall, as well as the depositing of waste soil into the Jaba river which killed all the fish and silted up the river mouth. Eight villages had to be relocated as a consequence. West notes that the 'well-known conservationist the Duke of Edinburgh . . . spent five hours at the Panguna mine but made no public comment about its effect on the island's ecology'.[28] The year before, a page of Prince Philip's engagement book, as revealed for a biographer, shows a half-hour meeting with the late Sir Val Duncan, then the driving force behind RTZ.[29] This probably concerned some charitable project the Duke was interested in.

Despite indications that the Queen may have held shares in RTZ, the determined secrecy about the shareholdings prevents us from being certain. What we can do is to examine, as a hypothetical example, the implications of the Queen's investing in a controversial company like RTZ. (We should bear in mind that RTZ is not the only company whose activities have attracted sustained criticism.) Had it become known that she held shares in such a company, it would seriously damage her image as the head and promoter of the multi-racial Commonwealth, particularly as she was in the 1980s very often compared favourably with Mrs Thatcher, and her 'uncaring' attitude to the Commonwealth.

RTZ has considerable mining interests in South Africa, which with-drew from the Commonwealth in 1961 over apartheid. These investments have recently been much expanded with the 1988 acquisition of BP's mines there, the most profitable of which made £32 million in 1987. But the most controversial of all RTZ's operations has been its uranium mine at Rössing, Namibia. South Africa's administration of Namibia, which finally ended in March 1990, was one of the most condemned in the world. Namibia had the distinction that in no other country had the ruling régime been declared illegal by the International Court of Justice, in a verdict of 1971.

The Catholic Institute of International Relations produced a study of mining in Namibia in 1983. It concluded that 'throughout the mines, church sources report that miners see the companies as part and parcel of the colonial occupation', while RTZ's subsidiary, Rössing Uranium:

has become the focal point of opposition to foreign investment in Namibia, for two main reasons. First, the mine was opened in 1976 with the full knowledge of the ruling of the International Court of Justice that South Africa's occupation was illegal;* and second, Western power authorities, all of which work closely with their governments, are the principal customers. There is also the fear that Rössing uranium may be being used (along with South Africa's own supplies) in the development of nuclear weapons by South Africa.[30]

RTZ's subsidiary worked closely with the South African government. In fact, the South African state-owned Industrial Development Corporation in 1983 had a 13 per cent shareholding in Rössing, and had made loans to the company of about £20 million.[31] Rössing Uranium was also excused paying tax in its first five years of operation. It is therefore a little difficult to credit the RTZ Chairman's statement in 1989 that the company had always supported independence for Namibia. What this may boil down to is that, as the uranium market became tougher and the international climate became less tolerant of apartheid in the late 1980s, South Africa's continued rule of Namibia became bad for business. Its formal ending still leaves Namibia, economically, largely dependent on South Africa. In this changing climate, Rössing did at last recognize the miners' union in 1988.

In 1982, Rössing represented only 4.5 per cent of the RTZ group's assets, but contributed no less than 26 per cent to its profits. An expanded RTZ is much less dependent on Rössing, but in 1988 made £23 million profits from its 46.5 per cent stake in its Namibian subsidiary.

In our hypothetical example, the disclosure of the Queen's RTZ

---

* None of this is mentioned in 'The Rössing Fact Book', put out by the company in 1989. The period of setting up the mine is described purely in terms of the engineering feat involved. Since then, the glossy pamphlet describes the company's role largely in terms of the benefits Rössing Uranium has conferred upon Namibia.

shareholdings would have led to adverse comment, especially during 1978–84 when her former private secretary, with whom she worked so closely on Commonwealth affairs, was on the board. Pressure would have been placed on her, as it was successfully on Church bodies, local authorities and the like. These are all thought to be publicly accountable in some sense and not just to be concerned with making as much money as possible. For instance, the Church of England Commissioners disposed of their RTZ shareholdings in 1976 because of the company's role in Namibia. Does the Queen have a general 'ethical' investment policy which clearly indicates to her investment advisers (Barings) that they should not invest in companies which break international law, bolster apartheid or engage in other unpleasant activities? If she had, one would have thought it would have been 'leaked' to a friendly newspaper by now.

But even companies which might not positively breach any ethical code are involved in the ordinary, everyday, 'normal' exploitation of their workforce. The Queen, and others of her family, would emerge in a very different light if it were known to company employees that the royals were shareholders in the company they worked for. Owning shares is not simply an act of possession, though that is the only 'activity' required of the shareholder. It means drawing dividends from the efforts of those who toil for this or that company. If the latter knew of this 'relationship', it might well dampen their enthusiasm for the monarchy. Some might write to the Queen, putting her on the spot by asking for her help in, say, preventing a factory closure or improving pay.

The very carefully constructed system of secrecy which surrounds the royal shareholdings is the other side of the coin from the royal limelight. There we have the saturation coverage of royal activities, like those for the Save the Children Fund (of which the Queen is patron and Princess Anne is president).

Effective propaganda/public relations depends not only on influencing what is publicly stated, but equally in keeping certain sensitive information publicly unstated. Of course, the royal press officers cannot fully control press intrusion into the royals' personal lives. Irritating and sometimes distressing though this no doubt is to the royals most affected, this kind of publicity rarely challenges the basic mystique of royalty. Revelations of their shareholdings might do exactly that.

Conclusion

Ending the Queen's Tax Exemption and
Other Financial Privileges

'If we can reduce dishonesty, selfishness and injustice, the nineties can become a time of peace and tranquillity . . . and a time for working together for the benefit of our planet as a whole.'
The Queen, speech at a Save the Children fund-raising event, December 1989

This book has concentrated on matters of royal finance and taxation, but has not, one hopes, been narrowly economic. For instance, an examination of the mysteries of Crown immunity have allowed us to understand how the Queen is allowed to discriminate, despite the Sex Discrimination Act and the Race Relations Act (see also Appendix B). Also mysterious, but documented throughout, has been a recurring element in the royal state of mind – feeling hard-up amongst prodigious luxury and wealth. We have discovered the special relationship between the monarch and the Treasury and how this department has struggled to ease royal financial anxieties. We have seen how Edward Peacock, as private financial adviser to George V, took on a political role during the political crisis of 1931. In examining various forms of royal wealth – the works of art, jewels and archives – we have seen how they are used to project a suitably regal image.

When investigating the relationship with the Treasury, we have commented upon the double standard operated in government. Government effectively allocates a higher moral worth to the rich, including royalty, than to ordinary people, when it comes to spending public money. This is a major reason why the financial privileges of the royal family should be ended, as well as the saving to the tax-payer this would afford. It is not a question of being vindictive to an institution that one disagrees with, but of demanding a different set of priorities from government.

Therefore it is argued that the Queen, the richest person in the country, should be treated like everyone else and be liable to income tax, capital gains tax and inheritance tax on her private fortune. This appears not unreasonable when one knows that monarchs used to pay income tax on their private fortune during a period of nearly a hundred years. The fact that this tax-paying past and the manner of its ending have been covered up suggests that monarchs too have realized their exemption is unreasonable. Even if invoking Crown immunity could make it seem reasonable, the meaning of Crown immunity should not be stretched to cover the Duchy of Cornwall.

It is even dubious whether the Duchy of Cornwall is owned by the Prince of Wales, for similar reasons to those laid out in Chapter 10, which argued that the Queen did not own the Duchy of Lancaster. Both duchies should be handed over to the state or, at the very least, should be taxed as normal. The Queen's Privy Purse and the Prince of Wales could be funded from the Queen's private resources. And as long as the Duchy of Lancaster is in royal hands, the Queen should hand over to the Duchy's Benevolent Fund the millions she has withdrawn from the Duchy as a result of those dying intestate without relatives in Lancashire. The bulk of the art treasures should be handed over to the state, as has occurred with other monarchies in Europe. Jewels given to royalty on state occasions should similarly be surrendered. This would still leave a sizeable collection in the Queen's hands. And the Bank of England Nominees arrangement should be withdrawn.

The monarch now has a vast fortune. If royal relatives find the income from their own inherited wealth insufficient, and find it beneath their dignity to work as others do, then perhaps the Queen should pay the 'expenses' incurred in their attending various functions. At the same time, they could pay rent to the state for their luxurious accommodation at Kensington Palace and elsewhere, which, if nominally owned by the sovereign, is maintained by the state. Nearly all these changes could be brought about by the government of the day 'advising' the monarch to accept them.

The government could also do what we know the Treasury greatly feared in 1936 – transfer the audit of the Civil List from the Treasury to the auditor and Comptroller-General who heads the National Audit

Office. The latter might think that the Civil List paid the wages of staff, who for a lot of their time, e.g., at Balmoral and Sandringham, were performing personal duties for the royal family, and not simply helping them perform their public role.

Ending the many financial privileges of the monarch and her family will not by itself end the double standard operated by government and society, but it would be a step in the right direction.

In June 1991, Granada TV's World in Action team made a programme based largely on the findings of this book. (I worked as a consultant for the programme with Paul Lashmar as researcher and Brian Blake as producer.) The circumstances of the Queen's tax exemption attracted a great deal of publicity in Britain and many other countries.

It was publicly known that the Queen did not pay income tax on her private income. Therefore it came as a great surprise to learn that the monarch used to pay such tax and had only comparatively recently and secretly escaped from paying it. Moreover, for the first time it was argued that the Queen's immunity from practically all taxation was based on an outdated view of her constitutional position. Even a bare outline of the facts and arguments, which was all that was possible in the programme and consequent media coverage, brought forth the demand across a wide spectrum of opinion that the Queen should cough up.

Leader articles in the *Independent on Sunday*, the *Guardian* and the *Financial Times* (and the *Sunday People* earlier in the year, and more gently voiced in the *Mail on Sunday* in 1990) were clear that she should be taxed on her private fortune.

The editor of the *Sunday Times*, Andrew Neil, was most emphatic on his LBC radio programme that there was no possible reason, especially given the new findings, why the Queen should not pay. The *Daily Mail* carried a long article by an Oxford academic making much the same point; and Keith Waterhouse in the same paper found it 'disagreeable' that the Queen received this 'spectacular form of tax relief'. Peter Tory's column in the *Daily Express* said that 'if the monarchy doesn't wish to be chased into the hills it ought fairly quickly to volunteer to pay taxes'. *Today*'s article was headlined 'The biggest tax loophole in history'. The Palace stayed virtually silent when it came to saying anything on the record to journalists. The government likewise.

A few defenders of the monarchy did take the field. Charles Moore in the *Spectator* felt it was 'unspeakable puritanism' to tax the Queen, though his own paper, the *Daily Telegraph*, subsequently registered that the controversy over the tax immunity was damaging to the monarchy. For Mr Moore, the fact that the monarchy only recently escaped paying tax through 'discreet deals' is not a cause for criticism. Rather he admires their 'cunning' in getting away with it and making it appear that the exemption was 'traditional'. This is one part of Mr Moore's generally romantic justification of the monarchy which might not go down too well in Buckingham Palace.

Also in the *Telegraph*, Mr Moore (Eton and Cambridge), Hugo Vickers (Eton), and Winston Churchill (Eton and Oxford), in a letter to the paper, together with the Hon. Christopher Monckton (Harrow and Cambridge) of the *Evening Standard*, all felt that the Queen need not pay income tax because of the money the state gains from the monarch's surrender of the Crown Lands back in 1760. This was the first time this argument had been publicly employed to justify the tax exemption. It had only ever been used to maintain that government expenditure on the monarchy was really paid for out of these estates, and even that the state made a profit from the monarchy. As was noted in Chapter 6, this is a threadbare argument, even for that purpose. It used not to be accepted even by the Treasury, and a Conservative Chancellor, R. A. Butler in 1952, went out of his way to disagree with those Tory backbenchers who propounded it during a debate on the Civil List. But no doubt some will continue to employ it for lack of any other justification for the tax exemption.

Lord St John of Fawsley (previously Norman St John Stevas, the former Conservative Cabinet minister), appearing on *World in Action*, termed it a 'constitutional impossibility' that the Queen should be taxed. Yet Lord St John, despite his knowledge (as an editor of the Collected Works of Walter Bagehot) of the Constitution, encapsulates a history of the confusion on the question of the Queen's taxation. In 1969 he wrote an article in which he reproached those who felt that she was not paying tax on her private income. He shared the common delusion fostered by the Palace and government that the Queen paid income tax. In the 1971 Civil List debates, despite Labour pressure on the subject, he could provide no reason why the Queen need not be taxed. Twenty years later he had decided that it was a 'constitutional impossibility' that the Queen could be taxed. But then he went on to argue that, in other terms, this privilege was 'difficult to defend'. Employing exquisite understatement, he mentioned that, 'I don't think myself it's totally acceptable in the modern world.' He thought 'at some time in the future' the 'exemption will be waived, or modified'. The *Daily Mirror* considered this, coming from such a devout monarchist as Lord St John, 'an opinion as devastating as the Rev. Ian Paisley siding with the Pope'.

Another devoted monarchist, Harold Brooks-Baker of *Burke's Peerage*, also showed some inconsistency in his statements on this matter. In July 1991 on Radio 4 he confidently justified the tax exemption, maintaining that the Queen already paid 'one of the largest tax bills' in the country by surrendering the Crown Estate revenue. Yet in April he had told the *Sunday People*, 'if the Queen doesn't volunteer to pay taxes, then the future of the monarchy is threatened'. This may have something to do with his rather peculiar notion that eighteen monarchies have been deposed in the last 200 years 'largely because of tax related problems'. It is hard to see the overthrow of the Tsar or the Kaiser in such terms, but that is another matter. In June on ITN he thought 'the monarch will surprise the people by making a statement [on the tax issue] through her advisers in the near future'. The implication he appeared to be making was that, for the general good, she would grasp the nettle and volunteer to pay.

By coincidence, a week after the *World in Action* programme, the Liberal Democrat MP Simon Hughes was due to introduce a ten-minute bill in the Commons which sought to tax the Queen on her private income. (Tony Benn's Commonwealth Bill, aimed at overhauling the Constitution, had also included a clause to end the tax privileges of the Queen.) After Mr Hughes spoke, no one sought to defend the Queen's tax exemption and the bill was passed (as a ten-minute bill this had only a symbolic significance, but he plans to introduce it as a private member's bill in 1992). The government tactic mirrored the Palace's: to say nothing and sit it out. As a tactic, there is no doubt something to be said for it, but it is not one generally used by those who feel they have strong arguments in their favour.

In general, the picture that filtered back to me from journalists was that it was extremely difficult to get a Conservative MP to defend the tax exemption. Apart from Winston Churchill and his *Daily Telegraph* letter, I could discover only one other who did so publicly. This was Sir John Stokes, who appeared on BBC TV News, saying that he was a supporter of 'hierarchy' in society, and any tampering with the Queen's privilege would interfere with that.

It would seem perhaps only a matter of time before the current situation is ended. Yet some hope for the Queen in preserving her tax privileges was provided by the helpful silence maintained by the Labour Front Bench. A 'Labour source' was quoted in the *Sunday Times* as saying that it would be 'political suicide' for them to insist the Queen should be taxed. A Labour frontbencher evinced the same fear. The reasoning behind it is difficult to discover; 79 per cent of those in an *Independent on Sunday* poll thought the Queen should be taxed on her private fortune, and not just Simon Hughes but also Anthony Beaumont-Dark, the Conservative MP, have spoken out on the matter. Both of these are defending constituencies with a majority of less than 3,000 over their Labour rival. Clearly they feel that their outspoken public stance will do them no harm in the difficult situation of defending their seats at the next election. Given that large parts of the press which normally support the Conservative Party also feel that the Queen should pay tax, Labour need hardly feel worried that they will be accused of adopting a 'loony left' policy.

Perhaps the Queen may volunteer to pay income tax, as some have suggested she should. She may even volunteer to pay income tax at the full rate (40 per cent is currently the higher rate of taxation, which would apply to virtually all her income). This would put pressure on Prince Charles to do likewise, as his 'voluntary contribution' is only at 25 per cent of his Duchy profits. The Queen volunteering to pay could be engineered between the two main party leaders, though of course it will be difficult for it to be announced as an 'act of grace', or by some such courtly language, for it would appear as bowing to adverse publicity. Such a gesture would do much to undercut the outrageous double standard by which the Queen's tax privileges are allowed. Yet, because it maintained the constitutional fiction of appearing voluntary, it would still leave the Queen as being above the law. And is there any reason why, in John Major's 'classless society', she should not pay in the same fashion as everyone else?

Appendix A

The Effect of the Monarchy on Tourism and Trade

A very common argument states that even if the monarchy isn't so cheap, one should consider how the monarchy brings money into the country. Indeed, in surveys of British attitudes towards the monarchy, the benefit to tourism and trade is the most commonly cited advantage of having a royal family.[1]

Tourism

Reasons why tourists come to Britain depend on a variety of factors. The most recent *Overseas Visitors Survey* conducted by the British Tourist Authority[2] lists twelve activities, from which visitors are asked to choose those which 'were of particular importance to you in deciding to visit Great Britain'. From the list 41 per cent chose 'visiting historic sites, houses, cathedrals etc.' and 38 per cent 'visiting historic cities or towns' (visitors could pick more than one activity). The survey did not ask about the royal family, nor has any other such survey. Undeniably, Britain's heritage is of major importance in bringing people to Britain, but this of course includes much more than just Buckingham Palace, Windsor Castle and so on.

Those tourists who travel to Windsor can see a good deal of the Castle. But in London, where tourists from abroad spend most of their time, Buckingham Palace offers admission only to the small Queen's Gallery and on two days a week to the Royal Mews, where the carriages are put on display. Most tourists in London traditionally have done no more than stand outside the railings at Buckingham Palace. The actual work

239

of keeping the tourists happy is done by the soldiers, who take their turn at Changing the Guard. At the height of the summer crowds, unless the expectant tourist is one of the small minority at the very front, near the railings, he or she will not see very much. The chance of their seeing any of the royals themselves is slight indeed.

Were the monarchy to be abolished, it would be possible for the tourists to have virtually complete access to the untenanted royal Palaces. Versailles in France is a wonderful tourist attraction, and long before Glasnost the Soviets were happy to capitalize on the tourist appeal of the Tsar's palaces. The most popular tourist attraction in Britain where it is necessary to enter the building complex remains the Tower of London,[3] which has long been vacated by Britain's monarchs. It is now run by a government body, the Historic Royal Palaces Agency (which also organizes the more minor attraction of the State Apartments at Kensington Palace).

In the British Tourist Authority's *Strategy for Growth 1986–90*, 'Heritage and Culture' is mentioned as one of the thirteen strengths of the British Tourist industry; but of the twelve elements considered under that heading the Royal Family is only one. It is possible that, because there is a surviving monarchy and aristocracy in Britain, this generates more interest in the history than if these institutions had been abolished as in most European countries. But it is really impossible to tell. Also, the picture of a backward, tradition-bound Britain which might attract more tourists may, at the same time, adversely affect the image abroad of British industry (what is left of it). Exports would more probably be helped by the image of Britain as a more modern and efficient country, not a living museum.

The *Overseas Visitors Survey* asks only about activities, and therefore leaves out other factors which encourage visits. The fact that English is the dominant international language is not therefore mentioned as a factor in attracting visitors. For Americans, who are the biggest group coming to the UK, it is a big plus. Britain is also conveniently located for Americans, on the western side of Europe, as a convenient jumping-off point to other parts of Europe. Even when it comes to ties of sentiment, the fact that Britain was a wartime ally and that many older American males were stationed here during the war, and subsequently, may be more significant than the monarchy.

Tourism has not been as successful a money-earner, recently, as is popularly imagined. The National Economic Development Office in a 1990 report identified tourism as one of the five major industries where urgent action was needed to correct the basic problems which produce Britain's large balance of payments deficit. The deficit on tourism amounted to £2.5 billion for 1989.[4] In other words, British tourists spend more abroad than foreign tourists spend here. Those who feel that the monarchy is important in this matter would, if they were consistent, be thinking about what more the royals could be doing to attract tourists. On the other hand, *The Times* commented that there seemed to be no link between big royal occasions like royal weddings and increases in the volume of tourists.[5]

Trade

Royal visits abroad are seen as a means of generating trade. However, Britain's fifth largest export market is the Republic of Ireland,[6] with a population of only 3 million. Therefore, per head of population, Ireland is easily Britain's greatest trading success. Yet members of the British royal family do not set foot in the Republic. Similarly, although Japan's Emperor until his death in 1988 was Hirohito, widely thought of as a war criminal in easily Britain, this did not stop British people buying Japanese goods. By and large, trade has more to do with economics than sentiment about the monarch of the country whose exports one buys.

Edgar Wilson, in *The Myth of British Monarchy*, using the statistics on trade from 1971 to 1984, suggests that more often than not a royal visit to a particular country is followed by a decline in that country buying British goods. The idea that the monarchy benefits trade seems to have arisen when Britain's share of world trade started to decline. Under the present Queen, as Wilson points out, it has slipped disastrously. It would be foolish in the extreme to blame her for this, just as foolish as it is to think that the royals generate demand for British goods and services. That the monarchy might have a relatively marginal effect on boosting tourism is possible, but not proven. But the argument that the monarchy encourages people abroad to buy British goods is a complete non-starter.

Appendix B

Race and Sex Discrimination at Court

In the mid-1970s, at about the same time as the Companies Act was being repelled, action was taken which prevented other government legislation from troubling the Queen. This concerned the legislation which outlawed sex and race discrimination. The preferred image of the monarchy is that somehow, along with its tradition, it is adapting to the new world, and that it is really quite progressive, in its own way. The reality of the Queen's Court is very different.

Douglas Keay, in his 1983 book on the relationship between the monarchy and the media, notes that Australia, New Zealand and Canada have taken it in turns to supply one of the two assistant press secretaries. Usually it is a civil servant seconded for two years or more. Keay tells us that in 1959 a Ghanaian held the post for all of two months, in advance of a proposed visit by the Queen to newly independent Ghana. Keay adds that 'there was a move much more recently, backed by Prince Charles, for another black person to take up the position, but in the end this came to nothing'.*[1] Nor has there been any change since Keay wrote. The white

---

* One would probably not have expected Charles's father to have intervened in the same way, if his speeches are any guide to his attitudes. On his return from a tour of South America in 1962, he observed that the continent 'has very considerable resources and a rapidly growing population of which quite a large proportion is of European descent. This means that there is no practical reason why it should not reach the same state of industrial development as Europe or the United States.' The nearby West Indies was somehow not so fortunate. In 1969, Prince Philip told an interviewer that in the West Indies, 'the climate and the possibilities are such that an ambition level can be very low. You have three pigs and sixteen banana trees and you have everything you want, and to do better than that the effort is so great that people stick at that level.'

Commonwealth rota has seen a New Zealand press secretary in post, Warwick Hutchings, followed by a Canadian, Vic Chapman (1983–7), and an Australian, Geoffrey Crawford, who is the present incumbent. It appears then that the exclusion of a press secretary from the black Commonwealth is a matter of policy.

Before the brief Ghanaian presence, there had been a Nigerian equerry at Court for a few weeks in 1956, again prior to a visit to that person's country. I have noticed two military officers with Asian names listed as holding minor honorary Court positions for a few years in the 1960s, which may or may not have required their presence at the occasional Court ceremony. There is also, presently, one out of the thirty-six Chaplains to the Queen who is black, the Antiguan Rev David Tonge, whose parish is in Worcestershire. Such a position in the Royal Household is also fairly nominal. Perhaps there have been a few other appointments of this order. But this is bearing in mind that during her reign the Queen has been responsible for over a thousand Court appointments, major and minor. In 1983, even Lady Elizabeth Longford, one of the most flattering of all the Queen's biographers, felt constrained to issue a polite reminder to the Queen. She pointed out that the Nigerian equerry was said to be the first non-white person at Court since Queen Victoria, but that 'many years later people are still hoping that a post might be found for someone from her black Commonwealth, high up on her permanent staff'.[2]

In her Christmas broadcasts, the Queen often waxes lyrical about the Commonwealth. Her mild, conventional expression of 'concern' for the poorer (i.e. African, Asian, and Caribbean) nations within the Commonwealth in the 1983 broadcast was too 'progressive' for the anti-immigration MP Enoch Powell.[3] And in response to Powell, Patrick Keatley in the *Guardian* defended her broadcast and was impressed by her liberal credentials, describing her as 'Third World minded'.[4] But he did not consider the virtual exclusion of courtiers from the 'Third World' countries of the Commonwealth.

In fact, the supposedly modernized monarchy of Elizabeth II can be compared to that of her great-great-grandmother, Queen Victoria, whose name is a byword for things old-fashioned. The latter, as part of the romantic notions she held about *her* Indian Empire and the devotion in which she supposed her Indian subjects held her, appointed an Indian Muslim to the Court late in her reign. Abdul Karim (known as 'the Munshi') achieved much influence with Victoria, though this often led to conflicts between him and the ladies and gentlemen of the Household. The accusations against him as being an intriguer may be correct, but so was Victoria's accusation against her Court of 'race prejudice'.[5] Earlier still, one may recall that George I's personal secretary was Turkish (a portrait of him, dressed in the manner of an English gentleman, survives in the Royal Collection).[6]

Why, in thirty-nine years, has the Queen not made a significant black or Asian appointment?

A source close to the Queen has recently confirmed that there are at present no non-white 'Members of the Household'. The Royal Household as a whole comprises three levels. The term Members of the Household does not refer, as one might think, to everyone who works in the Household. It only covers the top level, who are sometimes described as 'courtiers'. There are nearly 400 Members of the Household, of which about fifty are full-time employees, the involvement of the remainder shading from part-time to nominal. It is not simply a question, as Longford put it, of finding a senior place in the Household for someone from the black Commonwealth. Not only is the Commonwealth multi-racial; so too is Britain. Moreover, Britain is still a country which discriminates. As a recent report of the Employment Institute concluded, greater unemployment rates for ethnic minorities than for whites 'cannot be explained by differences in levels of qualifications'. A survey of black British graduates showed they are prevented from obtaining jobs of the same level as their white counterparts.[7] The Employment Institute argues that one cannot expect real change 'without a serious assault on racial discrimination' in employment.[8]

Many of those who believe that the monarchy is there to set a good example would hope that the Queen would quietly but firmly set a multi-racial example. The Civil Service is not ideal in this respect, but at least it has got the message that something must be done. In 1990, it created a special and relatively senior post in the Cabinet Office to promote equal opportunities for ethnic minorities in the Civil Service itself. This includes working with government departments to 'attract suitable candidates of ethnic minority origin, especially at senior levels where they are currently under-represented'.[9]

Douglas Houghton had in 1971 proposed that a Department of the Crown be formed to run the monarchy. There was even a measure of sympathy for this proposal on the Tory side. If it had been implemented,

245

then all three parts of the Household would largely have come under Civil Service control. As such, there could have been at least some deferential suggestions to the Household that it open up recruitment at all levels to both non-whites and also to women. However, Houghton was rebuffed by Lord Cobbold, representing the Queen. Cobbold felt that 'the dignity of the monarchy' requires that 'the Queen is controlling her own Household'.[10]

As things stand, could the Queen not be in danger of attracting complaints of discrimination under the Race Relations Act and, as we shall see, the Sex Discrimination Act as well?*

As the diligent reader will now know, the principle of Crown immunity is said to mean that an Act of Parliament does not apply to the monarch 'unless Parliament says so either explicitly or by inevitable inference'. It did so unequivocally in the 1968 Race Relations Act (RRA), because the latter stated 'this Act binds the Crown'[11] and, from the official point of view, 'the Crown' includes the Queen, in addition to Ministers of the Crown, government departments etc. A more modern interpretation of the law, which has been argued by this author in relation to taxation, is that the Queen should generally be bound by Acts of Parliament in the modern era, even if she or the Crown is not mentioned. Yet from either point of view, the Queen was bound by the 1968 RRA, which for good measure also specified the Duchies of Cornwall and Lancaster.

In the Queen's case, enforcement of the Act would not be through the courts. By a 1947 Act (Crown Proceedings Act), the monarch can never be a defendant in 'her' own courts,[12] and no exception to this was made in the RRA. The procedure for dealing with complaints against the Queen was revealed in a Home Office document. Any allegation against her as an employer or landlord would be referred to the Home Secretary for consideration. That minister, without going to court, would have the power to 'advise' the monarch to conform to the RRA.

Of course, in the wider society there is not just discrimination on grounds of race but also against women. The Sex Discrimination Act (SDA) of 1975 at least constituted an official recognition of that fact.

* This type of legislation has not been very effective in practice. It is usually difficult to prove discrimination, and those who have been refused a job because of their race or sex will usually need to devote their energies to finding employment, rather than proving discrimination. But the Acts have some significant symbolic value in officially outlawing race and sex discrimination and defining in exact terms what constitutes discrimination.

That the Queen discriminates on grounds of sex is obvious, if only from some of the job titles. The administrative head of much of the work at the Palaces is the Master of the Household, who is assisted by a Deputy Master. These are not honorary positions, but actual jobs. (Conceivably, these positions could be filled by women, despite their titles, but this has never happened.) Also, the overall Head of the Household is always the Lord Chamberlain.

There has never been a woman in the most influential of all the jobs at Court, that of private secretary. Nor has there been a female as deputy or assistant private secretary. Similarly, there has yet to be a woman appointed as Keeper of the Privy Purse, Chief Press Secretary, Surveyor of the Queen's Pictures, Crown Equerry, Royal Librarian or to any comparable position. The list of all the Members of the Household is published annually in the *Civil Service Year Book* and in *Whitaker's Almanac*, and one can see quite easily that women are not selected for certain posts. One could envisage circumstances in which all this could have been, legally, quite embarrassing.

As with the RRA, it was intended that the SDA should cover public employment. But the clause that was inserted in the SDA was not 'this Act binds the Crown', as in the earlier RRA. Instead, we find that the Act specifies Ministers of the Crown, those holding statutory offices under the Crown, government departments and practically everything and everyone else who would come under the Crown – except for the Queen and the Duchies.

The Home Office document mentioned earlier comments on the fact that now (1975) it was illegal for the Queen to discriminate on grounds of race, but perfectly legal for her to do so on grounds of sex. A Home Office minister would need an excuse to cover this contradiction 'if the question of the comparison between the Crown application provisions [in the two measures] is raised'. The document offers two excuses.

First, 'it is constitutionally inappropriate and derogatory to Her Majesty's position to make it possible for proceedings to be brought against her in her own courts'. Yet this was not a genuine reason for exempting her from the SDA. The document acknowledges that, though covered by the RRA, the Queen could not be taken to court under that Act. In fact, a special amendment had been introduced in 1968 by the Home Office to ensure that this could never happen.[13] The SDA was similarly drafted and even if the Queen had been clearly bound by the Act, she could not have ended up in court.

Second, the Home Office argued that it was more suitable that the RRA applied to the Queen, because of its 'different enforcement arrangements'. This refers to the role of the old Race Relations Board as a clearing house for all complaints of discrimination, making it possible to hand any against the Queen to the Home Secretary. It could offer some much-needed protection to the Queen, as an intermediary body 'interposed between the courts and the complainant', whereas the SDA set up the Equal Opportunities Commission, which works on a different basis, allowing complainants to approach industrial tribunals and courts *directly* for redress of their grievances. But this argument neglects the fact that the Equal Opportunities Commission is involved as an intermediary in many sex-discrimination complaints. And in any case, it would hardly be difficult to devise a procedure to replicate the one applicable under the 1968 RRA, whereby any sex-discrimination complaints could be dealt with by the Home Secretary.

The difference between the SDA and the RRA would seem to have more to do with protecting the Queen from any embarrassment. The SDA raised the problem of the greater obviousness of discrimination on grounds of sex in the Royal Household, which is highlighted by several male job titles and the personnel listings in the *Civil Service Year Book* and *Whitaker's Almanac*. Perhaps also there was the general desire to repulse any further legislation which might interfere with the Queen's control of her household.

It will be remembered that the Queen does not simply react to legislative proposals, like those concerning sex discrimination, after they are published. As Sir Geoffrey Howe told the Commons in 1973, there is a mechanism which allows the Queen to push for changes in proposed legislation before it reaches a final form to be put before Parliament. Howe was referring to the Companies Bill of 1973, which could have made the Queen's shareholdings public, but his description obviously applies more generally: 'The advisers of the Queen, as they do as a matter of routine, examined the [Companies] Bill to see whether it contained inadvertently or otherwise, any curtailment of the Royal Prerogative.'[14] Or perhaps the problem with the SDA was spotted at an earlier stage, inside the Home Office, the responsible ministry.

For a brief period after the 1975 SDA, the Queen was still covered by the 1968 RRA. As we have seen, this inconsistency would be very difficult to justify if anyone had asked about it, but the Home Office soon had an opportunity to resolve the matter, in a new RRA passed in 1976. Then the SDA clause concerning the Crown was inserted. Thus the new RRA did not cover the Queen, but practically every other part of 'the Crown'. As with the tax exemption and the anonymity of her shareholdings, the Queen maintains her privileges, if indeed the right to maintain discriminatory practices is a privilege. It is certainly difficult to fit it into the image of the modernizing monarchy, ever adapting to changing circumstances.

Of course, some may try to justify the social composition of the Court in terms of its tradition, which should not be eroded by too much modernization. It is simply recruiting Members of the Household in the same way as it always has done. However, it would be impolitic for the monarchy to mount such a defence. What both Gordon Franklin, the personnel officer, and Charles Anson, the Press Secretary, told me is that the Royal Household is an equal opportunities employer, which operates an equal opportunities programme.[15] Now, the aim of any such programme is firstly to identify any imbalance in recruitment on sex, racial or other grounds such as physical disability. Once identified, recruitment and promotion should be organized to ensure the elimination of any practices which discriminate, even if they did so without conscious intent. The tendency for the Queen to recruit Members of the Household so heavily from the aristocracy, the diplomatic service and the officer class, particularly the Household Regiments, is just such a practice. One does not expect an institution based on birth readily to come to terms with an equal opportunities programme. But the unwillingness to change seems little short of arrogance.

Most Members of the Household are not employees in the strict sense, and therefore the reference to legislation and equal opportunities is not directly relevant in their cases. But the same general principles apply. For instance, the job of the ten Gentleman Ushers, and the greater number of 'Extra' (or reserve) Gentleman Ushers, is to make sure on various occasions when large numbers of guests arrive at the Palace that they do not get lost. They perform this task on an occasional basis. But there is no reason why there should not be 'Lady' Ushers, even if the usual requirement, that they should be former military officers, is maintained.

Below the all-white Members of the Household in the Palace hierarchy are the officials (lower-level administrators and clerks.) Royal-watcher Andrew Morton's assessment in 1990 was that there had never been an official who was not white.[16] Below the officials and clerks come the staff who are the largest category, comprising footmen, housemaids, chefs, chauffeurs, those who look after the horses and carriages etc. When I spoke to Mr Franklin, he told me that there are some non-white employees in the Royal Household, paid from the Civil List. He had a record of how many, but he did not feel it proper to tell me. It would seem safe to assume that there are not many. There was a young black female secretary employed in the early 1980s in Prince Charles's office at the Palace, but she did not stay long. Stephen Barry, Charles's valet for eleven years, stated in 1985 that since she left, 'you never see a black face'.[17] John Barratt was private secretary to Lord Mountbatten from 1965 to 1979 and to Prince and Princess Michael of Kent, 1981–83. He records that 'although members of the royal family would pledge themselves as non-racist, there were no black faces among the staff at Buckingham Palace in my day.'[18] In the late 1980s, there was one black footman and no more than a few others. Morton claimed that the position of ethnic minorities 'in the palace hierarchy is symbolised by the fact that the job of serving coffee to the royal servants is performed by West Indian women.'

Two job adverts for staff grade appointments at the Palace were discovered by the press in the late 1980s. One was for a footman/valet placed with the Job Centre in King's Lynn, Norfolk, a few miles from Sandringham. Another for various staff jobs at the Palace was displayed at another Job Centre, in Truro in Cornwall.[19] Both are areas where there are hardly any black people. One is not suggesting that a black person becoming a footman or a valet, especially at the wages on offer, would constitute an advance for black people in this country. But that is no reason why the choice should not be available to them.

At Balmoral in 1988, the Balmoral Estate looked to members of the Commonwealth staying in London to help out in the refreshment room and souvenir shop. An advert appeared in *New Zealand News (UK)*, a free London paper for Antipodeans in London.[20] When I rang up Balmoral in 1989 to enquire about some matter, expecting to hear a Scottish voice on the other end, I was somewhat startled to hear a cheery 'down-under' accent from remote rural Scotland. If the Queen's Estate could not recruit locally, why could there not just as easily be a policy of recruiting some employees from the black Commonwealth?

Thanks to Crown immunity, the Race Relations Act no longer applies to the Royal Household. This immunity, perhaps, is also needed to save the Queen, as head of the multi-racial Commonwealth and a multi-racial Britain, from infringing the Trade Descriptions Act.

Notes and References

The following collections of unpublished papers are referred to in the notes below:

Asquith Papers, Bodleian Library, Oxford
Balfour Papers, British Library
Crown Estate Papers, Public Record Office, Chancery Lane
Dalton Papers, British Library of Political and Economic Science
J. C. C. Davidson Papers, House of Lords Record Office
Dilke Papers, British Library
Gladstone Papers, British Library
Gerald S. Graham Papers, Queen's University Archives, Kingston, Ontario
Sir Edward Hamilton, Papers, British Library
Sir William Harcourt Papers, Bodleian Library, Oxford
Hicks-Beach Papers, Gloucester Records Office
Hopkins Papers, Public Record Office, Kew
Marquess of Lincolnshire Papers, Diaries, Bodleian Library, Oxford
Lloyd George Papers, House of Lords Record Office
MacDonald Papers, Public Record Office, Kew.
Monckton Papers, Bodleian Library, Oxford
Russell Papers, Public Record Office, Kew
Sandars Papers, Bodleian Library, Oxford
Treasury Papers, Public Record Office, Kew

Introduction

1 *The Monarchy in Sweden* (Swedish Institute, 1986); Meirion and

253

Susie Harries, *Sheathing the Sword: The Demilitarisation of Japan* (Hamilton, 1987), p. 82; David Yallop, *In God's Name* (Corgi, 1985), pp. 150–56.

2 NMR asked: do you 'agree or disagree' that 'the Queen should pay income tax on income generated by her wealth? for the *Independent on Sunday* (24 February 1991). See also *Sunday Times*, 21 January 1990.

3 *Daily Mirror*, 27 July 1989.

4 Treasury Papers, T160/631/F14542 (PRO), Memorandum, 7 March 1936.

5 *Hansard*, 9 May 1901, col. 1202.

6 *New Statesman*, 28 May 1971.

7 Ibid., 10 December 1971.

8 Walter Bagehot, *The English Constitution* (Fontana, 1963), p. 95.

9 Ibid.

10 See Chapter 7.

11 *Guardian*, 5 April 1990.

12 Information provided by Embassy of German Federal Republic in 1987. Allowance is made for inflation since 1987.

13 *The Times*, 16 January 1987.

14 Inland Revenue Statistics (1989), Tables 1.1 and 1.4.

15 Annual Report, Save the Children Fund (1988/9).

1: William III to Victoria

1 Christopher Hill, *Reformation to Industrial Revolution* (Weidenfeld & Nicolson, 1967), p. 15.

2 Paul Einzig, *The Control of the Purse* (Secker & Warburg, 1959), p. 132.

3 E. A. Reitan, 'From Revenue to Civil List, 1689–1702: The Revolution Settlement and the "Mixed and Balanced" Constitution', *The Historical Journal*, xiii (1971), p. 572.

4 Some of the Hereditary Revenues such as beer duties were voted by Parliament in 1660 to compensate for the abolition of military tenures.

5 E. A. Reitan, 'The Civil List in Eighteenth-Century British Politics: Parliamentary Supremacy versus the Independence of the Crown', *The Historical Journal*, ix (1966), pp. 318–37.

6 Treasury Papers, T171/331 (PRO), 'Civil List Historical Note'.

7 Willie Hamilton in *My Queen and I* (Quartet, 1975), p. 32, compounds a number of errors in his history of the Civil List. He and many other authors believe that George III in 1760 received the first modern form of the Civil List, which was no longer responsible for civilian government expenditure, whereas in fact, for the first decades of that King's reign, the bulk of civil expenditure was met from the Civil List. Hamilton also makes other important factual errors in this and other contexts and it is to be regretted that the book has to be read with a degree of caution. In spite of this it was, in 1975, something of an eye-opener.

8 Roger Fulford, *The Prince Consort* (Macmillan, 1949), p. 70.

9 See George III's message to the House of Commons, *Hansard's Parliamentary Debates*, 1800–01, xxxv, col. 386, and the actual debates, cols 387–90.

10 The preamble to the Act (c. 88) refers to his having bought land privately.

11 Russell Papers, PRO 30/22 8c.

12 Tyler Whittle, *Victoria & Albert at Home* (Routledge & Kegan Paul, 1980), p. 12.

13 Philip Magnus, *King Edward VII* (Penguin, 1967), p. 358. Figure of £200,000 from Robert Rhodes James, *Albert Prince Consort* (Hamish Hamilton, 1985), p. 143.

14 Ronald W. Clark, *Balmoral – Queen Victoria's Highland Home* (Thames & Hudson, 1981), p. 29; see also Rhodes James, op. cit., p. 183.

15 Suzy Menkes, *The Royal Jewels* (Grafton, 1985), p. 11.

16 Elizabeth Longford, *Victoria R I* (Pan, 1966), pp. 286, 486, gives the lower figure of a quarter of a million. It is the editors of Victoria's correspondence who give the figure of half a million pounds. See A. C. Benson and Viscount Esher, ed., *The Letters of Queen Victoria*, first series, ii (John Murray, 1907), p. 475n. Because Esher was a royal insider privy to most royal secrets his figure is preferred.

17 Thea Holme, *Chelsea* (Hamish Hamilton, 1972), p. 115. Some authors have spelt his name Nield, but in his will it is spelt Neild.

18 Benson and Esher, op. cit., ii, p. 475.

19 The Balmoral Estates Act, which confirmed the legality of the purchase, was dated 17 June 1852.

20 David Duff, *Whisper Louise* (Frederick Muller, 1974), p. 57; see also Tyler Whittle, op. cit., pp. 8–12.

21 Duff, op. cit., pp. 58–9.

22 Clark, op. cit., pp. 59–60. Victoria also managed to restrict railway development along the boundaries of her estate; see ibid., p. 82.

23 Ibid., p. 44.

24 Ibid., p. 46.

25 Albert to Mr Gladstone, 18 July 1853, in Philip Guedella, ed., *The Queen and Mr Gladstone*, i (Hodder & Stoughton, 1933), p. 104.

26 Gladstone Papers, Add. Ms. 44280, 24 July 1862.

27 T1/16155/8735 (PRO).

28 Lytton Strachey, *Queen Victoria* (Penguin, 1971), p. 200.

29 Longford, op. cit., p. 479.

30 Magnus, op. cit., p. 272.

31 Gladstone Papers, Add. Ms. 44301, Lowe to Gladstone, 29 November 1871. The figure of £509,000 saved is from the same reference; a Cabinet memorandum, Add. Ms. 44617, gives a higher figure, of £573,554.

32 Speech at Newcastle on 6 November 1871, printed as *Cost of the Crown*, p. 7. The inadequate evidence was from a pamphlet of the Liverpool Financial Reform Association. Its secretary had written to the Treasury for details of the Queen's tax-paying. The Treasury had brushed him off with a 'no comment' reply and he wrongly concluded she did not pay.

33 Gladstone Papers, Add. Ms. 44301, Gladstone to Lowe, 25 November 1871; Gladstone Papers, Add. MS. 44541, Gladstone to Lord Granville, 1 December 1871.

34 Gladstone Papers, Add. Ms. 44301, Lowe to Gladstone, 25 and 29 November 1871.

35 Victoria to Gladstone, 19 November 1871, Guedella, ed., op. cit., p. 309. Andrew Morton is therefore wrong to state that Gladstone 'was forced to remind her that she did escape this unpopular tax' in *Theirs is the Kingdom* (Michael O'Mara, 1989), p. 50.

36 Cited in Dilke Papers, Add. Ms. 43943.

37 Victoria's private secretary to Gladstone, 7 December 1871, Guedella, ed., op. cit., p. 315.

38 Dilke Papers, op. cit.

39 'Civil List Notes' in T250/2, pp. 68–73, 96–8 (PRO).

40 On the relationship of Crown immunity to the Royal Prerogative, see note 45, below.

41 According to Harry Street, *Government Liability* (Cambridge University Press), Chapter 6, this rule has come to be applied more strictly, especially since 1870. Between the mid-sixteenth century and the early eighteenth, the Crown was occasionally held by the Courts to be bound by statutes, even when not named in them.

42 H. A. L. Fisher, ed., *The Collected Papers of F. W. Maitland*, iii (Cambridge University Press, 1911), p. 257.

43 Ibid., p. 258.

44 [1978] AC 359.

45 Report from the Select Committee on the Civil List, 1971–2 (29), xxiv, Appendix 12. However, Sir William Wade states that Crown immunity 'has nothing to do with the Royal Prerogative'. Instead he describes it as a 'long-standing rule' for interpreting statutes. This does not greatly affect the case made in this chapter, as one is still talking of the 'rights' of the Crown. If anything it strengthens the chapter's argument by not seeing Crown immunity as deriving from royal power, but from another source, the Common Law. In any case Wade concedes that, in certain important legal cases involving the Crown and taxation, ' "prerogative" is sometimes used in a loose sense' to suggest that Crown immunity from taxation is part of the Royal Prerogative (*Administrative Law*, Clarendon Press, 6th edn, 1988, p. 827). Another authority takes a middling view, that Crown immunity is 'in its origin a prerogative immunity [but] can also be formulated as a particular rule of statutory interpretation'; see Stanley de Smith and Rodney Brazier, *Constitutional and Administrative Law*, 6th edn (Penguin, 1989), p. 134.

2: Edward VII, 1901–10

1 Select Committee on Public Monies, pp. 119–20, Parliamentary Papers, 1856, xv, 5.

2 Hamilton Diaries, 9 May 1901.

3 A. C. Benson and Viscount Esher, ed., *The Letters of Queen Victoria*, first series, i (John Murray, 1907), pp. 486–7.

4 This author shares many of Tam Nairn's doubts about ever being

able to pin down what is or is not a convention. See his *The Enchanted Glass* (Radius, 1988), p. 362.

5 'Civil List Notes', p. 29, in T168/52 (PRO).

6 Philip Magnus, *King Edward VII* (Penguin, 1967), p. 357.

7 Hamilton Diaries, 3 and 4 March 1901.

8 Dudley W. R. Bahlman, *The Diary of Sir Edward Walter Hamilton, 1880–85*, i (Clarendon Press, Oxford, 1972), p. xv.

9 Hamilton Diaries, 30 January 1901.

10 Ibid., 10 February 1901.

11 Ibid., 25 September 1905.

12 Ibid., 13 February 1901.

13 Ibid., 14 February 1901.

14 Hicks-Beach Papers, PCC/71, Sir Michael Hicks-Beach to the King, 19 February 1901.

15 Ibid., Knollys (Edward VII's private secretary) to Hicks-Beach, 20 February 1901.

16 Ibid., Knollys to Hicks-Beach, 8 May and 11 June 1901.

17 Balfour Papers, Add. Ms. 49691, Balfour to Lord Salisbury, 26 January 1901. Hamilton Diaries, 30 May, 6 and 11 June 1901.

18 Hicks-Beach Papers, op. cit., Knollys to Hicks-Beach, 11 June 1901.

19 Sandars Papers, c. 718, Knollys to Lord Salisbury, 15 June 1901.

20 Balfour Papers, op. cit., Lord Salisbury to Balfour, 4 July (?) 1901.

21 Harcourt Papers, Knollys to Harcourt, 18 July 1901.

22 Sandars Papers, op. cit., Knollys to Lord Salisbury, 15 June 1901.

23 Asquith Papers, vol. 94, *f*162, memorandum, 8 May 1910.

24 Hicks-Beach Papers, op. cit., dictated by the King to Hicks-Beach, 21 March 1901.

25 Hamilton Diaries, 19 February 1901.

26 *Hansard*, 9 May 1901, col. 1202.

27 Hamilton Diaries, 9 January 1904; also Knollys to Hamilton, 14 January 1904, Add. Ms. 48606.

28 Hamilton Diaries, 29 April and 15 June 1904.

29 Ibid., 15 March 1901.

30 T168/71 (PRO).

31 Hamilton Diaries, 28 and 29 January, 2 February 1905; also Balfour Papers, Add. Ms. 49763, Sandars to Balfour, 21 January 1905.

32 Hamilton Diaries, 29 January 1905.

33 Magnus, op. cit., p. 357.

34 Hamilton Diaries, 15 and 24 June 1904.

35 Paul Ferris, *The House of Northcliffe* (Weidenfeld & Nicolson, 1971), pp. 122–5.

36 *The Cecil King Diary, 1970–74* (Jonathan Cape, 1975), 16 February 1974.

37 Geoffrey Harmsworth and Reginald Pound, *Northcliffe* (Cassell, 1959), p. 295.

38 Balfour Papers, Add. Ms. 49683, Edward VII to Balfour, 25 December 1903.

39 Balfour Papers, Add. Ms. 49685, letter of 4 December (?) 1905; see also G. R. Searle, *Corruption in British Politics, 1895–1930* (Clarendon Press, Oxford, 1987), pp. 93–4.

40 Hamilton Diaries, 2 February 1905.

41 Gordon Brook-Shepherd, *Uncle of Europe* (Collins, 1975), p. 139.

42 Balfour Papers, Add. Ms. 49683, Knollys to Sandars, 24 June 1903.

43 Bahlman, op. cit., i, p. 128.

44 Magnus, op. cit., p. 303. See also Stanley Jackson, *The Sassoons* (Heinemann, 1968), p. 86 etc.

45 Balfour Papers, Add. Ms. 49683, Knollys to Balfour, 21 November 1903.

46 Paul Foot, *Race and Immigration in British Politics* (Penguin, 1965), p. 91.

47 Ibid.

48 Magnus, op. cit., p. 306.

49 *The Times*, 12 January 1907.

50 Lincolnshire Diaries, 3 February 1907. Carington (later Marquess of Lincolnshire) as quoted here differs from how he is cited in Magnus's biography, p. 477. Magnus has added various bits to the original diary, which makes Carington sound more damning still about the affair.

51 Magnus, op. cit., p. 357.

52 Brook-Shepherd, op. cit., p. 132. Morton, op. cit., also quotes from the Cassel Papers.

53 Jamie Caplin, *The Rise of the Plutocrats: Wealth and Power in Edwardian England* (Constable, 1978), pp. 207–8.

54 *Daily Telegraph*, 10 June 1971.

55 Wigram Diaries, quoted in Francis Watson, 'The Death of George V', *History Today* (December 1986).
56 Edward David, ed., *Inside Asquith's Cabinet, From the Diaries of Charles Hobhouse* (John Murray, 1977), 30 June 1910.

3: George V, 1910–36

1 Civil List Act, 1910.
2 Report from the Select Committee on the Civil List, 1935–6 (74) v.719.
3 Maurice Bruce, *The Coming of the Welfare State*, 4th edn (Batsford, 1968), p. 179.
4 Skilled worker: Department of Employment, *British Labour Statistics* (HMSO, 1971), Tables 1 and 36; Sandringham labourer: Marquess of Lincolnshire Diaries, 4 December 1913 (Bodleian Library).
5 Asquith Papers, vol. 94, *f*162, Treasury memorandum, 8 May 1910.
6 Ibid.
7 *Hansard*, 22 July 1910, cols 1622–3.
8 'Civil List Notes', T250/2 (PRO).
9 Sandars Papers, memorandum, 10 May 1901. c. 718.
10 Asquith Papers, vol. 94, 8 May 1910.
11 Bruce K. Murray, *The People's Budget 1909–10* (Clarendon Press, Oxford, 1980).
12 Letter of 17 February 1916, T172/396 (PRO).
13 Ibid., Sir Frederick Ponsonby to Reginald McKenna, 2 March 1916.
14 Asquith Papers, vol. 4, Ponsonby to Asquith, 10 March 1916.
15 All figures for savings from the Civil List during George V's reign come from the 1936 Civil List Select Committee Report.
16 Sir John Wilson, Bt, *The Royal Philatelic Collection* (Dropmore Press, 1952), pp. 19–20, 24–5.
17 Lloyd George Papers, F/31/1/50, 20 November 1920.
18 Hamilton Diaries, February 1901.
19 Wilson, op. cit., p. 12.
20 Watson, op. cit., p. 30. Willie Hamilton, op. cit., also fails to mention the phenomenon of Civil List savings, which is surprising given the author's concentration on information in Parliamentary Papers and the fact that data on these savings are to be found in Select Committee Reports on the Civil List.
21 Lloyd George Papers, F/31/1/50, memorandum, 13 January 1921.

22 Ibid., 20 November 1920.

23 Menkes, op. cit., p. 80.

24 *Hansard*, 10 August 1921, col. 604.

25 T160/284/F.12544 (PRO).

26 M. M. Reese, *The Royal Office of Master of the Horse* (Threshold Books, 1976), p. 302.

27 Gladstone Papers, Loan 73/28, Prince Albert to Gladstone, 28 May 1854.

28 Gabriel Tschumi, *Royal Chef* (William Kimber, 1954), pp. 134, 137.

29 T160/701/F.5227 (PRO).

30 Watson, op. cit., p. 30.

31 Walter Guinness to Sir Warren Fisher, 19 November 1925, T161/258/ S.28132 (PRO).

32 Hamilton Diaries, 15 June 1904.

33 *Hansard*, Lords debates, 22 February 1884.

34 Royal Commission on the Housing of the Working Classes, 1884–5, vol. 30, pp. 588–96.

35 Lincolnshire Diaries, 4 December 1913. The figure of sixty labourers is given in the local press in 1923. If anything, there would have been more in 1913.

36 Ibid., 29 November 1913.

37 Ibid., 4 December 1913.

38 Reg Groves, *Sharpen the Sickle! The History of the Farmworkers' Union* (Porcupine Press, 1949), p. 145.

39 Alun Howkins, *Poor Labouring Men* (Routledge & Kegan Paul, 1985), p. 114.

40 Groves, op. cit., p. 144.

41 Lincolnshire Diaries, 26 February 1914. I am indebted to Kenneth Rose's *King George V* (Papermac, 1984) for the reference to the Lincolnshire Diaries. However, his account on pp. 100–1 could be taken to mean that there was a strike on the King's Home Farms, which there was not. The strikes on the Sandringham estate affected only his tenants.

42 *Norwich Mercury*, 25 January 1919.

43 Duke of Windsor, *A King's Story* (Pan, 1957), p. 283.

44 Groves, op. cit., pp. 172–7; see also G. D. H. Cole, *The British Working Class Movement 1789–1947* (Allen & Unwin, 1947), pp. 364, 403.

45 Groves, op. cit., pp. 176–7.
46 *Norfolk News and Weekly Press*, 31 March 1923.
47 Ibid.
48 *Norfolk Chronicle*, 13 April 1923.
49 Howkins, op. cit., pp. 172–4.
50 John Ramsden, ed., *Real Old Tory Politics: The Political Diaries of Sir Robert Sanders, Lord Bayford 1910–35* (Historians Press, 1984), 15 April 1923.
51 Groves, op. cit., p. 208.
52 William Burkitt, 'His Majesty the King as Farmer and Stockbreeder', *Transactions of The Highland Agricultural Society of Scotland* (1931), p. 10.

4: From Tax-payers to Tax-avoiders

1 T171/338 (PRO).
2 Gladstone Papers, Add. Ms. 44301, Lowe to Gladstone, 25 November 1871. *Re* Alice, see index of T108/3 (PRO), under 'Royal Family', no. 3269.
3 Lloyd George Papers, F/29/4, Lord Stamfordham to Lloyd George, 26 May 1920.
4 T171/338 (PRO).
5 David, ed., op. cit., 30 June 1910.
6 Georgina Battiscombe, *Queen Alexandra* (Sphere, 1972), p. 293.
7 Minute of Sir Robert Horne, Chancellor of the Exchequer, 3 August 1922, T171/331 (PRO).
8 Duchy of Cornwall Accounts, Parliamentary Papers.
9 Willie Hamilton, op. cit., pp. 217–18.
10 Report from the Select Committee on the Civil List, 1971–2 (29), xxiv, p. 45.
11 Willie Hamilton, op. cit., pp. 217–18.
12 'Taxation Questions', in T171/338 (PRO).
13 8 & 9 Geo. 5, c.40, Schedule A, Rule no. viii, 1 and 4.
14 Monckton Trustees Deposit 74, *ff.* 245–51 (Bodleian Library).
15 With no royal beneficiary, it was not considered necessary to extend this arrangement to the Crown Lands. See H. E. Davies of the Treasury to S. E. Minnis of the Inland Revenue, 7 July 1926, in T161/226 S.29642 (PRO).

16 'Taxation Questions', T171/338 (PRO).

17 Duchy of Cornwall accounts. For amounts withdrawn by the Prince, see Select Committee on Civil List, 1935–36(74) v.719, p. 39.

18 2 April 1936, T171/331 (PRO).

19 Voluntary contributions for fifteen years were £300,000. Net revenues for 1921–35 were £1,337,363, which has been calculated from the accounts. He would have been taxed on this figure, not the slightly lower total of the amounts he withdrew from the Duchy.

20 'Taxation Questions', T171/338 (PRO).

21 These accounts are at the House of Lords Record Office.

22 1 & 2 Vic., c. 101.

23 2 April 1936, T171/331 (PRO). Also, an examination of the accounts of 1921 compared to 1920, and of 1935 with 1936, when the voluntary contribution stopped, bears this out.

24 Andrew Duncan, *The Reality of Monarchy* (Heinemann, 1970), p. 180.

25 Willie Hamilton, op. cit., p. 240.

26 *Southwark Labour News*, August and September 1921. Frances Donaldson in her *Edward VIII* (Futura, 1976), p. 65, was far too keen to find that the Prince, soon after the First World War, became an ideal landlord. For instance, she says the Lambeth 'Labour Council presently declared him to be one of the best landlords in the country'. But there was not a Labour council elected in Lambeth until 1937. Nor, as far as one can gather, did the non-Labour councils heap praise upon the Prince.

27 Rose, op. cit., p. 379.

28 Kenneth Young, ed., *The Diaries and Letters of Sir Robert Bruce Lockhart*, i: *1915–38* (Macmillan, 1973), 8 October 1931.

29 MacDonald Papers, 30/69, 1314, PRO, MacDonald to Ponsonby, 5 September 1931.

30 Tschumi, op. cit., says he and about a hundred royal servants were made redundant in 1932 as part of the economy drive. But his memory is probably faulty here and the number pensioned off must have been far fewer. Were he right, the figures for staff pay in 1932 and 1933 would have dipped much more appreciably than they did.

31 Select Committee on Civil List, 1935–36(74) v.719.

32 'Taxation Questions', T171/338 (PRO).

33 Davidson Papers, Sir Ralph Harwood to Davidson, 23 March 1933.

34 Sir Robert Somerville, *History of the Duchy of Lancaster*, ii (Duchy of Lancaster, 1970), p. 444.
35 'Taxation Questions', T171/338 (PRO).
36 as note 32.
37 Menkes, op. cit., p. 53.

5: George V to George VI

1 'Taxation Questions', 1936, T171/331 (PRO).
2 *Bankers' Magazine*, October 1927, p. 461.
3 T160/429/F12276/01 (PRO).
4 Somerville, op. cit., ii, p. 461.
5 There has also been a clause written into income-tax legislation since its inception. This laid down that the Crown was exempt from taxation normally deducted at source 'in respect of the stock or dividends belonging to the Crown, in whatever name they may stand in the books of the Bank of England'. This is clearly a provision to stop the government taxing itself. This seems an extra safeguard on top of Crown immunity. None of the Treasury reports or other evidence, when arguing for the monarch's Crown immunity, ever refers to this provision.
6 Other royals were, however, liable (see T1/11999/33404 (PRO)), although after 1922 their surtax liability was greatly reduced by the automatic 80 per cent tax allowance.
7 John Gore, *King George V: A Personal Memoir* (Murray, 1941); see also Sir Harold Nicolson, *King George V: His Life and Reign* (Constable, 1952), p. 455n.
8 Graham Papers, Box 1, Collection 2170, Folders 10 and 16. These papers consist of a long essay by Peacock on his life, notes of Graham's interviews with Peacock, and other material, collected for a planned biography of Peacock.
9 Philip Ziegler, *The Sixth Great Power: Barings 1762–1929* (Collins, 1988), p. 358.
10 John Orbell, article on Peacock, *Dictionary of Business Biography*, iv (1985).
11 Graham Papers, op. cit., Folder 16.
12 Graham Papers, op. cit., Folder 10, interview with Lord Monckton.
13 Graham Papers, op. cit., Folder 16.

14 John Orbell, *Baring Brothers & Co. Ltd: A History to 1939* (Baring Brothers, 1985), pp. 82–3. Peacock was active for a charity for which the Prince of Wales was patron. But at that time his involvement was of less than two years' duration and not the type of work to earn so 'elevated' an honour as a GCVO (Knight Grand Cross of the Victorian Order).

15 Graham Papers, op. cit., Folder 16.

16 Philip Williamson, *The Formation of the National Government: British Politics 1929–31* (Cambridge University Ph.D, no. 14673), p. 411. See also his *National Crisis and National Government: British Politics, the Economy and Empire 1926–32* (Cambridge University Press).

17 Keith Middlemas and John Barnes, *Baldwin: A Biography* (Weidenfeld & Nicolson, 1969), p. 626.

18 Graham Papers, op. cit., Folder 16.

19 Ibid.

20 Obituary of Greig, *The Times*, 2 March 1953.

21 Watson, op. cit., p. 30.

22 Michael Bloch, *The Secret File of the Duke of Windsor* (Bantam Press, 1988), p. 46.

23 Philip Ziegler, *King Edward VIII* (Collins, 1990), pp. 246–7. John Colville, the Queen's private secretary before she came to the throne, gave a figure of £2 million split between the three younger brothers (*Daily Telegraph*, 10 June 1971).

24 Bloch, op. cit., p. 46.

25 Winston Churchill mentions a figure between £800,000 and £950,000; see Martin Gilbert, *Winston S. Churchill*, v, Companion vol. iii (Heinemann, 1982), p. 634. Two estimates mentioned in Ziegler, *Edward VIII*, p. 326, give £1.1 million.

26 28 April 1936, T171/331 (PRO).

27 How to answer possible Labour questions on savings from the Civil List was considered in 'Civil List Bill: Notes on Resolutions', Appendix E, p. 25, in T171/329 and also in T160/631/F14542 (PRO). Similarly, Mr Fellowes, the Secretary of the Select Committee, Fraser of the Treasury and Harwood for the King considered how to explain the large increase in money withdrawn by the King from the Duchy of Lancaster, without mentioning it had anything to do with the removal of income tax (T171/338).

28 Dalton Diaries (unpublished), 1 October 1931.

29 Memorandum of 12 March 1936, T171/331 (PRO).

30 Graham Papers, op. cit., Folder 16.

31 Ziegler, *Edward VIII*, p. 263. Somerville, op. cit., ii, p. 469.

32 Robert Rhodes James in his book on Davidson, *Memoirs of a Conservative* (Weidenfeld & Nicolson, 1969), pp. 412–13, refers to 'one incident' in 1936, concerning the Duchy, which had 'rather dismayed Davidson' about Edward VIII. These unseemly demands for money could well be the incident in question.

33 T171/331 (PRO).

34 T171/338 (PRO).

35 T171/329 (PRO). It seems that the food bill, which had been massively cut from £50,000 to £20,000, had climbed back up and been cut again. Sir Ralph Harwood, the Financial Secretary to the King, informed the latter in April 1936 that the cost of food had been reduced from £45,000 a year to £13,500 (Ziegler, *Edward VIII*, p. 260). Given the fall in prices, £45,000 was a much larger sum in 1936 than £50,000 was in 1921. Perhaps the pilfering that Harwood had helped root out fifteen years earlier had returned.

36 Middlemas and Barnes, op. cit., p. 978. J. Bryan III and Charles J. V. Murphy, in *The Windsor Story* (Granada, 1981), p. 664, say an across the board 10 per cent cut. See also F. J. Corbitt, *Fit For A King* (Odhams Press, 1956), p. 197.

37 Select Committee Report on the Civil List, 1936–7 (114), vi, p. 12; and Select Committee Report, 1951–2 (224), v, p. 13.

38 Frances Donaldson, *Edward VIII* (Futura, 1978), p. 186.

39 Ziegler, *Edward VIII*, pp. 376, 325. See also Bloch, op. cit., Ch. 2 especially.

40 Bloch, op. cit., p. 50.

41 Watson, op. cit., p. 30.

42 John Wheeler-Bennett, *King George VI: His Life and Reign* (Macmillan, 1958), p. 287.

43 Bloch, op. cit., pp. 45–6.

44 Ibid., pp. 49–50.

45 Graham Papers, op. cit., Folder 10. See also Ziegler, *Edward VIII*, p. 350, and Bloch, op. cit., pp. 44, 48.

46 Sarah Bradford, *George VI* (Fontana, 1991), p. 310.

47 Churchill to Lloyd George, 8 April 1937, in Gilbert, op. cit., v, companion vol. iii, p. 643.

48 Bradford, op. cit., p. 310.

49 Bloch, op. cit., p. 50.
50 Ziegler, *Edward VIII*, p. 350.
51 Bloch, op. cit., p. 51.
52 Ibid., p. 59.
53 Ibid., p. 58.
54 Ibid., p. 43.
55 Ziegler, *Edward VIII*, p. 327.
56 Bloch, op. cit., pp. 29–31.
57 William Gerhardie, *God's Fifth Column* (Hodder & Stoughton, 1981), p. 310.
58 Slee of Inland Revenue to Harwood, 19 January 1937. Copy in Hopkins Papers, T175/92, Part 2.
59 'Taxation Questions', T171/338 (PRO).
60 T160/763/F14755 (PRO).
61 *Hansard*, Written Answers, 20 June 1991, col. 313.
62 *Hansard*, 9 July 1952, col. 1430.
63 Graham Papers, op. cit., Folder 10.
64 24 March 1937, in Gilbert, op. cit., v, companion vol. iii.
65 Bloch, op. cit., p. 65.
66 Bryan and Murphy, op. cit., pp. 466, 642.
67 Bloch, op. cit., pp. 220, 227, 233, 246.
68 Ibid., p. 226.
69 Humphrey Jennings and Charles Madge, ed., *May 12 1937* (Faber & Faber, 1987), p. 34.
70 Hugh Cudlippe, *Publish and Be Damned* (Weidenfeld & Nicolson, 1953), p. 105.
71 Select Committee Report on the Civil List, 1951–2 (224), v.
72 T160/881/F16210 (PRO).
73 Corbitt, op. cit., p. 68.
74 Charles Stuart, ed., *The Reith Diaries* (Collins, 1975), 9 July 1941.
75 Leslie Field, *The Queen's Jewels: The Personal Collections of Elizabeth II* (Weidenfeld & Nicolson, 1987), p. 155.
76 Ibid., p. 157.
77 Dalton Diaries (unpublished), 18 October 1947, and Select Committee Report on Civil List, 1947–8 (18), vi.
78 Graham Papers, op. cit., Folder 16.
79 Ron Chernow, *The House of Morgan: The Secret History of Money and Power* (Simon & Schuster, 1990), pp. 551–2.

80 Dalton Papers 9/3, *ff.* 58–9, Dalton's Minute for Prime Minister, 27 October 1947.

81 Ibid.

82 *Hansard*, 17 December 1947, col. 1721.

83 Philip Williams, *Hugh Gaitskell* (Jonathan Cape, 1979), p. 251.

84 The evidence to the 1971 Select Committee, from the Deputy Treasurer to the Queen, states that 'all the Queen's clothes are borne from the Privy Purse'. This official did, however, argue that much of this expenditure was on account of official duties (para. 27).

85 Ben Pimlott, ed., *Political Diary of Hugh Dalton 1918–40, 1945–60* (Cape and LSE, 1986), 20 October 1947.

86 Tschumi, op. cit., pp. 168–9, and others. Civil Service Union evidence to Select Committee on Civil List, 1971, referred to difficulties in getting staff of 'right calibre'. John Dean, in *HRH Prince Philip, Duke of Edinburgh: A Portrait by His Valet* (Robert Hale, 1954), pp. 64, 167–9, complained about the low pay at Buckingham Palace.

87 Select Committee Report on Civil List, 1951–2 (224), v.

88 Report from the Select Committee on the Civil List, 1971–2 (29), xxiv, pp. 79, 82–3, 165.

89 Dean, op. cit., p. 65.

90 Select Committee Report on Civil List, 1951–2 (224), v, p. 13.

91 CREST 36/63 (PRO).

6: The Queen's Civil List, 1952–71

1 *Daily Telegraph*, 27 June and 5 July 1991.

2 *The Times*, 27 February 1991.

3 For example, Sir Charles Petrie, *The Modern British Monarchy* (Eyre & Spottiswoode, 1961), p. 211.

4 Consolidated Fund, Supplementary Statement, December 1990.

5 *The Economist*, 4 December 1971.

6 *Today*, 26 July 1990.

7 Hicks-Beach Papers, PCC/73.

8 Penny Junor, *Charles* (Sidgwick & Jackson, 1987), p. 5. The Prince greatly underestimated the income of the Crown Estate at £4 million p.a. Ms Junor thought he was referring to the profits of Balmoral and Sandringham, but this would appear unlikely in this context.

9 *Daily Telegraph*, 18 February 1991. The editorial also suggested

that the present monarch could reclaim the Crown Estate. But even in the most formal interpretation of the Queen's rights, this is ruled out by the 1952 Civil List Act, which states that, like other monarchs before her, she has surrendered these lands for her lifetime.

10 Lloyd George Papers, F/31/1/50.
11 Select Committee Report on the Civil List, 1935–36(74) v. p. 36.
12 Report from the Select Committee on the Civil List, 1971–2 (29), xxiv, p. 26.
13 Lloyd George Papers, F/31/1/50.
14 A. S. Foord, 'The Waning of "The Influence of the Crown"', *English Historical Review* (October 1947), p. 496.
15 E. A. Reitan, 'The Civil List in Eighteenth Century British Politics . . .' The Historical Journal (1966), p. 322.
16 *Hansard*, 9 July 1952, cols 1341, 1366, 1368–9, 1392. The backbenchers were Christopher Soames (later Lord Soames), Ronald Bell and Ralph Assheton.
17 Ibid.: Gaitskell, col. 1413; Butler, col. 1423.
18 Bow Group, *An Evolving Monarchy* (Bow Publications, March 1968), p. 20.
19 *Hansard*, 11 November 1969, col. 190.
20 *Daily Telegraph*, 28 March 1980; *Daily Express*, 19 April 1983 and 12 February 1987.
21 Appendix 18 of Select Committee Report, 1971–2 (29), xxiv, p. 126, para. 12.
22 Consolidated Fund, Supplementary Statement, December 1990. See also Noel Ing, *Bona Vacantia* (Butterworths, 1971).
23 T160/632/F14740 and T171/329 (PRO); see also a 1901 file, T1/9644B/ 3693 (PRO).
24 Post Office Act 1969, Sch. 8.
25 T632/F14740 (PRO).
26 Select Committee Report on the Civil List, 1951–2 (224), v. See also WORK 19/1193 (PRO).
27 Lord Tryon to Sir Norman Brook, 9 March 1959, WORK 19/1193.
28 Select Committee Report, 1971–2 (29), xxiv, p. 94, and *Hansard*, 11 November 1969, col. 186.
29 Select Committee Report, ibid.
30 Douglas Keay, *Royal Pursuit: The Palace, the Press and the People*

(Severn House, 1983), p. 20. The threefold distinction still exists: Buckingham Palace Press Office, 27 July 1989.

31 Select Committee Report, 1971–2 (29), xxiv, p. 79.

32 John Dean, *H.R.H. Prince Philip The Duke of Edinburgh, A Portrait by His Valet* (Robert Hale, 1954), pp. 158, 167–8.

33 Select Committee Report, 1971–2 (29), xxiv, p. 82, para. 635.

34 Ibid., pp. 81, 166.

35 Ibid., p. 94.

36 *Hansard*, 26 February 1975, col. 627.

37 Select Committee Report, 1971–2 (29), xxiv, p. 70, para. 560.

38 Royal Trustees Report, 16 January 1984.

39 Ibid., 1974, xix, 179.

40 Duncan, op. cit., pp. 171–2.

41 Basil Boothroyd, *Philip: An Informal Biography* (Longman, 1971), p. 142.

42 Barbara Castle, *The Castle Diaries, 1964–70* (Weidenfeld & Nicolson, 1984), p. 727.

43 Quoted in Richard Crossman: *The Diaries of a Cabinet Minister*, iii (Hamish Hamilton and Jonathan Cape, 1977), p. 724.

44 Figures calculated from Select Committee Reports, except that for Edward VIII, T171/329 (PRO), which also confirms figures for George V.

45 *Hansard*, 11 November 1969, cols 186, 192.

46 Select Committee Report, 1971–2 (29), xxiv. pp. xi–xii.

47 *Hansard*, 14 December 1971, cols 292–304.

48 Select Committee Report, 1971–2 (29), xxiv, p. 2; *Hansard*, 14 December 1971, col. 281.

49 *Daily Express*, 3 December 1971; *Observer*, 5 December 1971; *Daily Telegraph*, 4 December 1971.

50 *Hansard*, 14 December 1971, col. 337.

51 Stephen P. Barry, *Royal Service* (Macmillan, New York, 1983), p. 76.

52 Select Committee Report, 1971–2 (29), xxiv, pp. 24, 28.

53 Ibid., p. 2.

54 Ibid., p. 16.

55 *Hansard*, 14 December 1971, col. 302.

7: Hidden Subsidy

1 *Hansard*, 9 July 1952, col. 1430. A subsequent Chancellor of the Exchequer, Denis Healey, implied that the tax exemption was in place in 1952; see *Hansard*, 26 February 1975, col. 627.

2 All editions of COI booklet up to and including June 1971.

3 Dorothy Laird, *How the Queen Reigns* (Hodder & Stoughton, 1959), p. 341.

4 For example, Sir Charles Petrie, *The Modern British Monarchy* (Eyre & Spottiswoode, 1961), p. 210.

5 Stevas, in Jeremy Murray Brown, ed., *The Monarchy and its Future* (Allen & Unwin, 1969), p. 222.

6 Report from the Select Committee on the Civil List, 1971–2 (29), xxiv, Appendix 12, para. 12.

7 *The Economist*, 17 April 1971.

8 *Hansard*, 14 December 1971, col. 311.

9 *New Statesman*, 10 December 1971.

10 *Daily Telegraph*, 10 June 1971; *The Times*, 11 June 1971.

11 Memorandum, Select Committee Report, 1971–2 (29), xxiv, Appendix 12.

12 *The Times*, 9 December 1971.

13 *Sunday Telegraph*, 5 December 1971; *The Times*, 3 December 1971; *The Economist*, 4 December 1971; *Financial Times*, 3 December 1971; *Guardian*, 7 December 1971; *Daily Mirror*, 4 December 1971.

14 *Hansard*, 21 December 1971, col. 1326.

15 *Daily Mirror*, 22 December 1971.

16 *Hansard*, 19 January 1972, cols 500, 502. See also *Hansard*, 14 December 1971, cols 311–17 and 21 December, col. 1339.

17 Ibid., 21 July 1873, cols 709 (Solicitor-General), 697 (Gladstone).

18 Ibid., 9 May 1901, col. 1208.

19 *Hansard*, 21 December 1971, cols 1325 (Whitelaw), 1359 (St John Stevas).

20 Ibid., 19 January 1972, cols 510, 514.

21 Ibid., 14 December 1971, col. 389.

22 Ibid., col. 318.

23 Select Committee Report, 1971–2 (29), xxiv, Appendix 12.

24 Ibid., p. 45. The case is 9 App. Cas. 61. The acute reader will remember from the Prince of Wales's escaping income tax in

Chapter 4 that the Income Tax Acts specifically made the Crown liable to Schedule A as a landlord. Therefore one might wonder how certain bodies could seek Crown immunity from Schedule A. The difference is that in the many cases like this one, it was not a question of the Crown as landlord, merely as owner and occupier.

25 3 T.R. 519, in English Reports, vol. 100, p. 710.
26 H.A.L. Fisher, ed., op. cit. iii, p. 257.
27 Interview with John Griffith, 7 June 1991.
28 [1954] App. Cas. 584, 630.
29 Or, to be more precise, Barber, responding to Crossman, says the Queen did not ask for 'advice' about whether she should reveal her private fortune; see *Hansard*, 19 January 1972, col. 519.
30 Select Committee Report, 1971–2 (29), xxiv, p. 43.
31 *Hansard*, 26 February 1975, cols 588–9.
32 Opinion Research Centre for *Woman*, 4 November 1978.
33 *Daily Mirror*, 8 December 1971.
34 Select Committee Report, 1971–2 (29), xxiv, p. 43.
35 Most reports stated that the Queen was not paying the poll tax for the poorly paid live-in staff at Windsor, Holyroodhouse and Buckingham Palace, whose pay comes from the Civil List (e.g. *Daily Mirror*, 7 March 1990); the *Independent*, 4 July 1991, said she was paying.
36 Information provided by local councils from the valuation rolls.
37 Report of the Royal Trustees, 15 October 1990.
38 Select Committee Report, 1971–2 (29), xxiv, pp. 45, 51.
39 R. T. Bartlett, 'Taxation and the Royal Family – II', *British Tax Review*, 1983, pp. 138–57.
40 Select Committee Report, 1971–2 (29), xxiv, p. 53.
41 H. A. L. Fisher, ed., op. cit., iii, p. 259.
42 Duncan, op. cit., p. 180.
43 Duchy of Cornwall Accounts, 1982.
44 Ibid., 1990.
45 Select Committee Report, 1971–2 (29), xxiv, p. 45.
46 *Hansard*, 19 January 1972, col. 549, and 21 December 1971, cols 1350, 1354.
47 Select Committee Report, 1971–2 (29), xxiv, pp. 44–6.
48 P. Russell, op. cit., pp. 170–71, 157.

49 For example, Treasury memorandum, Appendix 12, Select Committee Report, 1971–2 (29), xxiv.
50 Ibid., p. 73.
51 Ibid., pp. 73–4.
52 *New Statesman*, 10 December 1971.
53 Select Committee Report, 1971–2 (29), xxiv, p. 75.
54 Brian Hoey, *Anne, The Princess Royal* (Grafton, 1990), p. 119.
55 Brian Masters, *Great Hostesses* (Constable, 1982), p. 105.
56 *Sunday Telegraph*, 5 December 1971.
57 Select Committee Report, 1971–2 (29), xxiv, p. 44.
58 *Woman's Hour*, BBC Radio 4, 13 April 1983.

8: Government Expenditure on the Monarchy, 1975 to the Present Day

1 *Daily Telegraph*, 7 February 1975.
2 Barbara Castle, *The Castle Diaries, 1974–76* (Weidenfeld & Nicolson, 1980), 11 February 1975.
3 Royal Trustees Report, 16 January 1984, p. 13.
4 *Hansard*, 14 December 1971, col. 386.
5 Ibid., 26 February 1975, col. 610.
6 *Castle Diaries, 1974–76*, p. 309n.
7 *Hansard*, 27 February 1975, written answers, col. 202.
8 Report from the Select Committee on the Civil List, 1971–2 (29), xxiv, p. 86, para. 13. See also *Hansard*, 21 December 1971, col. 1374.
9 Select Committee Report, 1971–2 (29), xxiv, pp. 11, 26.
10 The money paid over to the Belgian and Danish monarchs is index-linked, but these arrangements were set up in less controversial circumstances. These monarchies also cost far less.
11 *The Times*, 17 November 1976.
12 *Daily Telegraph*, 2 May 1977.
13 *Hansard*, 21 January 1980, written answers.
14 *Daily Express*, 22 January 1980.
15 *Guardian*, 27 March 1980.
16 *Sunday Telegraph*, 3 February 1980 and 28 March 1982; *Daily Express*, 22 January 1980.

17 Royal Trustees Report, 1984.
18 *Observer* and *Sunday Telegraph*, 28 March 1982.
19 Royal Trustees Report, 15 October 1990.
20 Consolidated Fund, Supplementary Statistics, 1989–90, p. 13.
21 *Sunday Telegraph*, 28 March 1982; *Hansard*, 26 February 1975, col. 626.
22 *Sunday Telegraph*, 13 February 1983.
23 *Guardian*, 22 July 1987 (Truro); *Today*, 17 February 1988 (Norfolk).
24 *Daily Mirror*, 14 November 1989.
25 Dean, op. cit., pp. 167–8; Stephen Barry, *Royal Secrets* (Villard Books, New York, 1985), p. 86.
26 *The Times*, 21 May 1987.
27 Royal Trustees Report, 1974, in Reports, Accounts Papers, xix, 179.
28 *Hansard*, 14 December 1971, col. 380.
29 *Observer*, 4 September 1988. Information on *Britannia* from COI's *Monarchy in Britain* and Select Committee Report, 1971–2 (29), xxiv, p. 101.
30 Royal Trustees Report, 15 October 1990.
31 *Sunday Telegraph*, 3 February 1980.
32 *Guardian*, 4 November 1987 (confirmed by Ministry of Defence spokesman).
33 *Observer*, 4 September 1988.
34 *Daily Mirror*, 6 October 1987.
35 CAB 24/277, Piece 155 (PRO).
36 *The Times*, 9 October 1951.
37 *Daily Mirror*, 12 April 1982; *Daily Express*, 12 February 1987.
38 *Royal Heritage: The Queen and Prince Philip*, BBC TV programme made in 1980.
39 *Daily Express*, 12 February 1987.
40 Up to and including 1980, refits were £28,396,000 in 1980 prices; see *Hansard*, 5 February 1980. Further refits cost £6 million in 1984 and £19 million in 1987.
41 *Guardian*, 10 March 1989.
42 Ministry of Defence spokesman to author, 9 August 1989.
43 Royal Trustees Report, 15 October, 1990.
44 *Guardian*, 8 April 1981.
45 Royal Trustees Report, 15 October 1990.

46 *Sunday Times*, 17 March 1985; *Today*, 27 February 1989.
47 Ronald W. Clark, *Balmoral: Queen Victoria's Highland Home* (Thames & Hudson, 1981), p. 83.
48 *Sunday Telegraph*, 30 May 1971.
49 Supply Estimates 1989–90, class XIX, vote 1, A1(3).
50 Ibid., p. 86; *Hansard*, 12 February 1975, col. 374, and 4 December 1975, cols 1984–5.
51 Bill Curling, *All The Queen's Horses* (Chatto & Windus, 1978), p. 114.
52 Anthony Howard, *RAB: The Life of R. A. Butler* (Papermac, 1987), p. 356.
53 *Stroud News and Journal*, 20 October 1977.
54 *Guardian*, 6 January 1978.
55 *Daily Telegraph*, 4 January 1987.
56 *Daily Mirror*, 27 September 1982.
57 *Guardian*, 4 November 1987; *Daily Mirror*, 6 November 1987.
58 *Hansard*, 24 July 1990, cols 299–300.
59 *Sunday Times*, 29 July 1990.
60 *Hansard*, 26 February 1975, cols 609–12.
61 Robert Harris, *The Making of Neil Kinnock* (Faber, 1984).
62 Quoted in the *Sunday Times* article. A few years ago, Neil Kinnock also found 'greatness' to be a quality possessed by the Queen. See *The Times*, 31 July 1986.

9: The Queen's Wealth and Its Uses

1 *Fortune*,12 September 1988.
2 Menkes, op. cit., p. viii; Field, op. cit., p. 17.
3 Morton, op. cit., pp. 120, 170.
4 Report from the Select Committee on the Civil List, 1971–2 (29), xxiv, p. 2.
5 'Schedule of Houses and Apartments The Property of the Crown', in CREST 36/63 (PRO).
6 Select Committee Report, 1971–2 (29), xxiv, p. 3.
7 Ibid.
8 Philip Ziegler, *Mountbatten: The Official Biography* (Collins, 1985), p. 684.
9 Ibid., pp. 683–4.

10 *Daily Telegraph*, 10 June 1971.

11 *Evening News*, 10 June 1971.

12 Select Committee Report, 1971–2 (29), xxiv, p. 4.

13 WORK 19/1263 (PRO).

14 Sir Oliver Millar, *The Queen's Pictures* (Weidenfeld & Nicolson, 1977), p. 202.

15 Ibid., p. 206.

16 J. H. Plumb and Sir Huw Wheldon, *Royal Heritage: The Story of Britain's Royal Builders and Collectors* (BBC, 1977), p. 9.

17 J. H. Plumb and Sir Huw Wheldon, *Royal Heritage: The Reign of Elizabeth II* (BBC, 1981), p. 16.

18 Ibid., p. 172

19 Millar, op. cit., p. 216.

20 Bow Group, op. cit., p. 19; *Daily Telegraph*, 1 December 1987. See also *Guardian*, 24 April 1991.

21 *Guardian*, 14 August 1985.

22 Millar, op. cit., p. 13.

23 Plumb and Wheldon, *Elizabeth II*, p. 177.

24 Plumb and Wheldon, *Royal Builders and Collectors*, p. 114.

25 Sir Lionel Cust, *Van Dyck* (George Bell, 1906), p. 88, and (George Bell, 1900), p. 107.

26 Ellis Waterhouse, *Painting in Britain, 1530–1790* (Pelican, 1953), pp. 46–51.

27 Millar, op. cit., p. 217; BBC TV programme, *Royal Heritage: Elizabeth II and Prince Philip*.

28 *Guardian*, 5 November 1987.

29 Roy Strong, *Cecil Beaton: Royal Portraits* (Thames & Hudson), p. 24; *Sunday Times*, 24 July 1988.

30 Field, op. cit., p. 108.

31 Strong, op. cit., p. 9.

32 James Lees-Milne, *Harold Nicolson*, ii (Chatto & Windus, 1981), p. 223.

33 *Daily Mirror*, 7 December 1984.

34 Harold Nicolson to Vita Sackville-West, 8 June 1948, in Stanley Olson, ed., *Harold Nicolson: Diaries and Letters 1930–64* (Collins, 1980), p. 334.

35 The same letter as note 34, in Nigel Nicolson, ed., *Harold Nicolson: Diaries and Letters, 1945–62* (Collins, 1968), p. 142.

36 Lees-Milne, op. cit., ii, p. 223.
37 *New Statesman*, 16 August 1952.
38 The misquoting of the memorandum is pointed out in Michael and Eleanor Brock, ed., *H. H. Asquith, Letters to Venetia Stanley* (Oxford University Press, 1982), p. 46n. Those interested further in how Nicolson's biography was put together would no doubt profit from an examination of his *original* diaries at Balliol College, Oxford.
39 Roy Jenkins, *Asquith* (Collins, 1964), preface; A. J. P. Taylor in *Observer*, 25 October 1981.
40 Lees-Milne, op. cit., ii, p. 268.
41 *Observer*, 12 October 1958.
42 Lord Twining, *A History of the Crown Jewels of Europe* (Batsford, 1960), p. xxix.
43 Michael Alexander and Sushila Anand, *Queen Victoria's Maharajah: Duleep Singh 1838–93* (Weidenfeld & Nicolson, 1980), pp. 46–7, 49.
44 Field, op. cit., p. 28.
45 Kenneth J. Mears, *The Tower of London* (Phaidon, 1988), p. 146.
46 Ibid., p. 152.
47 Field, op. cit., p. 17.
48 Menkes, op. cit., 3rd edn (1987), p. 131.
49 Ibid., p. 133.
50 Magnus, op. cit., p. 173.
51 Menkes, op. cit., p. 38.
52 Robert Blake, *Disraeli* (Eyre & Spottiswoode, 1966), p. 562.
53 H. H. Dodwell, ed., *Cambridge History of India*, vi (1958), p. 300.
54 Menkes, op. cit., p. 7.
55 Balfour Papers, Add. Ms. 49686, February 1905, *ff*18–22; Anne Edwards, *Matriarch* (Coronet, 1986), p. 154.
56 Menkes, op. cit., p. vii.
57 Rose, op. cit., pp. 131–2.
58 Menkes, op. cit., pp. vii, p. 71.
59 Field, op. cit., pp. 35, 112.
60 Masters, op. cit., p. 105.
61 Field, op. cit., p. 91.
62 Menkes, op. cit., p. 80.
63 Ibid., pp. 53, 199. However, Field, op. cit., p. 16, disputes that Queen Mary did not pay the full price to her Russian relatives.

64 Ibid., pp. 53, 103, 146.

65 For King Faisal's gift of a diamond tiara in 1967, see Menkes, p. 152; for King Khalid's present of a necklace in 1979, see Field, p. 57.

66 *Sunday Times*, Colour Supplement, 30 December 1979.

67 Report of the Royal Trustees, 1984. Select Committee Report, 1971–2 (29), xxiv, p. xxxvii.

68 *My Turn: The Memoirs of Nancy Reagan* (Weidenfeld & Nicolson, 1989), pp. 262–3.

69 Menkes, op. cit., p. 151; Field, op. cit., p. 18.

70 Menkes, op. cit., p. 119.

71 Ibid., p. viii.

72 Select Committee Report, 1971–2 (29), xxiv, p. 3.

73 Menkes, op. cit., p. viii.

74 Conversation with Suzy Menkes, April 1989. This denial seems to be repeated by Brigadier Mears, the Deputy Governor of the Tower, who refers only to the 'State Collection' at the Tower and 'the jewellery worn by Elizabeth II [which] is from her personal collection' (Mears, op. cit., p. 150). In my conversation with a representative of the Lord Chamberlain's Office on 20 September 1989, it took quite some time for him to come round to the idea that there were some jewels belonging to the Crown in the hands of the Queen. For quite a while he insisted, like Mears, that there was simply a twofold classification between private jewels in the hands of the Queen and state jewels in the Tower.

75 Menkes, op. cit., pp. 132, 145; Field op. cit., pp. 18–19.

76 Menkes, op. cit., p. 136.

77 *Guardian*, 29 December 1988.

78 Menkes, op. cit., p. 101.

79 Ibid., pp. 153–4; see also Field, op. cit., p. 91.

80 Conversation with Professor Fred Halliday, 27 July 1989. See also *Guardian*, 1 January 1990, on the 'continuing British military adviser presence in Oman'.

81 Figures from *African Economic Handbook* (Euromonitor Publications, 1986), Table 6.4, and *Western Europe 1989: A Political and Economic Survey* (Europa Publications, 1988), p. 512.

82 Menkes, op. cit., 3rd edn, p. 177.

10: The Duchy of Lancaster

1 *Estates, predominantly agricultural in nature*:

	Approx. acreage
Northamptonshire and Lincolnshire	2,865
Staffordshire, Cheshire and Shropshire	13,353
Lancashire	10,920
Yorkshire	9,318
	36,456

In addition there are 3,145 acres of woodland. Single holdings (e.g. not forming part of an estate) of commercial property are located in Leeds, Leicester, Bradford, Lewes and London (other than the Savoy estate in the Strand area). Information from *Hansard*, Written Answers, 12 November 1987, cols 219–20.

2 *The Times*, 23 June 1965.

3 C. H. Knowles, *Simon de Montfort 1265–1965* (Historical Association, 1965).

4 Somerville, op. cit., i (1953), p. 5.

5 Ibid., p. 69.

6 Ibid., p. 139.

7 Ibid., ii, p. 101; see also i, p. 261. Though his book does not seem to support the view, Somerville himself believes that the Duchy belongs to the monarch. Conversation with Sir Robert Somerville, 4 September 1989.

8 Report from the Select Committee on the Civil List, 1971–2 (29), xxiv, p. 115. The officials who briefed the Chancellor of the Duchy for the Civil List debates of 1910 saw the flaw in the 1399 Charter and pinned their case on that of Edward IV in 1461. The principles laid down in that Charter are at great variance with the 1399 and 1485 Charters, favoured by the 1971 Duchy evidence. See *Hansard*, 22 July 1910, col. 1665.

9 Similarly with the preamble to one of the many Duchy of Lancaster Acts, that of 1779, which mentions that the King owns the Duchy; this too came before the 1800 Crown Private Estates Act. More promising for the official view is the 1811 Regency Act, which passed on the monarch's power to the Prince Regent when George III's mind was

279

beyond repair. This lays down that the Duchy revenues were to go to the King's Privy Purse, though in fact they seem to have ended up with the Prince Regent. This Act, though, lapsed with George III's death in 1820. It did not settle matters, for, as we shall see, William IV still had to fight to retain the Duchy in 1830.

10 Somerville, op. cit., i, p. 318, and S. T. Bindoff, *Tudor England* (Pelican, 1950), Chapter 9.

11 Somerville op. cit., p. 28.

12 Robert Somerville, *Duchy of Lancaster* (Duchy of Lancaster, 1946) p. 8; Duchy of Lancaster Act 1988 and preceding Commons debates.

13 Somerville, *History of the Duchy of Lancaster*, ii, p. 104.

14 Somerville, *Duchy of Lancaster Office Holders* (Phillimore, 1972).

15 Select Committee Report, 1971, p. 66.

16 A. S. Foord, 'The Waning of "The Influence of the Crown" ', *English Historical Review* (1947), p. 491; see also E. A. Reitan, 'The Civil List in Eighteenth Century British Politics . . .', The Historical Journal, 1966, p. 323n.

17 Henry, Earl Grey, ed., *The Reform Act, 1832: Correspondence of the late Earl Grey with H. M. King William IV* . . . (John Murray, 1867), pp. 9–12.

18 Somerville, *History of the Duchy of Lancaster*, ii, pp. 384–5.

19 Ibid., p. 395.

20 Ibid.; see also *Hansard*, House of Lords, 1894, fourth series, vol. 26, col. 1551.

21 *Hansard*, Standing Committee G, 17 November 1987, col. 10.

22 Ibid., 21 January 1988, col. 1213.

23 Ibid., Standing Committee G, 17 November 1987, cols 9–12.

24 Select Committee Report, 1971–2 (29), xxiv, pp. 2–4.

25 Even the Treasury in the post-war period found the Duchy an 'excrescence in the body politic', preferring government to run 'on an even level'. Sir Robert Somerville in conversation with author, 4 September 1989.

26 Ibid.

27 Select Committee Report, 1971–2 (29), xxiv, p. 65.

28 *Hansard*, Standing Committee G, 17 November 1987, col. 11 (Clarke); *Hansard*, 25 July 1873, col. 1005 (Gladstone).

29 Lloyd George Papers, F/29/2, Lord Stamfordham to Captain F. E. Guest, 8 February 1918.

30 Somerville, *History of the Duchy of Lancaster*, ii, p. 353.

31 Select Committee Report, 1971–2 (29), xxiv, p. 64.

32 Ing, op. cit.

33 Somerville, *History of the Duchy of Lancaster*, ii, p. 473.

34 Figures for the Duchies come from their accounts for the relevant years. For the rest of the country, see Parliamentary Papers, Finance Accounts of the UK, Accounts and Finance, vol. i, for appropriate year.

35 The Duchy would probably have preferred to sell the rights to its lucrative devolution income to the government, as in 1882, when the Treasury bought out certain minor rights to *Bona Vacantia* outside Lancashire for £15,000 (1991: about £750,000); see Somerville, *History of the Duchy of Lancaster*, ii, p. 411. If the modern Duchy could have cashed in their income from devolutions, or if there was legislation removing this form of income, they would be looking for the annual average of the last few years, about £1 million, multiplied by at least ten. However, a £10 million pay out would have been a great risk to the Queen's image. Also, because the Duchy of Cornwall gave over its much smaller devolution income to a Benevolent Fund, that made it much harder for the Queen's Duchy to seek compensation for giving up this source of income.

36 *Hansard*, Written Answers, 12 November 1987, col. 219.

37 *Hansard*, 21 January 1988, col. 1207.

38 Robert Somerville, *The Savoy, Manor: Hospital: Chapel* (Duchy of Lancaster, 1960).

39 Figures are from Duchy accounts.

40 *Hansard*, 26 October 1987, col. 13.

41 Ibid., 16 February 1972.

42 *Guardian*, 21 March 1990.

43 Field, op. cit., pp. 36, 37, 139.

44 As regards the situation in 1971, Lord Cobbold listed the other uses to which the Duchy revenues had been put, apart from the Queen's current personal expenditure (Select Committee, p. 3). They were used for charitable donations and a 'pension fund for past and present employees of the Queen and her family not otherwise provided for'; 'for welfare and amenity purposes for the Staff of the Royal Household'; and 'to create a contingency reserve' for the Civil List. Further contributions to the contingency reserve may not be necessary

since 1975, except for fairly minor expenditure, because after that date the government increased the Civil List annually to more or less cover inflation. The 1990 arrangements for the Civil List aim to do likewise. When, in fact, there were deficits on the Civil List in the 1980s, they were covered by the Royal Palaces Presentation Fund, as described in Chapter 8. As regards occupational pensions, the Queen has to pay only for those she privately employs at Sandringham and Balmoral. The government pays the occupational pensions of the large majority of staff who had been paid from the Civil List. One is intrigued by Cobbold's mention of pensions to members of her family. It is not known what is paid out by the Queen in charitable donations for welfare and amenity purposes for the Staff of the Royal Household.

45 *A King's Story* (Pan, 1957), p. 283.

11: Private Estates and Racehorses

1 *Mail on Sunday*, 'You Magazine', 14 August 1988. See also the Balmoral Estate Office's own pamphlet, *Balmoral Castle* (Pilgrim Press, 1986).

2 Ralph Whitlock, *Royal Farmers* (Michael Joseph, 1980), p. 167.

3 *Sunday Times*, 22 July 1990. Conversation with Book Trust representative, July 1990. The rule is that the royals do not accept presents given by firms wishing to promote their products. However, it was pointed out to me that the publishers did not present the books and that it is Book Trust which makes the selection. It is, however, a charity mostly funded by publishers.

4 Barry, *Royal Service*, p. 29.

5 From the Consolidated Fund.

6 Harcourt Papers, Ms. Dep. 6, ff. 69–70, Victoria to Harcourt, 5 June 1894.

7 Asquith Papers, vol. 23, *f* 291.

8 Appendix 12.

9 Bartlett, 'Taxation and Royal Family – I', *British Tax Review*, pp. 106–12. Also conversation with author, 17 October 1989.

10 Christopher Warwick, *George and Marina: The Duke and Duchess of Kent* (Weidenfeld & Nicolson, 1988), p. 143; Giles St Aubyn, ed., *William of Gloucester: Pioneer Prince* (Frederick Muller, 1977),

pp. 84–5; Ms Ogilvy appeared on BBC 1's *Kilroy* in 1989.

11 Select Committee Report, 1971–2 (29), xxiv, p. 108; for the objections of civil servants, see WORK 19/1193 (PRO).

12 Barry, *Royal Secrets*, pp. 59–60.

13 *Daily Mail*, 2 March 1988.

14 Select Committee Report, 1971–2 (29), xxiv, p. xxxvi.

15 *Mail on Sunday*, 14 August 1988; Barry, *Royal Secrets*, p. 67.

16 Field, op. cit., p. 40. Two years later, during a state visit to France, the Queen was given another watch, very similar and nearly as small.

17 *The Times*, 12 March 1986.

18 *Daily Telegraph*, 21 April 1981.

19 *Daily Telegraph*, 19 December 1973; *The Times*, 28 December 1974; *Daily Telegraph*, 21 September 1978.

20 Willie Hamilton, op. cit., p. 234.

21 *Daily Telegraph*, 17 April 1974.

22 *Daily Express*, 27 January 1988.

23 *Sun*, 9 July 1988.

24 *Daily Express*, 4 October 1989.

25 19 January and 1 April 1959, WORK 19/1193 (PRO).

26 Whitlock, op. cit., p. 159.

27 *The Times*, 24 August 1987; *Today*, 31 May 1988.

28 *Daily Telegraph*, 29 December 1987.

29 Len Rush, *Captain of the Queen's Flight* (Bloomsbury, 1987).

30 Lord Carnarvon to author, 2 August 1990.

31 Elizabeth Longford, *Elizabeth R* (Coronet, 1984), p. 350.

32 *The Times*, 4 August 1956; Robert Lacey, *Majesty* (Sphere, 1978), p. 296; see also Kenneth Rose, *Kings, Queens and Courtiers* (Weidenfeld & Nicolson, 1985), under Duke of Richmond entry.

33 Duncan, op. cit., p. 279.

34 The *Daily Mirror*, 14 February 1983, says the Queen had thirteen out of the forty shares in Shirley Heights, but Lord Carnarvon told the author she has sold one or two shares over the years. Jocelyn de Moubray, in *The Thoroughbred Business* (Sidgwick & Jackson, 1987), p. 159, states that one share in the horse fetched £535,000 in 1986. But since then prices for top horses have dipped somewhat and the horse has got nearer his retirement age.

35 Bill Curling, *All The Queen's Horses* (Chatto & Windus, 1978), pp. 71, 114.

36 Tony Morris in *Racing Post*, 1 June 1989.
37 *Daily Mirror*, 27 September 1982.
38 Laird, op. cit., p. 60.
39 *Sporting Life*, 27 September 1982.
40 *Independent*, 25 March 1989.
41 *Sporting Life*, 5 January 1990.
42 *Racing Post*, 21 December 1989.
43 *Racing Post*, 13 December 1989.
44 *Guardian*, 22 July 1990.
45 Information from TGWU official Brian Cox, 29 November 1989. Richard Mackaness of the Trainers' Federation, though otherwise very helpful, would not confirm who the Federation's representatives were on the National Joint Council.
46 *Sporting Life*, 5 January 1990.
47 Information from Brian Cox.
48 Lord Carnarvon to author.
49 *Independent*, 25 March 1989.
50 Michael Varney with Max Marquis, *Bodyguard to Charles* (Robert Hale, 1989), p. 128.
51 Curling, op. cit., p. 71.
52 *Racing Post*, 12 May 1989.
53 Ibid., 14 March 1989.
54 *The Times*, 3 June 1989.
55 *Daily Mail*, 9 June 1989.
56 Lord Carnarvon to author.
57 Richard Baerlein, *Joe Mercer* (MacDonald, 1987), p. 115.
58 *Racing Post*, 1 June 1989.
59 Richard Baerlein in *Guardian*, 19 June 1989.
60 *Racing Post*, 1 June 1989.
61 Lord Carnarvon to author.
62 *Daily Mail*, 8 October 1984.

12: Private Investments

1 *Morning Star*, 22, 24, 25 February 1975.
2 Tony Benn, *Against the Tide, Diaries 1973–76* (Hutchinson, 1989), 24 February 1975, believed that this and earlier leaks could have been orchestrated as part of a 'dirty tricks campaign' to discredit the

Labour government, and that the Security Services were particularly out to get him. It was not paranoid for Benn to think along these lines, for it was during this period, as Peter Wright describes in *Spycatcher*, that a group of MI5 officers were attempting to destabilize the Labour government. However, it is unlikely that in the process they should want to discredit the Queen. Benn himself in his other writing stresses that the unelected parts of the state, like MI5, often feel their allegiance is to the monarch as the permanent symbol of the state, rather than to an elected Labour government.

3 *Hansard*, 26 February 1975, col. 622.
4 At least one expert in constitutional law sees Crown immunity as a long-standing rule of interpretation in law, and not part of the Royal Prerogative. See Chapter 1, note 45.
5 *Hansard*, 24 February 1975.
6 Ibid.
7 Section 27 (9).
8 *Guardian*, 22 April 1977.
9 *Hansard*, Written Answers, 21 April 1977.
10 *Financial Times*, 30 April 1987.
11 *Guardian*, 30 April 1987.
12 Ibid., 13 February 1986.
13 *Hansard*, Written Answers, 21 April 1977.
14 DTI Press Office, 1990; see also *Financial Times*, 30 April 1987.
15 *Guardian*, 21 June 1983.
16 *Guardian*, 22 April 1977.
17 *Observer*, 20 March 1983. Barings were also Prince William of Gloucester's executors; *Evening Standard*, 10 June 1974.
18 *Sunday Times*, 19 and 26 June 1988; *Hansard*, 5 July 1988, col. 536.
19 Ron Chernow, *The House of Morgan: The Secret History of Money and Power* (Simon & Schuster, 1990), p. 522. Richard Spiegelberg, *The City: Power without Accountability* (Blond & Briggs, 1973), p. 184, said that Morgan Grenfell 'look after a sizeable part of the Queen's private fortune'.
20 *The Times*, 9 January 1987; *News of the World*, 26 May 1985; *Woman*, 31 August 1985; *Daily Express*, 27 August 1985; *Fortune*, 12 October 1987.
21 *Sunday Times*, 2 April 1989; *Harpers and Queen*, February 1991.
22 *Independent*, 27 June 1991.

23 The method used by this author is not unlike that employed in Andrew Morton, op. cit., pp. 82–3. He also starts with Cobbold's 1971 statement and says that by 1989, *if* her shares had risen in value to the same extent as the top 700 companies since 1971, they would in 1989 be worth 'between £350 and £400 million'. But he did not tell us the 1971 figure from which he started. From what he told the *Sunday Times* in June 1991, it seems he started from £35 million and thought by that point the investments were worth £600 million. He is also confusing in saying that when *Fortune* estimated the Queen's shareholdings at about £2 billion, such a huge capital sum would yield dividends of only £18 million a year, which would be an incredibly low yield of under 1 per cent per annum.

24 Granada TV, *World in Action*, 24 June 1991.

25 *Sunday Times*, 8 October 1978.

26 Helen Cathcart, *The Queen in her Circle* (W.H. Allen, 1977), p. 159.

27 *Sunday Times*, 13 November 1977.

28 Richard West, *River of Tears: The Rise of the Rio Tinto Zinc Mining Corporation* (Earth Island, 1972), p. 118. The mine, though otherwise still very profitable, was closed in May 1989 after sabotage from local groups conducted against its electricity supply and the mine itself. There was also aboriginal anxiety over RTZ's Australian subsidiary and its plans to mine uranium in western Australia. There were claims that it had damaged sacred aboriginal sites in the Rudall River National Park. See *Observer*, 29 May 1988.

29 Basil Boothroyd, *Prince Philip: An Informal Biography* (Longman, 1971), p. 176.

30 *A Future for Namibia 3, Mining, Mines and Independence* (Catholic Institute for International Relations, 1983), pp. 26, 45.

31 Ibid., p. 37.

Appendix A: The Effect of the Monarchy on Tourism and Trade

1 Michael Billig, 'Rhetorical and Historical Aspects of Attitudes: the case of the British Monarchy', *Philosophical Psychology*, i (1988), pp. 95–6. One takes Billig's point that the reference to tourism and trade is little more than a rationalization. Adherence to the monarchy starts from a very young age and has relatively little to do with

such hard-headed or rational criteria as its contribution to Britain's balance of payments.

2 Information provided by BTA, 29 April 1991.
3 Survey by London Visitor and Convention Bureau, 1986.
4 *Guardian*, 5 April 1990.
5 *The Times*, 9 January 1987.
6 Department of Trade and Industry statistics for 1989.

Appendix B: Race and Sex Discrimination at Court

1 Keay, op. cit., p. 38.
2 Longford, op. cit., p. 212.
3 *Guardian*, 21 January 1984.
4 Ibid.
5 James Pope-Hennessy, *Queen Mary* (Allen & Unwin, 1959), pp. 345–6.
6 Plumb and Wheldon, *Elizabeth II*, p. 16.
7 John Brennan and Philip McGreevor, *Employment of Graduates from Ethnic Minorities* (Commission for Racial Equality, 1987).
8 *Employment Institute, Economic Report*, v, no. 4 (June 1990).
9 Job Description Form.
10 Report from the Select Committee on the Civil List, 1971–2 (29), xxiv, p. 28.
11 RRA, 1968, c. 71, s. 27 (1).
12 Crown Proceedings Act, 1947, c. 44, s. 40 (1). See also *The Monarchy in Britain* (COI, 1988), p. 9.
13 *Hansard*, House of Lords, 30 July 1968, col. 244.
14 *Hansard*, 26 February 1975, col. 622.
15 Conversation with Gordon Franklin, 25 October 1989; with Charles Anson, 31 July 1990.
16 *Sunday Times*, 28 January 1990.
17 Barry, op. cit., p. 41.
18 John Barratt with Jean Ritchie, *With the Greatest Respect* (Sidgwick & Jackson, 1991).
19 *Today*, 17 February 1988 (Norfolk); *Guardian*, 22 July 1987 (Cornwall).
20 *Evening Standard*, 29 January 1988.

Index

Abdulla, Prince Khaled, 218
Adams, Bill, 212
Adams, Frederick, 13*n*
Albert, Prince Consort, 10–15, 42, 105, 106
Alexander, Sir Ulick, 75, 86, 87
Alexandra, Princess, 39*n*, 135, 198, 203, 228
Alexandra, Queen, 21, 32, 52–3, 182, 184; photographs of, 172
Alice, Princess, 52
Allen, Sir Douglas, 133
Al Maktoum, Sheikh Hamdan, 211, 214, 215, 217
Al Maktoum, Sheikh Mohammed, 217
Andrew, Prince, *see* York, Duke of
Anne, Princess, xi, 101, 132, 135, 136, 140, 150, 151, 179–80, 209, 210, 232
Anne, Queen, 5
Anson, Charles, 121, 249
Armstrong, Robert, 221
art collections, Queen's, 159, 161, 163, 165–71
Arthur, Prince, Duke of Connaught, 15
Asquith, Herbert, 35, 37, 38, 124, 125*n*, 202
Aston Farm, Cherington, Gloucs, 151
Attlee, Clement, 76, 192, 194

Bagehot, Walter, 229, 236; *The English Constitution*, xiii
Balding, Ian, 212, 213
Baldwin, Stanley, 68, 69, 76
Balfour, A. J., 26, 28, 29
Balmoral Castle: Victoria and Albert buy, 11, 13–14; rents taxed, 16; Edward VII inherits, 21; rents taxed, 24; George V inherits, 32; maintenance costs, 45; rental income, 64; Edward VIII reduces costs, 73–4; tenancy surrendered to George VI, 75, 77, 78, 79; 'special accounts' not taxable, 80*n*; rents taxed, 81; food from estate not rationed, 85; Queen's holidays at, 110, 200–1, 203–4; rates and taxes on, 114, 128, 129–30, 202; security at, 148, 204; staff, 201–2, 204, 250; not self-supporting, 203, 207; public access to, 207
Bank of England, 66, 67, 68, 104, 223–4
Bank of England Nominees Ltd (BoEN), 222–5, 229 *and n.*

Barber, Anthony, 108, 116, 117, 121, 125, 134, 135, 139, 204
Baring Brothers (merchant bank), 66, 67, 69, 225–6, 232
Barnett, Joel (now Lord), 110
Barratt, John, 250
Barry, Stephen P.: *Royal Service*, 110, 204 *and n*, 208*n*, 250
Bartlett, Roy T., 129*n*, 131, 203
Beaton, Cecil, 172
Beaumont-Dark, Anthony, 155, 238
Beaverbrook, Lord, 28, 194
Beck, Edmund, 46, 48
Belfield, Richard, *see* Hird, Christopher
Bell, William, 179
Bevan, Aneurin, 87
Biffen, John, 140
biographies, official, 172–5
Blackburn, Lord, 123
Blake, (Lord), Robert, 118
Blewitt, Sir Shane, 111*n*
Bloch, Michael, 78 *and n*
Blunt, Sir Anthony, 167
BoEN, *see* Bank of England Nominees Ltd
Bona Vacantia, 98; in Duchy of Lancaster, 99*n*, 194–5
Bow Group, the, 98, 167–8
Boyd-Carpenter, John, 121
Bradford, Sarah: *George VI*, 76
Britannia, Royal Yacht, xv, 105, 109, 143, 144–6, 148
British Telecom, 148*n*
British Tourist Authority: *Overseas Visitors Survey*, 239, 240; *Strategy for Growth 1986–90*, 240
Brook-Shepherd, Gordon: *Uncle of Europe*, 31–2
Brooks-Baker, Harold, 237
Buckingham Palace, 75–6, 147, 161, 164, 239; *see also* Household staff; Queen's Gallery
Buckingham Palace Gardens, 88
Buckingham Palace Press Office, 140, 165; transferred from Civil List, 138, 149*n*
Burke, Edmund, 7, 192
Burkitt, William, 50
Bustino (Queen's horse), 217
Butler, R. A., 81, 97, 100, 101, 113, 114, 150–1, 236
Buxton, Noel, 50

288

INDEX

INDEX

A NOTE ON THE AUTHOR

Phillip Hall has conducted research on the British Monarchy and its full history for ten years. He lives in West London.